# European Regional Policy

# European Regional Policy

## The Impact of Structural Transfers and the Partnership Principle since the 1988 Reform

**Marco Schaub**

**Purdue University Press**
**West Lafayette, Indiana**

First U.S. edition published 2004 by Purdue University Press
www.thepress.purdue.edu

©Verlag Rüegger, Zurich/Chur, 2000. All rights reserved.
website: www.rueggerverlag.ch
email: info@rueggerverlag.ch

This edition not available in Europe.

Printed in the United States of America

ISBN 1-55753-354-7

Library of Congress Cataloging-in-Publication Data available

## Acknowledgements

I take this opportunity to express my thanks to all those who have contributed to this study. First of all, I am indebted to Professor Dieter Ruloff, Head of the Department of International Relations and Professor at the Centre for International Studies (CIS), on whom I could count whenever I needed advice and assistance during my work.[1] I also owe thanks to Professor Bruno S. Frey (Institute of Empirical Research in Economics, University of Zurich), who convinced me to proceed with my studies at university. This research was made possible in part by the generous grant of the Alfred und Bertha Zangger-Weber-Stiftung (Uster) which enabled me to work so independently. The Department of International Relations kindly provided me with all the infrastructure facilities.

I am also grateful to the many interview partners in the Directorate General of Regional Policy (DG-16) of the European Commission in Brussels; the Ministry of Economy and Finance in Madrid; the Junta of Andalusia; the Ministry of Equipment, Planning and Administration of the Territory in Lisbon; and the Commission of Regional Co-ordination Algarve from whom I received generous support while conducting the case studies. Particular thanks go to the following persons: Professor Jorge Gaspar (Director of the CEDRU and of the Geographic Institute, University of Lisbon), Professor Adriano Pimpão (Rector of the University, Algarve) and Juan Requejo (Director of Arenal Grupo Consultor, Seville). At all the institutes, I was warmly welcomed with my scientific investigations on European regional policy and the planned time for the interviews was spontaneously extended to discussions that lasted several hours, and which included snacks from the respective regional kitchens.

Chapters 8 to 10 were written while the author was a research fellow at the Institute of Regional Development (IDR) at the University of Seville, Spain. I benefited inestimably from discussions with Professor Carlos Roman and Carmela Velez who invited me to the institute in 1999. The informal exchange of ideas that characterises this privileged site impressed me as much as the energetic life of the Andalusian capital.

When it came to number crunching and statistical calculations I appreciated the valuable input of Markus Knell (Institute of Empirical Research in Economics, University of Zurich), Hans-Jörg Schmidt (Zürcher Kantonalbank) and Thomas Widmer (Institute of Political Science, University of Zurich). Much valuable feedback came from Professor Miguel Benito (Head of the Evaluation Unit in the DG-16, European Commission) and Professor Rui Nunes (University of Algarve).

---

[1]    Both institutes belong to the University of Zurich, Switzerland.

I would also like to thank all my colleagues at the institute in Zurich, in particular Christoph Achini, Stefan Brem, Stefano Bruno, Jazmín Seijas, Professor Ulrich Klöti, Stephan Kux, Sandra Lavenex and Roy Suter, who all provided me with valuable inputs and critical comments on earlier drafts. I highly valued the discussion circle of Professor Martin Gabriel (CIS) and his team, as well as the Ph.D. colloquium of the Institute of Political Science at the University of Zurich. Many thanks go to Marie-Ange Maurer who contributed much to the friendly atmosphere at the institute. It was a pleasure to work with Iona D'Souza and John Gysin, who helped me to mould the manuscript into the present form.

Finally, I would like to thank three persons: my parents for my education and university studies; and my partner Claudia, who continuously encouraged me in my research. She was the imperturbable pillar I needed for my work, especially at times when the development of this work looked un-sustainable.

Though I alone am responsible for the remaining shortcomings of this study, I can say with certainty that the final product would have been far less satisfactory without the inputs I received from all these colleagues along the way. I conclude by finding the willingness of researchers to devote their time and intellect to helping each other to improve the quality of their work one of the most rewarding features of academic life.

Marco Schaub
Zurich, February 2000

## Table of Contents

## List of Abbreviations

| | |
|---|---|
| AMAL | Associação de Municípios do Algarve (Association of Algarve municipalities) |
| BIC | Business Information Centre |
| CAP | Common Agricultural Policy |
| CCR | Comissão de Coordenação Região (Commission of Regional Co-ordination) |
| CCFSE | Comissão de Coordenação do Fundo Social Europeu (Commission of ESF Co-ordination) |
| CEA | Confederación de Empresarios de Andalusia (Entrepreneurial Confederation of Andalusia) |
| CEAL | Confederação dos Empresarios do Algarve (Entrepreneurial Confederationof Algarve) |
| CEDRU | Centro de Estudos e Desenvolvimento Regional e Urbano (Centre of Regional and Urban Development Studies) |
| CEEC | Central and Eastern European Countries |
| CEH | Consejería de Economía y Hacienda (Regional Ministry of Economy and Finance) |
| CEPI | Centro de Estudos de Problemas de Informação |
| CIS | Center for International Studies (University of Zurich) |
| CF | Cohesion Fund |
| CP | Consejería de la Presidencia (Regional Ministry of the Presidency) |
| CSF | Community Support Framework |
| CTAS | Consejería de Trabajo y Asuntos Sociales (Regional Ministry of Labour and Social Affairs) |
| CTI | Consejería de Trabajo e Industria (Regional Ministry of Labour and Industry) |
| DFG | Deutsche Forschungsgemeinschaft (German Research Society) |
| DG | Directorate General |
| DGAPP | Dirrección General de Análisis y Programación Presupuestaria (Directorate General of Budget Analysis and Programmation) |
| DGDR | Direcção-Geral do Desenvolvimento Regional (Directorate-General of Regional Development) |
| DRA | Delegação Região do Ambiente (Regional Delegation of the Ministry of Environment) |
| EAGGF | European Agricultural Guidance and Guarantee Fund |
| EC | European Community |
| ECSC | European Coal and Steel Community |
| ECU | European Currency Unit |
| EEC | European Economic Community |

| | |
|---|---|
| EIB | European Investment Bank |
| EIF | European Investment Fund |
| EIU | European Intelligence Unit |
| EMU | European Monetary Union |
| ERDF | European Regional Development Fund |
| ESECA | Sociedad de Estudios Económicos de Andalucía (Society of Economic Studies Andalusia) |
| ESF | European Social Fund |
| EU | European Union |
| FAMP | Federación Andaluza de Municipios y Provincias (Federation of Andalusian Municipalities and Provinces) |
| FCI | Fondo de Compensación (Interterritorial Compensation Fund) |
| FDI | Foreign Direct Investment |
| FEM | Fixed Effect Model |
| FGLS | Feasible Generalised Least Square |
| GAT | Gabinete de Apoio Técnica (Units of Technical Assistance) |
| GLS | Generalised Least Square |
| IDR | Instituto de Desarrollo Regional (Institute of Regional Development) |
| IEA | Instituto de Estadística de Andalucía (Statistical Institute of Andalusia) |
| IEFP | Instituto do Emprego e Formação Profissional (Institute of Employment and Professional Training) |
| IFA | Instituto de Fomento de Andalucía (Institute of Economic Promotion Andalusia) |
| INE | Instituto Nacional de Estatística (National Statistical Institute) |
| ISPA | Instrument for Structural Policies for Pre-Accession |
| JdA | Junta de Andalusia |
| LSDV | Least Square with Dummy Variables |
| MEANS | Means for Evaluating Actions of a Structural Nature |
| MEH | Ministério de Economía y Hacienda (Ministry of Economy and Finance) |
| MEPAT | Ministério do Equipamento, do Planeamento e da Administração do Território (Ministry of Equipment, Planning and Administration of the Territory) |
| MQE | Ministério Para a Qualificação e o Emprego (Ministry of Qualification and Employment) |
| NUTS | Nomenclature of Units for Territorial Statistics |
| OLS | Ordinary Least Square |
| OP | Operational Programme |
| PP | Partido Popular (Popular Party) |
| PPS | Purchasing Power Standard |
| PSD | Partido Social Democrático (Social Democratic Party) |

| | |
|---|---|
| PS | Partido Socialistico (Socialist Party) |
| PSOE | Partido Socialista Obrero Español (Spanish Socialist Worker's Party) |
| SAPARD | Special Accession Programme for Agriculture and Rural Development |
| R&D | Research and Development |
| RDP | Regional Development Plan |
| REM | Random Effect Model |
| SEDR | Secretaria de Estado do Desenvolvimento Regional (Secretary of State of Regional Development) |
| SEM | Single European Market |
| SME | Small and Medium-Sized Enterprises |
| SPD | Single Programming Document |
| w.y. | without year |

## List of Figures

## *List of Tables*

# 1 INTRODUCTION

## 1.1 Cohesion As Central Goal of European Regional Policy

This study is about European regional policy in southern Europe.[2] It aims to analyse the impact of both the increased structural transfers and the more decentralised regional policy process through the partnership principle, which were the two main features of the 1988 European regional policy reform. The reason for structural interventions lies in the success of European integration itself which has led to substantial economic benefits for the Union as a whole, but left behind (some) peripheral areas with socio-economic development significantly below the European Union (EU) average (Martin, Reiner 1998: 1). Nine out of the ten poorest European regions are located either in Greece, Portugal, Spain and southern Italy (European Commission 1998: 233f). The unequal spatial effects of European economic integration has been the reason for political conflict between central and peripheral parts since the very beginning at the Treaty of Rome (1957), with the peripheral member states demanding an active European regional policy including transfers from the rich to the poor. In the early years of European integration the market driven evolution was predominant, according to which the convergence[3] process was little more than a desired outcome of economic integration. However, the ratification of the Single European Act (SEA) in 1987 substantially changed the nature of the integration process by formally building into it the political goal of social and economic cohesion[4] (Amtsblatt der Europäischen Gemeinschaften 1987: Article 130a-e; Nanetti 1996: 59).

---

[2]  Throughout the text regional policy, structural policy and cohesion policy are used as synonyms.

[3]  The literature provides a range of definitions of convergence since the notion stands for the attempt to narrow the differences of *real*, *nominal* or *institutional* parameters (see also footnote 12). This study focuses on real convergence and defines this concept in accordance with Leonardi (1995: 34). Convergence is considered as "the process towards the end-product of socio-economic policies designed to reduce the socio-economic disparities that exist among regions within Europe." Regional and national economies converge if the initially weaker economies benefit from appropriate economic policies designed to spur development and if the economies of the peripheral states and regions grow at rates faster than those in the core areas. In this respect, real convergence is the process that leads to cohesion. Divergence, in contrast, is identified with the widening of disparities.

[4]  Cohesion is defined as the reduction in territorial inequalities within European society. The concept encompasses economic, social and political aspects of anti-disparity policies (Dinan 1998: 46). Economically, the idea is to permit all the regions to compete in the internal market by endowing them with the requisite infrastructure and skills (Keating 1995: 18). Politically, there is a need to demonstrate the value of Community membership in peripheral regions, and to ensure a fairer spread of the benefits of economic integration (Armstrong 1995: 23). This definition, however, makes it difficult to determine when sufficient cohesion is achieved. For practical purposes, a simple rule is to define cohesion as the degree of

The centrality of the cohesion objective in the SEA brought the concept of real convergence and sustainable regional development to the core of European regional policy. The European Commission, responsible for the conceptualisation of European regional policy, took the view that "the development of peripheral areas in the Community is as much a question of capital investment in economic and social infrastructure as it is one of developing adequate institutional structures, procedures and networks for the purpose of engaging in effective policy-making and implementation at the regional level" (Leonardi 1993: 18). Thus, the Commission built its cohesion policy, which was implemented in the 1988 European regional policy reform, on two pillars. Regional development should be entrusted to regional and local institutions,[5] and needed to be backed by a substantial increase in European structural transfers, the former meaning in fact a more decentralised approach to the European regional policy process.

**Figure 1-1: Evolution of European Regional Fund Allocations, 1989-1996**

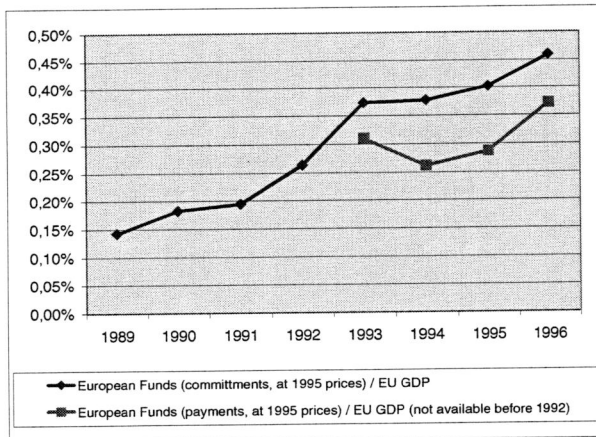

Note: Transfers consist of the following structural funds: the European Regional Development Fund (ERDF), the European Social Fund (ESF), the Guidance Section of the European Agricultural Gui-dance and Guarantee Fund (EAGGF), the Financial Instrument for Fishing Guidance (FIFG) and the Cohesion Fund (CF).

—◆—European Funds (committments, at 1995 prices) / EU GDP
—■—European Funds (payments, at 1995 prices) / EU GDP (not available before 1992)

*Source: own calculation (all transfers at 1995 prices); data from various annual reports of the structural funds (Directorate General XVI, European Commission).*

A look at the evolution of the structural transfers in relation to the EU GDP displays the increase of resources dedicated to the European cohesion goal (Figure 1-1). In absolute terms, the total flow of transfers in the Union was Euro 70 billion for the planning period 1989-1993. In the following period (1994-1999), the EU spent Euro

---

disparity between different regions within the European Community which is politically and socially tolerable. In the final analysis, this criteria is bound to be rather a political than an economic judgement, though economic criteria will figure prominently (Begg and Mayes 1993: 150).

5    Institution is defined narrowly. The notion includes public or private groups and organisations.

165 billion on structural development, and for the coming period (2000-2006) Euro 213 billion have been dedicated to structural funds. The share of structural funds in the total EU budget of 1992 amounted to 28 per cent, in 1996 it reached 33 per cent, and it will total 36 per cent from 2000 to 2006. Between 1989 and 1996, Euro 100 billion flowed into the Greek, Portuguese and Spanish economies, which is equivalent to 45 per cent of the entire European transfer sum for this period (European Commission 1997b: 154-177).

The involvement of regions in European regional policy, the second pillar of European cohesion policy, began in earnest with the Integrated Mediterranean Programmes (IMPs) in the late 1980s. A substantial step toward enhancing the regional level took place in 1988 with the reform of European regional policy. The introduction of the partnership principle involved "close collaboration between the Commission and all the relevant authorities at national, regional or local level appointed by each member state, at all stages in the programming" (European Commission 1993a: 19). This development shifted the European Commission's focus from a national development strategy to a multi-tiered one. The new funds regulation clearly spelled out the shared responsibilities for the implementation of regional policy among three levels of institution: the Commission, the national governments and the regions. While the trend towards greater interaction between the European Commission and regional actors throughout the 1980s and early 1990s is indisputable, it may be argued that this interaction was sought by the European Commission for technocratic reasons related to policy effectiveness, and not simply as an attempt to encourage the mobilisation of regional institutions (McAleavy and De Rynck 1997: 1). However, I provide evidence that the European Commission was indeed intending to raise regional institutional performance.[6] The reasons for the regional involvement in the European regional planning process was, on the one hand, the insufficient results with the traditional model based on the support of big, capital-intensive and vertically organised firms in the 1970s and 1980s (Garofoli 1992: 72). On the other hand, the Commission acknowledged the comparative advantage of regional institutions in responding to the demands of small and medium-size enterprises (SMEs), whose importance for employment increased in the 1980s (Europäische Kommission 1993: 29-31; 135-137; European Commission 1999c: 3).

More than ten years after the reform of the European regional policy, the success of this policy is far from clear. We know only little about the specific socio-economic impact of increased financial transfers and regions being more involved in the European regional policy process. A look at the performance of some regions reveals

---

[6]    Institutional performance is defined as the capacity of regional institutions to respond to the demands of the public and private environment.

that regional policy in southern Europe in different places and different fields has been highly effective, totally ineffective, and everything in between. The Spanish region of Extremadura is a positive example where a total of Euro 1,7 billion stands against an annual growth rate of 12,5 per cent (1989-1995).[7] European transfers were equally successful in the case of the Aegean Islands: Euro 2,6 billion brought an annual growth of over 11 per cent (same period). Conversely, the European regional policy has also been, at times, an unmitigated failure. In the case of the Spanish region Asturias, large-scale European financial transfers left no trace of progress: more than Euro 1,7 billion stand against a meagre annual GDP growth rate of 0,4 per cent (1989-1995). Things look worse in the case of the (administrative) Greek region "Peloponnese, Western and Continental Greece" where Euro 2,8 billion induced no growth at all (same period). Perhaps these differences can be expected in a complex field such as European regional policy that has spanned a quarter of a century, gone through a variety of reforms and a few hundred billion Euro in financial transfers. But hindsight is valuable only if it produces insight.

## 1.2   Review of Literature

An analysis of European regional policy is primarily approached from two perspectives.[8] Firstly, there is a major community of regional economists who have devoted effort to assessing the impact of cohesion policy on the process of economic convergence. Secondly, political scientists have questioned the implications of the mobilisation of sub-national actors on territorial politics.

Concerning the first perspective, the approaches that have searched for an explanation of the dynamic of regional growth (or the lack of it) can be divided into two basic categories from a theoretical point of view. The first one places emphasis on the process of convergence, and belongs to the neo-classical school of thought (Barro and Sala-i-Martin 1991; 1992; 1995; Mankiw, Romer and Weil 1992; Sala-i-Martin 1990; 1994; 1996a; 1996b). The second category is associated with the divergence school of thought – a less coherent theory focusing on economic phenomena such as economies of scale, external effects and transport costs (Krugman 1991a; 1991b; 1993a; 1993b; 1995; Martin, Ron 1999; Myrdal 1957; Rossi 1995; Walz 1996).[9] A review of empirical literature on the European cohesion pattern provides empirical evidence for the convergence hypothesis. European regional GDP *per capita* disparities (of the core member states) have indeed narrowed over time but at a decreasing rate since the 1980s (Armstrong 1995a; 1995b; Barro and Sala-i-Martin 1995; Button and Pentecost

---

7    All figures of GDP growth (PPS; at 1995 prices) come from the REGIO database (Eurostat).
8    The review of literature is limited to studies about European cohesion policy at the regional level in southern Europe.
9    For a detailed discussion of the two approaches see chapter 3.

1995; Cheshire and Carbonaro 1997; Dunford 1993; European Commission 1991; 1996b; Glen 1995; Leonardi 1995; Molle *et al.* 1980; Molle 1990b; Neven and Gouyette 1994; Sala-i-Martin 1996a; 1996b). Reiner Martin (1998) and Armstrong and Kervenoael (1997) make up for the four beneficiaries of the Cohesion Fund (CF; Spain, Greece, Portugal and Ireland) what has been analysed for the EU in general. The results indicate the same convergence pattern for the four countries.

Regional economists have also searched for factors explaining regional disparities. Investments in human capital and in infrastructure were found to have a positive influence on southern European regional economic development (Cutanda and Paricio 1994; De la Fuente and Vives 1995; Guerrero and Séro 1997; Mas *et al.* 1996; Martin, Reiner 1998).[10] Fagerberg and Verspagen (1996) found R&D expenses strongly influencing cohesion in their analysis of northern European regions. Easterly *et al.* (1993), Levine and Renelt (1992) as well as Rodríguez (1998) identified (national) macro-economic variables (gross fixed capital formation and share of international trade to GDP) as strongly determining regional economic performance. Rodríguez (1998) analysed political variables in a survey of all the EU regions. He found a lack of the relationship between regional economic growth and a variety of regional political factors (such as the political orientation of the main parties or electoral support). Some of the above-mentioned studies include measures financed by European structural funds. However, studies on the impact of European structural funds are rare. Guerrero (1997: 331f) found a positive relation between structural interventions (1989-1993) and cohesion for Andalusia (Spain). Barro and Sala-i-Martin (1995) and Sala-i-Martin (1996a) are pessimistic about the effectiveness of active regional policy, although they did not include structural transfers in their convergence study of European regions but drew this conclusion from transfer studies in the United States. Within the pan-European programme MEANS (Means for Evaluating Actions of a Structural Nature), the Commission itself has been heavily investing in order to improve evaluations of structural interventions (European Commission 1995g; 1995h; 1996a; 1999f; 1999g). As a result, the Commission recently started to assess regional macro-economic effects of the CF (but no other structural funds) investments in southern Europe (European Commission 1999d; 1999e). The main insight from these studies is that CF investments in infrastructure have a significant positive impact on private investment, regional income and the creation of employment.

Political scientists have focused less on growth and employment effects of European regional policy but investigated more the emergence of multi-level government in the context of structural funds. Extensive theoretical work and empirical studies reinforced

---

[10]  Nijkamp and Blaas (1995) came to the same conclusions for the Dutch regions.

the argument that EU regional policy is no longer dominated by national governments only but includes regional and supra-national actors (Hooghe 1996; Jouve and Négrier 1998; Knodt 1998a; 1998b; Kohler-Koch 1998; Kohler-Koch and Jachtenfuchs 1996; Marks 1996a; 1996b; Morata 1995; Morata and Munoz 1996). The drawback of this strongly process oriented, institutional approach is the neglect of the cohesion aspect so that the role of regional institutions for economic development has scarcely been investigated in the above-mentioned studies. The European Commission itself stresses the importance of functioning regional institutions for economic development, but provides no systematic evaluation approach in order to capture the influence of the European regional policy reform on institutional performance. Initial evaluations on institutional performance were conducted by Leonardi (1993), Morata (1993), Opello (1993) and Trigilia (1989), who all analysed how regional institutions were prepared in order to cope with increased competition in the Single European Market (SEM). The most comprehensive analytical framework of institutional performance was presented by Nanetti (1996). However, the empirical part of her research considers only the early 1990s when the implementation of the European regional policy reform had only just started which does not allow one to draw mid- and long-term conclusions of the impact of the partnership principle on institutional performance. Another approach, combining multi-level government and cohesion, was undertaken by Paraskevopoulos (1998), who analysed regional policy networks. His case study on the Aegean Islands revealed that European regional policy reform increased institutional performance, especially in terms of learning capacity and social capital (both prerequisites which the contemporary growth theory found to be important for economic development).

Striking the balance in the literature review, there are two areas which need deeper analysis. On the one hand, the impact of European structural transfers on cohesion at the regional level in the southern European member states should be enlightened. On the other hand, further research needs to be conducted on the implications of the partnership principle of the 1988 regional policy reform on institutional performance in order to understand better the role institutions play in economic growth and cohesion.

## 1.3  Research Questions

This research addresses the above two aspects of European regional policy since the 1988 reform: the impact of structural transfers on cohesion and the implications of the partnership principle on institutional performance. The research questions of this study will be treated with quantitative and qualitative methods using regional data from Greece, Portugal, southern Italy and Spain. The questions are as follows:

1. What has been the impact of European structural transfers on the convergence process of the poorer southern European regions?

2. Has the partnership principle effectively enhanced the performance of regional institutions in cohesion policy?

The relevance of these questions is two-fold. First of all, this study clarifies the convergence effect of European structural transfers in southern Europe. The result shows whether the billions of Euro currently flowing from Brussels to southern Europe should be interpreted as a side-payment for deeper economic integration or whether they have had a substantial growth effect. It is vital for the EU to know to what extent European regional policy has helped the less developed regions to catch up with the richer ones regarding the mandate to pursue cohesion. Secondly, this work can help to enlighten the relationship between the decentralised approach of European regional policy and the performance of regional institutions. The results will show whether the partnership principle of the 1988 European regional policy reform successfully promoted sustainable development.

The study combines both the perspectives of economic convergence and multi-level governance by focusing on the content as well as the politics of European regional policy. It aims to analyse cohesion effects of European regional policy at the macro-level but also asks how regional institutions have been doing their job in regional development at the micro-level. In this respect, territorial politics play an important role. The main interest, however, is neither the analysis of the configuration of territorial power relations between national, regional and European actors, nor the discussion of subsidiarity, which became popular with the promotion of a "Europe of the regions" and the establishment of the Committee of the Regions in 1993.[11] By investigating the spatial effects of economic integration, the study is entering the fields of economics and geography. I go beyond a purely macro-economic perspective, however, and do not aim to test a specific growth theory or development model.[12]

---

[11]   For an introduction to the concept of subsidiarity see e.g. Bullmann (1994); Dammeyer (1997); Hrbek (1996); Müller-Graf (1997); Schneider (1996).

[12]   Macro-economic aspects have been popular in the debate on nominal convergence and the Maastricht criteria (Dyson 1994; de Grauwe 1996; Scharrer 1987). Nominal convergence describes the attempt to narrow differences of monetary indicators such as convergence of monetary aggregates or interest rates and, on a limited scale, of growth rates through the synchronisation of business cycles (Aume and Niesr 1992: 96f). The goal of nominal convergence is stability of exchange rates and similar behaviour of economic policies. The relation between nominal and real convergence is a complex one. Even though nominal convergence can bring along the synchronisation of business cycles and, hence, a similar trend in growth rates, it cannot remove real economic disparities. Different regional unemployment and growth rates, or sectoral and regional variance in salary, are normally based on structural and institutional differences and hardly ever on monetary causes such as distorted exchange rates or interest rates (Harbrecht and Schmid 1987: 218; Hellmann 1987: 408; Pfeil 1993: 68-70). There is even strong evidence that nominal

I touch on fields that the reader may know from the debate on good governance (see e.g. Fuster 1997). My approach, however, is different from Third World development not only from a theoretical point of view but also because the southern European member states have carried out most of the political and administrative demands put forward by advocates of good governance.

## 1.4    Method

This study about the impact of European regional policy in southern Europe belongs to the category of the (*ex post*) policy evaluation study (van Evera 1997: 91). In the practice of regional policy evaluation a variety of impact assessment techniques have been developed.[13] I approach the topic of European regional policy reform from two sides. On the one hand, I use a macro-quantitative approach, applying a multiple regression technique on data of forty southern European regions, including seven Greek, seven Portuguese, eighteen Spanish and eight Italian regions.[14] This allows me to analyse the influence of European structural transfers on convergence (question 1). Moreover, two case studies on the Spanish region of Andalusia and the Algarve in Portugal help to comprehend how the European regional policy reform influenced institutional performance (question 2). The qualitative methodology applied in the two case studies helps to complement the understanding of cohesion in southern Europe. The combined approach of this study is an extension of existing studies on European regional policy which use either quantitative *or* qualitative methods. It also stands in contrast to the opinion that there is a logical contradiction between the two approaches as has recently been suggested in the growth debate between proponents of the "new geographical economics" and economic geographers (Krugman 1995; Martin, Ron 1999; *The Economist,* March 14th 1999: 104). These controversies obscure the fact that both quantitative and qualitative methods demand similar care in designing and conducting empirical research.

## 1.5    Structure

The analysis comprises eleven chapters. Each summarises the most important findings at the end of the chapter. Chapter 2 starts off with a summary of the evolution of

---

convergence of monetary aggregates has a negative impact on real convergence for some regions. Take the European Monetary Union (EMU) as an example: the actual stress on nominal convergence has a deflationary bias, not least as a consequence of the deficit and debt criteria. In order to squeeze the deficit at or below the required three per cent limit, governments massively lowered public demand and raised taxes. These factors led to prolonged recession in Europe, which itself is related to regional divergence because the cutback of production capacity (and, thus, the dismissal of the workforce) normally hit the periphery more than the core (Keating 1995: 6; Pintarits 1996: 149).

[13]    For an excellent survey on various quantitative and qualitative evaluation methods see the MEANS collection, which contains the results of a four-year European research programme on the evaluation of structural policies (European Commission 1999g).

European integration, with special reference to growing welfare disparities of the Union due to deeper economic integration. Chapter 2 also elaborates possible economic *rationales* for regional policy. Finally, the chapter provides a review of European regional policy, including its origins, the present operation and the plans recently announced by the Commission for the post-1999 period.

Chapter 3 analyses, from a theoretical point of view, whether economic integration is more likely to contribute to convergence or divergence of welfare conditions. Increasing cohesion is predicted by the neo-classical school of economic thinking (convergence theory), whereas the second line of reasoning is associated with the divergence school – a less coherent theory focusing on economic phenomena such as economies of scale, external effects and transport costs. On theoretical grounds, the dispute between the convergence and divergence theory remains unresolved, which leads to the empirical investigation of the convergence pattern. Therefore, a growth model is developed in order to estimate the convergence effect of European structural transfers. Chapter 4 elaborates empirical convergence concepts and operationalises the variables of the model developed in the preceding chapter. Chapter 5 presents the findings of the analysis and pits the results against the often stated criticism that European financial transfers act solely as side-payments to the poorer European member states for not blocking deeper economic integration.

Chapter 6 opens the field to the analysis of institutional aspects of European regional policy reform from a theoretical point of view. A model of ten regional roles in development, which allows us to capture institutional performance, is presented. Chapter 7 deals with methodological aspects of analysing institutional performance and justifies the selection of the case studies. Chapters 8 and 9 display the results of the two case studies on Andalusia and Algarve. Finally, chapter 10 compares the two case studies.

Chapter 11 summarises the main findings and provides recommendations for European regional policy in order to improve the catch-up prospects of the lagging, southern European areas.

---

[14] Appendix A.1 lists all regions.

# 2 ECONOMIC INTEGRATION AND EUROPEAN REGIONAL POLICY

This chapter provides background information on European economic integration and the European regional policy. The effects of European integration on spatial disparities are discussed in the first part of this chapter. The second part discusses the *rationale* of European regional policy. Section three presents the instruments of European regional policy. In section four, a brief history of regional policy including the latest developments in European regional policy in view of eastern enlargement is presented. Finally, a review is made of the principles on which the EU builds its structural policy since the European regional policy reform in 1988.

## 2.1 European Integration and Spatial Disparities

### 2.1.1 Stages and Economic Effects of European Integration

Integration is defined as the gradual elimination of economic barriers between countries. It is regarded as a continuum of ever-increasing integration where different stages can be distinguished (Dieckheuer 1997: 485f; Pfeil 1993: 7-18).[15] This view of integration stands in the tradition of the classical market theory, which is associated with the idea that the fusion of national markets leads to a quasi common market (Buschmann 1991: 8).[16] At the simplest level there is a free-trade area in which a group of countries remove tariff barriers among themselves, but retain their own individual tariff policies for trade with non-members (a well-known example is the European Free Trade Area (EFTA)). A customs union is a free-trade area in which members go one step further and set up a common policy for trade and tariffs with non-member countries. Beyond customs unions lie common markets. In a common market member states ensure complete free trade in goods and services amongst themselves, together with full internal mobility for labour and capital from one member state to another. In a monetary union, a common currency and a common monetary policy (sometimes also a fiscal policy) are established. The last stage in the integration process is a political union with all policy fields co-ordinated among the member states. The EU as it is currently constituted is a monetary union onto which a

---

[15] According to Frei (1983: 177f) and Unger (1995: 244-253), the European integration process consists of three dimensions. Integration as it is defined in this study belongs to the dimension of socio-economic interdependence. The other two dimensions of integration concern institutions and common awareness.

[16] Despite the fact that economic integration is based on economic theory, integration steps do necessarily have to be founded on economic reasons. The case of European integration, e.g., has been heavily influenced by political decisions (*The Economist*, September 21st 1996: 21-25).

number of policies such as agricultural, social, industrial and regional policy have been grafted.

The political argument for striving for an economically more integrated Europe is that the successful implementation of a new integration stage significantly boosts trade among member states (Dieckheuer 1997: 488, 491). The *rationale* of these integration benefits is that tougher competition leads to more efficient production and cheaper goods for consumers (Bretschger 1997b: 25-27). Economists distinguish between static and dynamic effects of economic integration of which not all are necessarily beneficial (Bretschger 1989: 247-249; 1997a: 2). Considering *static* effects, the benefits of trade creation, which is the replacement of expensive local production by cheaper imports from a partner member state, must be set against the problems caused by trade diversion, including the replacement of cheaper initial imports from a non-member by more expensive imports from a partner member state. *Dynamic* effects may spread over a longer period of time. They include effects such as the exploitation of economies of scale by bigger firms supplying a larger common market, the possibility of a whole range of external economies leading to reduced costs for companies, improved investment volumes and lower costs from greater competition but also pressure for corporate restructuring and unequal spatial diffusion of technological know-how.

### 2.1.2    Spatial Effects of Economic Integration

The spatial effects of economic integration are a controversial issue (see also Chapter 3). The current pattern of disparities reflects previous rounds of integration, the preparation for coming ones and the entry of new member states, all having their own distinctive effects. Structural changes and restructuring affect all the European regions when the static and dynamic effects of economic integration work through the system. Especially long-term dynamic effects are disturbing for disadvantaged peripheral regions. For they enhance corporate restructuring, occurring as firms adjust to a more competitive environment in which they must operate. Once firms in peripheral areas with high costs (due to the lack of smaller economies of scale) have to compete with low-cost firms from the core areas, they will be driven out of business or taken over by market leaders from the core. In each region we would expect to see some industries being run down or even closed while other industries expand and prosper (Leonardi 1995: 43; McDonald and Dearden 1992: 111).

The reason for spatial inequalities is that restructuring effects are not equally allocated. If a region is particularly heavily dependent on industries which are most likely to be affected by free trade, then economic integration will result in more painful restructuring effects (Rossi 1995: 2-4). In the case of e.g., SEM, the selective nature of trade barriers being removed meant that certain industries were more affected than others. This was particularly the case for industries which heavily relied on contracts from national governments (transport equipment, telecommunications, etc.) or other barriers such as technical product standards (electrical engineering or agricultural food products). There is evidence that the less developed European regions, notably in Greece, Ireland, Portugal and Spain, were heavily dependent on those industries that faced major restructuring after 1992 (Booz, Allen and Hamilton 1989).

### 2.1.3   Outlook: The Implications of the European Monetary Union

The European Monetary Union (EMU) is a continuation of the integration process that has taken place before. A further boost to integration is expected and new static and dynamic forces affecting the regions will be set in motion again. Exportation, for instance, will be easier with a single currency since transaction costs and exchange-risk premiums on interest rates will be eliminated (Aschinger 1996: 56; Dyson 1994: 316).

Only theoretical research has yet been conducted on the spatial effects of the EMU.[17] Again, there will be a balance of countervailing forces at work, some of which help peripheral areas, and others do not. In one respect, however, the EMU represents a distinctive break from previous processes. The EMU will remove two macro-policy instruments previously widely used to mitigate the consequences of depressed local economic conditions (Baltensperger and Jordan 1996: 89; Becker 1995: 89). No longer will peripheral member states be able to use exchange rate depreciation or massive public-sector deficit spending to protect or boost their flagging national economies (*The Economist*, November 9th 1996: 110). Any "incompetitive" European region (or nation) that does not undertake and succeed in reducing differential unit costs (particularly labour costs) will experience slower growth, lower exportations and thus a current account deficit (assuming importation are constant). If this is not accommodated by capital inflows there will be downward pressure on income levels, and subsequently increased unemployment (Berthold and Fehn 1997; Franz 1997: 23).

The European Commission's hope that wage flexibility might increase with EMU in response to employment conditions is fairly optimistic (Europäische Kommission 1994a: 43) as current European labour markets are rigid (except in the United Kingdom and to a certain extent in the Netherlands; *The Economist*, May 22nd 1999: 97f). For the time being, there is no reason to suppose that the European regions will experience increased wage flexibility either in the short or medium term (McDonald and Dearden 1992: 113). Less competitive economies with inflexible labour markets will, thus, suffer periods of high unemployment with the onset of EMU (*The Economist*, October 11th 1997: 17, 25-27).

---

[17]   The research on spatial effects of EMU is usually based on the theory of optimum currency area. For an introduction to the theory of optimum currency area see Mittendorf (1994); Mundell (1961).

## 2.2    The Case for European Regional Policy

The preceding chapters revealed that economic integration does not guarantee equal spatial distribution of welfare gains. This provides *rationales* for public policies designed to promote regional convergence. The literature lists a range of arguments, mixing social, political and economic reasoning when it comes to *rationales* for European regional policy.[18] The most frequently stated ones are:

(1) The flattening of "unjust" spatial income distributions (*equity* or fairness argument). It is considered unacceptable for political reasons that people of similar characteristics have different incomes depending on their place of residence.[19] A frequently heard reason for the equality argument is that regions which gain from integration should pay for the market access they obtain. According to this argumentation, the benefits of a bigger integrated market implies for richer economies the obligation to assist partners who lose relatively from the integration process (Begg and Mayes 1993: 152).

(2) The easing of *adjustment* problems for economies undergoing major transformations or shocks. The idea of an adjustment policy is to equip the less developed regions with basic assets such as infrastructure, services, technological capabilities or workforce skills, so that they are able to compete with the core of Europe (Artobolewsky 1997: 29f; Aume and Niesr 1992: 120).

(3) Welfare increases due to the activation of previously unused factors of production (*efficiency* argument; De la Fuente and Vives 1995: 15).

(4) The optimisation of the spatial allocation of production (e.g. by internalising *external* agglomeration *effects*; Pintarits 1996: 67).

The last two points are purely economic arguments for regional policy. *Rationale* (3) concerns the employment of unused resources. In areas where economic activity is insufficient some factors of production, notably labour, are likely to remain unused or underused. Regional policy, so the argument goes, can reintegrate these factors of production into the economic process, thereby increasing aggregate welfare (Eichengreen *et al.* 1995: 2-6). This approach, however, requires (a) that the surplus factors of production are too immobile to move to other parts of the integration area and (b) that the costs to activate them are lower than the welfare gains obtainable from their activation (Martin, Reiner 1998: 74).

---

[18]  Regional policy is defined as the "set of measures by which governments and interest groups try to influence the geographical distribution of economic activity" (Leonardi 1995: 4).

[19]  The complete elimination of disparities within the EU is a somewhat idealistic view of European regional policy. Nevertheless, an equal spatial distribution of income levels is politically highly desired (Caesar 1987: 269).

Condition (a) is by and large fulfilled in the EU as labour mobility is low. Condition (b) is more difficult to tackle and requires the introduction of agglomeration externalities (*rationale* 4). In the absence of external effects and on the basis of the assumption of rational behaviour, the market outcome must be the optimal spatial allocation of resources. In the presence of externalities, however, private welfare optimising behaviour is no longer equal to social welfare optimisation (Frey and Kirchgässner 1994: 236-239). A private decision to locate a company in the centre of an agglomeration, for instance, can lead to negative side-effects such as an increase in traffic congestion. The investor does not have to pay other economic costs (the increase in congestion) which arise from his decision because these costs are external to him. Most authors are careful in assessing the welfare implications of regional market failures, because it is not immediately clear whether they provide positive benefits or cause external costs that rise in the case of regional policy (Franzmeyer 1994: 208). Summing up, it is difficult to find clear economic *rationales* in favour of regional policy. Equity arguments for regional policy seem to be more powerful than efficiency arguments.

## 2.3 The Funds of European Regional Policy

In most European countries twenty to forty per cent of income differentials between regions are reduced through the workings of *direct* central public finance (Artobolewsky 1997: 116-123; European Commission 1996: 55; 1998: XIV). This happens inter-regionally as a result of fiscal federalism, or between individuals as a result of the tax and benefit system (Tsoulakis 1991: 233). No such built-in stabilisers exist on the European level, however, there is a range of indirect financial compensations.[20] The main instruments of European regional policy are the European Social Fund (ESF), the European Regional Development Fund (ERDF), the Cohesion Fund (CF), the Guidance Section of the European Agricultural Guidance and Guarantee Fund (EAGGF) and the Financial Instrument for Fisheries Guidance (FIFG). Further European aid-giving bodies which are related to European regional policy are the European Coal and Steel Community (ESCS) and the European Investment Bank (EIB), including (since 1992) the European Investment Fund (EIF). Whilst these funds are covered separately it should be borne in mind that some schemes have been financed jointly, e.g. ERDF subsidies on EIB loans.

*(1) The European Social Fund (ESF):* Originally this fund was not a proper instrument of regional policy. Through a major turning point in its activities during the 1970s its

---

[20] According to the theory of fiscal federalism and public choice theory, transfers should be as close as possible to the individuals concerned because they are thereby most effective. In the absence of a system of direct (interpersonal) compensation as in the case of the EU, inter-regional transfers are an adequate tool to rectify disparities (Teutemann 1993: 397).

priorities progressed to create full and better employment, the improvement of living and working conditions, and the participation by employees in the process of decision-making. Today, the ESF targets its expenditure mainly on two groups. These are young people seeking to join the labour market for the first time, and older, long-term unemployed workers. In addition, the fund provides assistance to migrant workers, the disabled, women returning to employment, and workers adversely affected by new technology (Harrop 1989: 118). Compared to the member states' engagement in social policy (e.g., health and social welfare), the ESF is still concerned with a very narrow field of social policy (Harrop 1996: 121).

*(2) The European Regional Development Fund (ERDF):* The ERDF was established in 1975 after the decision to enlarge the Community. Today, the ERDF is the central element of European regional policy. ERDF assistance is oriented to a variety of projects, ranging from infrastructure development (e.g., building roads and communication networks) to developing and redeveloping indigenous economic capacity (e.g., projects concerned with the conversion of traditional industries, job-training facilities, business information projects). It also supports energy and water engineering projects (Artobolewsky 1997: 94; Leonard 1998: 153f).[21]

*(3) The Cohesion Fund (CF):* This fund was established at the Edinburgh summit in December 1992 in order to meet the promise of the Maastricht Treaty, in which the cohesion goal of 1986 (SEA) had been reinforced. The Cohesion Fund's goal was to offset the expected costs of EMU for the poorest countries as the Monetary Union would remove two macro-policy instruments (exchange rate depreciation and public-sector deficit spending), previously widely used to mitigate the consequences of depressed economic conditions. In order to facilitate the adjustments to EMU, Euro 15 billion for the 1994-1999 period were devoted to the benefit of member states with a *per capita* GDP of less than 90 per cent of the EU average. The beneficiaries were, of course, those countries that promoted the Cohesion Fund most, namely Spain, Portugal, Greece and Ireland. At the Berlin summit in March 1999, it was decided to add another Euro 18 billion to the Cohesion Fund (Rist 1999: 23). Transfers of the Cohesion Fund finance investments were either in infrastructure (such as transport, energy and telecommunication projects) or environment (such as sewage plants or reforestation).

*(4) The Guidance Section of the European Agricultural Guidance and Guarantee Fund (EAGGF):* This fund, with an annual budget of about Euro 1 billion in the 1980s and 1990s (Artobolewsky 1997: 95), finances development in crisis agrarian regions. Structural measures have generally given farmers a minimum of 25 per cent of the

---

[21]   For the functioning of the ERDF see Chapter 2.5.4.

total cost of projects for the modernisation of farms, rationalisation, improvement of processing and marketing. The EAGGF helps with movement of workers from the land and also supplies funds to mountain and hill farming in less favoured areas (Harrop 1989: 115). Compared to the spending on the Common Agricultural Policy (CAP), which consists mainly of guaranteeing prices, the assistance to agrarian problem regions is a minor component of activity, and it cannot undo the negative effects of the CAP on cohesion.[22]

*(5) The Financial Instrument for Fisheries Guidance (FIFG):* The main task of the FIFG is to improve industry structures and their competitiveness world-wide as well as to achieve a sustainable balance between fishing efforts and resources, which are currently under threat from the overcapacity of the Community fleet. To achieve these goals, existing financial instruments – various multi-annual programmes – were regrouped in 1993 in a single "financial instrument for fisheries guidance". The FIFG was then integrated into the general system of the structural funds. It now has a dual role, contributing firstly to the operation of a common market in fishery products and attaining objective 5(a), the adjustment of fisheries structures (www.europa.eu.int).

*(6) The European Coal and Steel Community (ECSC):* The coal industry's fortunes have fluctuated greatly in the post-war period with initial expansion to fuel Europe's industrial recovery giving way to contraction as greater energy choices emerged between different fuels in a competitive multi-fuel situation (unlike in agriculture, the EC has pursued a low-cost energy policy). In the 1960s when the Community enjoyed high economic growth it imported cheap oil on a large scale and also found it cheaper to purchase coal from some low-cost world suppliers. While the energy policy chosen appeared judicious at that time from a macro-economic perspective, it resulted in massive regional and structural decline in coal mining areas at the micro-economic level (Harrop 1989: 113). This was the field of the ECSC, which has made loans to both the coal and the iron (steel) industry to finance investment projects and schemes for conversion and modernisation. Grants have also been made to assist the redeployment of workers. Today, the ECSC is no longer viewed as an instrument of European regional policy (Harrop 1996: 88).

*(7) The European Investment Bank (EIB), including the European Investment Facility (EIF):* Contributing to balanced regional development within the EU remains a cornerstone of the bank's lending activity besides credits to the Third World. In

---

[22] The CAP has not met earlier expectations regarding its redistributive role. Not only have income differentials in the agricultural sector remained large but the CAP has in fact contributed to the worsening of regional inequalities (Tsoulakis 1991: 238). A study of the European Parliament (1991) which evaluated the impact of the CAP on cohesion at the national level came to the same conclusion. Expectations that the CAP would be reformed in the context of the Agenda 2000 proved to be wrong. The Council did not agree on profound reform of the CAP (*The Economist*, October 17th 1998: 35).

channelling resources from the capital markets to finance a huge range of investment in less favoured areas, the EIB works in close association with the European Commission to ensure an optimum mix between EIB loans and EU grant aid (Thibaut 1996: 79). The EIB has been empowered to provide loans for projects which fall into the following categories: developing lagging regions, modernising, developing new activities, and supporting projects of common interest to member states (Harrop 1996: 92f). The Maastricht Treaty (1992) led to the creation of the EIF, a credit facility, organically linked with the EIB. The facility is designed to ease the financing of projects in peripheral parts of the EU which involve a higher credit risk than the standard operations of the EIB (Martin, Reiner 1998: 83f).

## 2.4    European Regional Policy: Past and Present

### 2.4.1    The Beginning of European Regional Policy (1970s)

The preamble of the Treaty of Rome (1957) mentioned the need to reduce regional disparities but it included only few redistributive mechanisms (preamble of the Treaty of Rome; Bieber 1997: 8). The European Social Fund (ESF) and the European Investment Bank (EIB), both established by the Treaty, were not primarily intended to promote cohesion but were nonetheless expected to help the EC's poorer regions. Similarly, Article 92-3 of the Rome Treaty declared that national subsidies were compatible with a common market if they promoted "the economic development of areas where the standard of living is abnormally low or where there is serious underemployment". Apart from those concessions, the prevailing attitude in 1957 was that the common market would, of its own accord, "promote throughout the Community a harmonious development of economic activities" and thereby lessen disparities between the rich and poor regions.

European regional policy really took off after the enlargement to nine members (1973), with the recognition of particularly severe regional problems in the UK and Ireland. After two years of negotiations the ERDF was created in 1975, though only meagre financial resources were devoted to it. 856 million units of account were set aside for a three-year period (1975-1977), despite the Commission's original request, itself very modest, for 1500 million units of account. Apart from its limited resources, there were two major criticisms (Keating and Jones 1985: 39f). Firstly, there was not enough concentration of spending on the most disadvantaged countries. Secondly, the European funds were not additional since member states used financing mechanisms to reduce national expenditures on structural policy.

The European Commission made several attempts to reform this early system of regional assistance. The aim of the Commission was to create a more encompassing regional policy where it would have an increased role vis-à-vis the national authorities. In order to achieve this goal, it was of crucial importance to move away from the member state quotas for ERDF funds. The Commission launched attempts to scrap them in 1978 and 1985 but the European Council left the quota system more or less intact. The member states were not yet willing to change a system that suited them well and allowed national governments to retain the initiative in regional policy-making (Martin, Reiner 1998: 81).

### 2.4.2 The Move to Programmes (post-1985)

Probably the most important reason for the overhaul of the original system was the southern enlargement of the EC. The enlargement not only increased regional disparities but led also to demands of the existing southern member states (Italy, France and Greece) to be compensated for their willingness to accept the widening of the Community (Pintarits 1996: 68; Stadlmann 1986: 130). The so-called Integrated Mediterranean Programmes (IMP) were designed to satisfy these demands. The IMPs, launched in 1985, moved beyond the precious project-based approach and towards a more encompassing programme-type policy. They thus became "pioneer" programmes for the large-scale 1988 European regional policy reform (Bianchi 1993: 62). The innovatory aspects of the IMPs included an integrated approach to development, careful consideration of environmental aspects, the involvement of SMEs and the coming together of different regional groups to participate in the planning process. There was to be a partnership between the regions, the member state and the EC. Each level of government contributed financially, with the major contribution being given by the Community. Some private finance was also forthcoming, mainly in France, to a lesser extent in Italy and in a minor way in Greece (Harrop 1996: 97).

The results were generally beneficial where regions already possessed a planning system. Northern Italian regions, e.g., fell into this category. On the contrary, southern Italian regions such as Sicily, Campania and Calabria, which lacked a planning system, were less successful. The deficiencies were most apparent in Greece where a highly centralised political system frustrated the operation of the IMPs. At least, the IMPs resulted in a re-division of the country from the 55 prefectures down to six regions to administer the IMPs. However, there was insufficient decentralisation and too much of a top-down approach by central parties, both in planning and controlling the expenditure (Harrop 1996: 97). Overall, the experience of IMPs and their deficiencies pointed the way forward in reforming the structural funds in 1988, as they showed the need to concentrate spending and to have a regionally balanced partnership (Leonardi 1993: 235).

### 2.4.3 Major Reform of the Structural Funds (1988)

Economic, political and moral arguments underpinned the Commission's efforts to promote cohesion after the EC's southern enlargement. Jacques Delors, a former president of the European Commission, had long been aware of the growing rich-poor

divide in the Community through the southern enlargement. The poorest regions in
Greece and Portugal had a *per capita* gross regional product of around 40 per cent of
the Community average while the poorest region (Calabria) of the nine members
between 1973 and 1981 came in at 59 per cent of the average. The Commission's
programme for 1985 cautioned that regional disparities "could become a permanent
source of political confrontation" and urged that the south be given "a fairer share of
the benefits of economic development" (Commission 1985: 15). Additional pressure
for reform came from the SEM project launched with the SEA in 1986. The poorer
member states demanded financial assistance by the EU in order to be able to increase
their economic competitiveness. The rich northern member states were willing to
satisfy these demands in order to make sure that integration would proceed
(Böckenförde 1997). Furthermore, inequalities in income endangered the European
ideal of promoting peace through economic development (Bellers and Häckel 1990:
287; Pfeil 1993: 6).

The Commission advocated a substantial redistribution of resources to the
Community's less-prosperous regions during the 1985 intergovernmental conference
(IGC). The Commission's emphasis on cohesion raised the prospect of a sizeable
budgetary hike and lowered the attractivity of the SEM programme. The IGC deferred
a decision about increasing the amount of structural funds until later but committed
member states to promoting economic cohesion. As a result Article 23 of the SEA
added a new title to the Treaty of Rome: "economic and social cohesion" (Amtsblatt
der Europäischen Gemeinschaften 1987). This committed the Community to "reducing
disparities between the various regions and the backwardness of the least favoured
nations". It also called for the co-ordination between other EC policies and cohesion,
and obliged the Council to reform the structural funds within a year of the SEA's
implementation, on the basis of a Commission proposal (Bachtler and Turok 1997:
348).

In February 1987 the Commission introduced a five-year budgetary package to impose
budgetary discipline and to control agricultural spending. The so-called Delors I
package also proposed a doubling in real terms of the resources available for the
structural funds (making a total of Euro 60 billion available from 1989 to 1993). A
fierce battle between proponents of market liberalisation (mainly England) and
southern European countries was eventually resolved at the special Brussels summit in
February 1988 thanks to Helmut Kohl's (the former German Bundeskanzler) *largesse*
that Germany would contribute most of the proposed budgetary increase (Dinan 1998:
48). With the agreement to double the combined size of the three structural funds, the
European Commission reached the first pillar of its cohesion strategy.

In 1988, the Council also adopted regulations reforming European regional policy
since substantially increasing the structural funds was not enough to redress regional

imbalances. The 1988 reform sought to turn the structural funds into effective instruments of economic development with the regions becoming an important partner in European regional policy (second pillar of cohesion strategy). The most important elements of the reform were arranged around four guiding principles, namely programming, concentration, additionality and partnership. These principles, which underwent minor changes in the second (1994-1999) and third (2000-2006) budgetary packages, are discussed below (see Chapter 2.5).

### 2.4.4 Monetary Union and the Creation of the Cohesion Fund (1993)

Moves towards the EMU in the late 1980s raised concerns in the EC's poorer countries similar to their concerns earlier in the decade. As the EMU would deprive member states of their ability to devalue, it could worsen the balance-of-payments difficulties of poorer countries (Baltensperger and Jordan 1996: 89). During the IGC in Edinburgh (December 1992), Ireland, Spain and Portugal attached the highest priority to the strengthening of structural policy. Felipe Gonzáles, the Spanish prime minister and the poor countries' standard-bearer, fought tenaciously in the run-up to the Maastricht summit to win a greater Community commitment to cohesion. A special protocol supplemented the Rome Treaty's cohesion provision at Spain's insistence. The Delors II package which was finally approved at the Edinburgh summit covered the costs of implementing the Cohesion Fund. The new financial perspective agreed to at the summit nearly tripled Community assistance for the least prosperous countries from Euro 7.7 billion in 1988 to over Euro 21.36 billion in 1993.[23] In 1999 the structural funds topped Euro 30 billion (both at 1992 prices and including payments of the Cohesion Fund).

### 2.4.5 Outlook: The Implications of the Agenda 2000

At the Berlin summit in March 1999, the European Council approved the *Agenda 2000*, which included the financial package for the 2000-2006 period. A total of Euro 213 billion (at 1999 prices) is available for European regional policy over the entire period, including Euro 18 billion devoted to the Cohesion Fund. Despite the initial statements by the Commission to lower the percentage of eligible population, the ratio of beneficiaries is still above 50 per cent. A step towards greater concentration of structural fund assistance in areas of greatest need was the substantial reduction in the number of objectives to three (European Commission 1999a: 8f).

Another challenge to the structural funds in the period 2000-2006 is the response to the future enlargement of the Union. The costs of cohesion in an enlarged EU with numerous poor central and eastern European countries (CEEC) are potentially prohibitive since the gap in output between these countries and the EU average is

---

[23] These figures display payments of the entire Union (not only to the southern European countries).

considerable, although most of the CEECs have been experiencing a period of economic recovery since 1993. The *per capita* GDP in the majority of the CEECs is less than forty per cent of the EU average (*Inforegio Newsletter* 1999/61). Major problems exist, moreover, in most CEECs owing to the disparities between the urban and rural areas or because of the fact that the regions are heavily dependent on traditional industries and agriculture (Dinan 1998: 51). In order to face the challenge of potential new CEECs, the Commission foresees structural expenditure of Euro 1'040 million a year (at 1999 prices) over the period from 2000 to 2006. The funds are divided evenly between environmental and transport infrastructure projects (*Inforegio Newsletter* 1999/66). There will be three instruments assisting the applicant countries until they join the EU. The PHARE aims, firstly, at the consolidation of institutions, the participation of CEECs in Community programmes, regional and social development, industrial restructuring and the development of the small-business sector. The ISPA (Instrument for Structural Policies for Pre-Accession), secondly, targets the development of transport and environmental infrastructure. Finally, the SAPARD (Special Accession Programme for Agriculture and Rural Development) is used for rural development and the modernisation of agriculture.

All in all, the *Agenda 2000* makes the effects of the eastern enlargement of European regional policy appear less dramatic than it is sometimes prophesied (Weise 1997: 179). While regional policy is certainly not an insurmountable obstacle for enlargement, the Commission's assumption that regional policy expenditures in the CEECs can be fully financed by means of savings and growth-generated resources has to be regarded with some caution, because minor changes in the expected growth rates can significantly alter the outcomes of the scenarios on which the *Agenda 2000* is based.

## 2.5    Principles of European Regional Policy

The 1988 reform (and to a smaller extent the 1994 and 2000 regulations) radically revised structural policy by introducing a number of new principles and strengthening existing ones.[24] These were concentration, additionality, partnership and programming. The principles are still at the heart of today's European regional policy.

### 2.5.1    Concentration

One of the guiding principles of the 1988 reform was the concentration of financial transfers on those parts of the EU which were in greatest need of structural support. Prior to the reform, areas eligible for national regional support qualified automatically

---

[24]   The main changes between the 1989-1993 and the 1994-1999 regulations concerned the strengthening of monitoring and evaluations, a reinforcement of the partnership principle, eligibility criteria, programming periods and administrative procedures. For a detailed comparison see European Commission (1993a), Michie and Fitzgerald (1997: 20) or Wishlade (1996: 49f).

for assistance from the European structural funds. With the reform, however, the Commission developed its own regional policy objectives, which underwent changes in each planning period (see Table 2-1). There were two main reasons for this change. Firstly, the definition of eligible regions on a European level ensured that member states did not unduly expand their national eligibility coverage in an attempt to maximise European structural support payments (Martin, Reiner 1994: 85). Secondly, a European rather than national perspective as to what constitutes a regional problem was useful for a policy aimed at the reduction of socio-economic disparities at the Union level (European Commission 1998: XIV-XVI).

**Table 2-1: European Regional Policy Objectives**

| First Community Support Framework (1989-1993) | **Fund** |
|---|---|
| 1    Development of structurally backward regions | ERDF, ESF, EAGGF |
| 2    Reconverting regions in industrial decline | ERDF, ESF |
| 3    Combating long-term unemployment | ESF |
| 4    Combating youth unemployment | ESF |
| 5a    Adjustment of agricultural structures | EAGGF |
| 5b    Development of rural areas | ERDF, ESF, EAGGF |
| **Second Community Support Framework (1994-1999)** | **Fund** |
| 1    Development of structurally backward regions | ERDF, ESF, EAGGF |
| 2    Reconverting regions in industrial decline | ERDF, ESF |
| 3    Combating long-term and youth unemployment | ESF |
| 4    Facilitating structural change | ESF |
| 5a    Adjustment of agricultural structures, including the fisheries sector | EAGGF, FIFG |
| 5b    Development of rural areas | ERDF, ESF, EAGGF |
| 6    Development of sparsely populated regions[25] | ERDF, ESF, EAGGF, FIFG |
| **Third Community Support Framework (2000-2006)** | **Fund** |
| 1    Development of lagging regions (including former objective 1 and 6 regions) | ERDF, ESF, EAGGF, FIFG |
| 2    Support for areas facing structural difficulties (including former objective 2, 5a and 5b regions) | ERDF, ESF |
| 3    Support for the adaptation and modernisation of policies and systems of education, training and employment (incl. former objective 3 and 4 regions) | ESF |

*Source: European Commission (1995f: I; 1999a: 8f); McDonald and Dearden (1992: 107).*

The objectives can be divided into two different categories. As far as the 1994-1999 period is concerned, objectives 1, 2, 5b and 6 were *regional*, that is they referred to certain eligible areas. Under objectives 3, 4 and 5a, however, it is possible to fund activities in the entire Union. These objectives were therefore called *horizontal*

---

[25]    This objective was added to the five existing ones when Sweden and Finland joined the EU since they could not claim financial transfers from any other fund.

(Martin, Reiner 1998: 85f). A set of designation criteria was developed in order to make the designation process for region-specific objectives more transparent. The most precise criteria were set up for designation of objective 1 regions. The *per capita* income in these regions, expressed in purchasing power standards (PPS), had to be less than 75 per cent of the Community average for at least three consecutive years. Moreover, objective 1 status could only be granted to the Nomenclature of Units for Territorial Statistics (NUTS) II regions in order to prevent the "creation" of low-income regions by disregarding regional frontiers. The regulation, however, allowed for exceptions from these rules.

The designation criteria for the other objectives were less strict. In order to qualify for objective 2 status regions had to have a greater unemployment rate and a higher share of industrial employment than the EU average. Moreover, industrial employment had to be in decline. These criteria needed to be satisfied for a couple of years but the number of years was not exactly defined in the regulations. The designation should be based on NUTS III regions but parts of NUTS III regions can also qualify. The criteria for objective 5b regions were a low level of socio-economic development, a high share of agricultural employment and a low level of agricultural income. Extensions of the eligibility criteria were possible once again and none of the criteria was quantified which left a leeway for "political" designations. The same criticism holds for all horizontal objectives (McDonald and Dearden 1992: 107f; Wishlade 1996: 34-38).

The development of regional policy objective areas and the concentration on objective 1 regions (which receive more than two thirds of the available resources) significantly improved the effectiveness of European regional policy, because objective 1 regions were arguably those parts of the EU which were in greatest need of structural support. The level of spatial concentration, however, has frequently been regarded as insufficient. For example, more than 50 per cent of the EU population currently lives in eligible areas despite the explicit aim of the 1988 reform to limit the geographical availability of EU regional assistance (Samland 1997). Moreover, the quantitatively defined criteria for objective 1 regions was eroded in 1994 through the addition of further regions to the objective 1 list, which neither corresponded with NUTS II level regions nor was their relative *per capita* income below 75 per cent of the EU average. The effectiveness and efficiency of the use of the remaining third of the structural funds has also been put into question because the objectives 2 and 5b designation policies were flexible and the resources devoted to the horizontal objectives (3, 4, 5a) were not used to assist the poorest regions of the EU (Martin, Reiner 1998: 88).

### 2.5.2   Additionality

The additionality principle dates back to the pre-1989 period and is valid for all structural funds except the CF. It was designed to make sure that EU funding increases total expenditures for structural purposes. In the light of the negative experiences with additionality during the pre-1989 period the principle was explicitly incorporated into the Co-ordination Regulation of the European regional policy reform. Despite its increased legal profile, it has been difficult to put the additionality principle into practice and it remains doubtful whether subtle attempts to evade the additionality principle have been detected (Martin, Reiner 1998: 91).

The additionality rules are different for projects financed by the Cohesion Fund where European funding can cover up to 85 per cent of the total project costs. This is in effect a departure from the principle of additionality, although an intended one, since the CF was designed to enable poorer member states to improve their infrastructure endowments and to launch environmental projects without putting further strains on their national budgets in the run up to EMU (Martin, Reiner 1998: 92).

### 2.5.3 Partnership

The designers of the 1988 reform realised that the successful implementation of EU regional policy depended on close co-operation between European, national and regional institutions in order to overcome the formidable information problems created by the involvement of various layers of administration as well as various sections within these layers (Dinan 1998: 48; see also Chapter 6.1.2). Partnership, a principle and a set of organisational structures, lay at the core of the 1988 reform and was thought to include public and private actors (Hooghe 1996a: 89). The form and intensity of partnership between different levels of government depended on the funds involved and especially on the phases of the programming process. Further aspects of partnership are therefore discussed in the next section together with the programming principle.

### 2.5.4 Programming

The structural funds reform involved a major switch from project-related assistance to programme assistance and decentralised management. This placed the emphasis on planning and continuity, rather than on *ad hoc* activities and improved the coherence between individual measures. Whereas under the old system the Commission dealt with thousands of separate projects, the Commission now oversees a much smaller number of programmes (Bachtler and Turok 1997: 362). A major improvement came from the co-ordination between the different institutions involved at EU, member state and regional level.

The programming process can be disaggregated into different subphases, depending on the instrument of cohesion policy.[26] The *Cohesion Fund* has operated outside the

---

[26] I present here the EU standard process of the programming principle. Peculiarities in the case of Andalusia and Algarve will be discussed in Chapters 8 and 9. Regions are usually only involved in the European planning process which consists of the following sub-phases: planning, negotiation, formulation,

structural funds and involved the Commission and each member state executive in the recipient countries in bilateral relationships that largely exclude regional governments (Marks 1996a: 399). The CF actually worked contrary to the programming approach, which aimed at reducing the complexity of structural funds management. For the CF financed single projects and did not bundle them into coherent programmes.

A little less than ten per cent of structural spending between 1994 and 1999 was determined autonomously by the Commission as *Community Initiatives* (CI), with 80 per cent earmarked at objective 1 regions (Harrop 1996: 118-120). CIs were multi-regional programmes targeted at specific problem areas such as cross-border (and transnational) co-operation, reconversion of declining coal-mining regions or promoting communications and infrastructure in the most peripheral regions (Martin, Reiner 1998: 90; Michie and Fitzgerald 1997: 24f). The ERDF which is largely responsible for financing CIs paid close attention to the expressed demands and implicit needs of national and regional constituencies but the formulation of policy was expressly monopolised by the Commission. The Commission determined the content and the timing of the initiatives and selectively mobilised actors, including regional governments, to help formulate and support initiatives (Hooghe and Keating 1994: 63).

The bulk of structural funds was organised in *Community Support Frameworks* (CSFs), economic development plans for each of the participating member states and constituent regions (Wishlade 1996: 34). More than any other EU policy, structural policy reached directly into the member states' competencies, directly engaging regional governments and private actors with the Commission and member state governments. The result of this approach was a diverse relationship across individual member states and regions concerned with decision-making in structural programming joined by the participation of one common actor, the European Commission (Marks 1996a: 400). In the planning period 1989-1993, CSFs were operationalised in a four-stage process. Firstly, regional or national development plans were formulated for each recipient country. Secondly, these were negotiated by representatives of the member state and the Commission into legally binding CSFs. Thirdly, the CSFs provided the basis for Operational Programmes (OPs) composed of specific development projects. In a fourth step, the OPs were implemented and monitored.[27]

---

implementation and monitoring of structural interventions. There has been no or only negligible participation in the other two main phases: the creation of the budgetary envelope of European regional policy and the design of institutions (Marks 1996a: 390).

[27]  The 1994 reform brought a reduction in the number of planning stages from four to three, with member states able to submit development plans (stage 1) and the programmes relating to them (stage 3) simultaneously. In response, the Commission had to adopt a single decision, the so-called Single

*Stage 1:* The first stage of structural programming involved the formulation of regional development plans by member state governments that became the basis of negotiation with the Commission. Central executives controlled the access of regional actors in most member states. They were serving in their traditional capacity as the sole intermediary between domestic political interests and European politics. There were wide variations in the extent to which central executives were willing or able to use their intermediary role to ignore regional demands (Marks 1996a: 400f).

*Stage 2:* At the second stage of structural programming, regional development plans were hammered into formal contracts (CSFs) allocating EU resources in negotiation between individual member states and the Commission (Martin, Reiner 1998: 88). These negotiations were conducted behind closed doors and they feature dimly, if at all, in scholarly descriptions of cohesion policy. Although we lack hard evidence and good secondary sources, it seems clear that these negotiations elevated the indulgence of those actors present at the bargaining table at the expense of those not represented (Marks 1996a: 401-403).

*Stage 3:* At the third stage of structural programming, the CSFs were negotiated into OPs, which detailed specific projects that would be funded to achieve the general priorities set out in the CSFs.[28] The institutional framework in stage 3 was quite different from that in stage 2, as the logic of stage 3 reflected the need on the part of the central executives to gain legitimacy and, above all, information from diverse actors on the ground. While it was possible for central executives to determine autonomously the general priorities that structured the regional or national development plans of stage 1, the conception of concrete projects placed much greater demands on local knowledge and resources (Martin, Reiner 1998: 89). It was at stages 3 and 4 (implementation and monitoring) that the principle of partnership between the Commission, local, regional and national authorities stood the best chance of realisation (Marks 1996a: 403-405).

*Stage 4:* The final stage of structural programming was the implementation and monitoring of CSFs/OPs. Given the diverse character of the projects that were carried out in individual regions, ranging from infrastructure development (e.g., building roads

---

Programming Document (SPD), comprising the details of CSFs and OPs set out separately beforehand (Wishlade 1996: 50).

[28] The regulations for the 2000-2006 period included two new elements. Firstly, OPs and SPDs will no longer contain details on the measures to be funded, as it was the case of the 1994-1999 period. Secondly, the member states or regions must adopt new, complementary programming documents for each programme after the adoption of the OPs and SPDs. The combination of these new elements reflects the Commission's desire to ensure a clearer division of responsibilities and a stronger application of the principle of subsidiarity: the European Commission supervises compliance with the strategic priorities but the management of the programmes is more decentralised (European Commission 1999b: 15).

and other communication networks) to developing or redeveloping indigenous economic capacity (e.g., projects concerned with the conversion of traditional industries, job-training facilities, business information projects), a variety of public and private actors participated in the implementation and monitoring stage of structural programming (Marks 1996a: 405f).

## 2.6   Synopsis

European economic integration inherits both adjustment costs and unequal distribution of welfare gains when static and dynamic integration effects ripple through European economies. These disparities provide *rationales* for regional policy intervention which are either based on equity reasons, adjustment costs, the efficiency argument or external agglomeration effects. In contrast to the member states, the EU supports only indirect financial compensation schemes which are financed by the European Social Fund (ESF), the European Regional Development Fund (ERDF), the Cohesion Fund (CF), the Guidance Section of the European Agricultural Guidance and Guarantee Fund (EAGGF) and the Financial Instrument for Fisheries Guidance (FIFG). Furthermore, the European Coal and Steel Community (ESCS) and the European Investment Bank (EIB), including (since 1992) the European Investment Fund (EIF) are relevant to European regional policy.

European regional policy started with small financial means. Today, over 35 per cent of the European budget flows into structural policies. A major change in the management of the European funds came with the 1988 (and to a lesser extent with the 1994) European regional policy reform when, on the one hand, spending on lagging regions was massively increased and, on the other one, four guiding principles – concentration, additionality, partnership and programming – were introduced. Partnership is the most central one in terms of my research question as it allows regional institutions to participate in the European regional planning process.

# 3 A CONVERGENCE MODEL OF FINANCIAL TRANSFERS (MACRO-LEVEL)

Economists have been unable to agree whether regions within an economically integrated area will tend to converge to a common level of per capita income. This chapter provides an overview of the convergence and divergence approaches of economic theory. Convergence theory, based on neo-classical economic reasoning is presented in the first section. It predicts that factor incomes (capital and labour) in all parts of an integration area will eventually converge provided that sufficiently strong adjustment mechanisms exist within the integration area. The second section presents concepts of the divergence theory. This approach predicts an increasingly uneven spatial distribution of economic activity due to economic phenomena such as technology, external agglomeration effects and transport costs. The third section analyses how European financial transfers influence the convergence process. Finally, a convergence model is presented which aims at answering the question of whether the European financial transfers have helped the southern European regions to catch up with the northern regions. The model is based on the neo-classical convergence theory including a range of variables detected by divergence theory.

## 3.1 Neo-Classical Convergence Theory

### 3.1.1 The Solow Model

The neo-classical theory is based on a set of rigid assumptions. The most important ones are (Bretschger 1996: 46-52; Pintarits 1996: 151):

(1) production technologies are identical and exogenously given across economies;
(2) returns of scale are constant;
(3) production factors are substitutes.

Based on those assumptions, the neo-classical convergence mechanism was first formalised by Solow.[29] His analysis builds on the following Cobb-Douglas production function:

$$y_t = A_t K_t^{\alpha} L_t^{1-\alpha} \qquad \text{with } 0 < \alpha < 1 \qquad (1)$$

The notation is standard: $y$ is output, $K$ capital, $L$ labour and $A$ is the level of technology used in the economy. The neo-classical theory assumes that technology spreads rapidly and can therefore be regarded as identical in all regions (assumption 1). Changes in the technology variable are exogenously determined (Quah 1993: 426).

---

[29] For mathematical details of the Solow model see Appendix A.2.

Assumption (2), constant returns of scale, means that a doubling of both production factors together exactly doubles the output. Individually, however, the production factors yield decreasing returns of scale (Mankiw, Romer and Weil 1992: 409f). In other words, the more that one production factor is used as input while keeping the other constant, the lower is the marginal return from this increase.

The assumptions in the Solow model lead to the conclusion that there is an optimal ratio – an equilibrium – between capital and labour, the so-called steady-state (denoted as k*; Schmidt 1997: 7-11). Once the steady-state is reached, per capita growth is only possible by technological progress, assumed to be exogenous to the economy. The identity of k and k*, however, is assumed to be the exception rather than the rule. Whenever locations are imperfectly integrated, spatial differences in relative factor endowments are likely to exist which explains spatial disparities in wages and unemployment (Bretschger 1995: 26-33). If, for example, an economy uses a production technology which requires relatively more capital than the economy has at its disposal, production cannot be efficient because labour has to act as an imperfect substitute for capital (assumption 3). The relative scarcity or abundance of capital are a strong incentive to adjust the capital stock until k equals the technologically determined optimal level of k* (Jones 1998: 28f). Nevertheless, changes in the saving rate or the growth rate of the workforce take time. Alternative and faster adjustment mechanisms are factor movements, since goods and services can be regarded as transformed factors of production, or movements of goods between regions (Martin, Reiner 1998: 20). The longevity of the convergence process of an economy from k to k* means that the interesting aspect of the neo-classical convergence model lies in the dynamic towards the long-term steady-state (and not in the steady-state itself!).

### 3.1.2    Absolute and Conditional β-Convergence

Provided that the existing adjustment mechanisms are sufficient and production technologies identical, neo-classical growth theory predicts convergence of factor incomes. The neo-classical convergence hypothesis is based on the following argument. If several economies differ only in stock of capital per effective unit of labour ($k$), poor economies with small capital intensity will grow faster than rich economies until each economy has reached the (same) steady-state $k*$ (Schmidt 1997: 12). During this transitional process, there is a "catching-up" of the less developed economies. This catching-up of economies among each other is known as the hypothesis of absolute β-convergence (Barro and Sala-i-Martin 1992: 232; Sala-i-Martin 1994: 741; 1996a: 1021; 1996b: 1326f).[30] Statistically, there is absolute β-

---

[30]    In fact, the neo-classical convergence model implies another type of convergence: the convergence of economies towards the steady-state. However, absolute convergence is defined usually as the catching-up of poorer economies.

convergence in a cross-section of economies if we find a negative relationship between the growth rate of income per capita and the initial level of income.

In empirical testing, the hypothesis of absolute β-convergence often does not hold (Grossmann and Helpmann 1994: 27; Mankiw *et al.* 1992: 12f). However, this does not deny the *raison d'être* of neo-classical convergence theory because the model predicts only conditional (and not absolute) convergence (Barro and Sala-i-Martin 1991: 128; Sala-i-Martin 1996b: 1330). Only if we take two identical economies (remember that each economy normally has its own steady-state), then economies converge to a common steady-state. Within the Solow model, there are already three possibilities of making a difference between two economies (capital intensity, labour and the level of technology). For example, a "poor" economy with low capital intensity might have a smaller growth of output than a "rich" economy because the "poor" economy is closer to its steady-state.

Considering the various parameters influencing economic development, we can state the hypothesis of conditional β-convergence, which means that each economy converges to its respective steady-state according to individual parameters. Statistically, we say that a set of economies displays conditional β-convergence if the partial correlation between growth and initial income is negative (Sala-i-Martin 1990: 129; Schmidt 1997: 14f). In other words, if we run a cross-sectional regression of growth on initial income, holding constant a number of additional variables, and we find that the coefficient on initial income is negative, then we say that the economies in the data set display conditional β-convergence. If the coefficient of initial income is negative in an univariate regression, then we say that the data set displays absolute convergence.

To test the hypothesis of conditional convergence one has to, somehow, hold constant the steady-state of each economy. There are two different ways of holding constant the steady-state (Sala-i-Martin 1996b: 1027; Schmidt 1997: 13, 164-171). The first is to restrict the convergence study to sets of economies for which the assumptions of similar steady-states is not unrealistic. For example, because we think that the technology level, institutions and tastes of most African economies are very different from those of Europe and Japan, the assumption that these economies converge to a common steady-state is not realistic. The geographical, technological and institutional differences across the southern European economies, however, are probably smaller. The second way to hold the steady-state constant is to introduce variables which stand proxy for the steady-state of an economy in a regression analysis. The problem, thus, is to find variables which stand proxy for the steady-state.

### 3.1.3    Adjustment Mechanisms and Factor Price Equalisation

The role of government in neo-classical convergence theory is limited. The most important task of the state is the creation of a "market-friendly" economic environment which is of crucial importance for adjustment mechanisms to work properly (Frenkel 1989: 242). In the following the economic integration affects of these adjustment mechanisms will be analysed.

Imagine a model world with two locations, two goods and two production factors (capital and labour). Location 1 (the core, C) is relatively well endowed with capital ($k_t^c > k*$) and location 2 (the periphery, P) is relatively well endowed with labour ($k_t^p < k*$). If the core specialises in the good that is most efficiently produced by making relatively intensive use of capital whereas the periphery produces the labour-intensive good, the two locations can trade their products until the product mix best suits their local needs (Armstrong 1997: 32). Reasoning along these lines serves as the basis of the Heckscher-Ohlin-Samuelson model of international trade. Locations specialise in the production and export of the good, which requires relatively intensive use of the location's relatively abundant factor of production (Heckscher-Ohlin-Samuelson theorem; Molle 1990a: 128-136; Pintarits 1996: 150). According to the theory, the remuneration for the factors of production is the same in both locations because the relative scarcity or abundance of the factors is equalised due to trade (factor price equalisation theorem). In practice, however, factor price equalisation is the exception rather than the rule. There are various reasons for the difference between theory and reality (Rossi 1992: 111-136). Firstly, the theory denies the existence of artificial (e.g., regulations) and natural barriers (e.g., language) to trade. Secondly, not all production factors are fully mobile, neither between different economic sectors, nor within regions. Even in the long run, substantial parts of the labour force will not be able to move from, say shipbuilding to software development, and they will not be willing to move from Andalusia to Madrid just to find employment.

It was argued above that trade in goods and services leads to an exchange of production factors between regions. This implies that factor movements can substitute goods movements whenever trade is impossible or too expensive because of high transport and transaction costs (Martin, Reiner 1998: 21). Within the neo-classical theory, it can be demonstrated that inter-regional factor movements also lead to convergence. Imagine again the relatively labour-abundant periphery ($k_t^p < k*$) and the relatively capital-abundant core ($k_t^c > k*$). The initial equilibrium wage in C will be higher than in P. Looking at migration, it can be assumed that people move to two regions where wages are higher as long as the costs of migration are lower than the income difference the migrants can realise. Provided that neither capital movements nor trade between the two locations are possible, immigration from the periphery to the core increases the relative labour supply in the core and decreases it in the periphery. As a result the equilibrium wage level in the core decreases to a new equilibrium wage which is identical in both regions. Since the improved production input factor intensities $k_{t+1}^P$ and $k_{t+1}^C$ are now closer or equal to the optimum capital-labour ratios, production in both regions will become more efficient and output will increase both in the periphery and the core (McDonald and Dearden 1992: 101).

Within the EU, however, the level of interregional factor mobility across borders is limited. Each year only 0,5 per cent of the EU population moves from one country to another, mainly because of substantial costs of migration such as language problems and social hardships that arise from settling in an unfamiliar cultural surrounding or the separation of families (Martin, Reiner 1998: 23). Quite often these costs outweigh the potential benefits from moving to a different location. As far as capital mobility is concerned, one has to distinguish between financial and physical capital mobility. It is mainly the physical capital mobility, e.g. foreign direct investments (FDI), that can contribute to factor price equalisation across locations (Blomström and Kokko 1997: 32). Economic integration theory predicts an increase of such flows and empirical research on intra-European FDI flows shows indeed evidence for an upward trend in capital mobility between different parts of the Union. Moreover, the southern member states are net recipients of FDI whereas Germany and the UK are net investors (Europäische Kommission 1994b: 88). This suggests that the ratio between capital and labour within the EU will become more equal over time although the mobility of physical capital is still quite limited.

## 3.2 Divergence Theory

New approaches of economic theory relax the rigid assumptions of neo-classical theory. In the following, some of the concepts used to explain a divergent economic development between different locations are reviewed in order to identify variables that stand proxy for different steady-states.[31] On the basis of these concepts, those forms of governmental intervention are analysed that might invoke an alteration in the spatial distribution of economic activity.

### 3.2.1 Technological Differences between Locations

A first strand of divergence theory is based on the argument that technological progress does not spread evenly across locations which leads to spatial inequalities of the level of technological development (Guerrero and Seró 1997: 381). It can, for example, be assumed that factor productivity in the core (C) is absolutely superior to factor productivity in the periphery (P), which implies that any given combination of

---

[31]  Some of the divergence concepts use similar variables but follow different arguments. In general, the search for controlling variables was based on the EU regions with the poorest data availability. In the case of the southern European regions, this meant limitations for the specification of the model. In practice, the search for variables influencing convergence was guided largely by pragmatic thoughts of data availability.

input factors will produce a higher output in C than in P. The production factors in C are therefore better paid and as long as the factor proportions do not become too unfavourable in C, it is beneficial for both production factors to emigrate to the core. Whereas in the neo-classical theory factor mobility equalised factor returns it now becomes a source of divergence. Assuming that capital and labour are fully mobile the periphery faces a total outflow of production factors in the long run unless immobile, location-specific factors are taken into account. Once the mobile factors of capital and (mobile) labour have become sufficiently scarce in P, wages and capital returns will equalise across both locations. The return for immobile factors in the core, however, will be higher than the return for immobile factors in the periphery (Rossi 1995: 47).

Not only factor movements but also trade between locations can be a source of divergence if we allow for technological differences. Imagine again regions C and P producing two different goods with two factors of production. There is not only inter-regional trade but also inter-regional factor mobility. C has a technological advantage over P in the production of a specific good and will export it to P. The rate of return for the factor used relatively intensively in the production of this good will be higher in C than in P, which causes factors used relatively intensively in the production of the traded good to move from P to C. Trade thus creates a previously absent factor endowment difference which further amplifies the trade flow (Martin, Reiner 1998: 25).

Although this is a simplified model, it has real life relevance to it. Imagine, for example, capital being removed from peripheral parts of an integration area in order to be invested in more central locations where industries have acquired superior production skills. Immobile factors are left behind and the ratio between mobile and immobile factors in the periphery becomes more and more unfavourable. This means that factor prices in the periphery, at least for immobile factors, will be significantly below those in the core which works against cohesion (Armstrong 1997: 33f). The implications for European regional policy are obvious. It is important to close technological gaps by improving the endogenous technological potential of disadvantaged regions. This should prevent disruptive outflows of mobile production factors from technologically disadvantaged regions (Guerrero and Seró 1997: 382; Verspagen 1994: 158-160).

The "technology-gap perspective" is in fact an application of the Schumpeterian thinking which takes into account the following factors: the impact of differences in innovative efforts across regions, the potential for imitation and the capacity to exploit advances in technology, whether developed indigenously or elsewhere in the world (Fagerberg and Verspagen 1996: 438). The opportunity of lagging economies is seen in the cheap imitation and free spillovers of already existing technologies, because the costs and losses of testing and developing new products and processes can be avoided by the imitators. Assuming that European regional policy devotes its resources to raise a region's capacity to exploit technology spillovers, the technology gap is supposed to lead to a catching-up of the poorer economies (Rossi 1995: 48).

## 3.2.2    External Effects of Agglomerations

This section drops the neo-classical assumption of constant returns of scale. Proponents of external agglomeration effects argue that firms benefit from other firms' positive external effects (spillovers) when there is a certain concentration of economic activity (Bretschger 1995: 85). There are three categories of positive externalities (Schmidt 1997: 126). Firstly, there exist advantages owing to a concentrated labour market with skilled labour forces that tend to be more economically active, better educated, and younger than those in the periphery. Secondly, sector specific inputs for production, and a large range of business facilities are available such as road, rail and telecommunications systems. And thirdly, there are technological spillovers owing to the proximity of knowledge. However, to view cumulative growth effects of European agglomeration as potentially explosive is too extreme since agglomeration has also negative external effects, e.g., the congestion of urban areas, the overuse of transport facilities and the rise in factor prices (labour, land-prices, etc.; Schmidt 1997: 128).

In order to understand agglomeration effects, one can imagine a model with two regions, core (C) and periphery (P), which are identical in everything but their size. Because of this difference, the marginal return and compensation of input factors in the bigger region C is higher than in P. If capital and labour can move from the periphery to the core, the size of C and hence its productivity advantage will increase even further along with the wage and interest rate gap between P and C. This process stops when the scarcity of location-specific factors A and corresponding redistribution effects eventually decrease the periphery-core differences in mobile factors' return to such an extent that this difference is no longer a sufficient incentive for mobile factors to move to C (Martin, Reiner 1998: 27). The predictions of this model are therefore quite similar to the situation where we assumed the technological differences between core and periphery. External agglomeration effects will have a negative effect on cohesion.

Which policy recommendations can be derived from the existence of external effects? In a situation where social factor returns do not equal private returns public interventions might be required to maximise collective welfare. If positive effects dominate, the public intervention should in principle try to promote these activities leading to positive externalities which in turn might result in aggregate welfare gains. From a regional policy point of view, however, things look different. External effects are likely to increase the dichotomy between core and periphery. Public policies designed to reduce spatial imbalances should therefore try to compensate for the relative disadvantages that peripheral regions face owing to positive external effects in the core.

### 3.2.3    New Growth Theory and Endogenous Technological Progress

The term "new growth theory" refers to a group of approaches that tries to overcome the shortcomings of the neo-classical assumptions. Solow's theory explains the transition to a long run steady-state, but the long-run steady-state growth itself is exogenous in the theory. New growth theories try to endogenise technology. In these models the stock of capital and, in extensions, the stock of human capital becomes a crucial factor for the growth performance, which also alters the likely impact of economic integration on growth (Bretschger 1996a: 7-9). Neo-classical economists argue that economic integration mainly results in a one-off optimisation of the inter-regional allocation of resources without a lasting change in the pre-integration growth path. New growth theorists, however, argue that integration leads to an increase of the available capital stock, increased social returns to capital and hence a permanent increase in the growth rate (Bretschger 1996b: 300-303). New growth theory also assumes that technological progress depends crucially on human capital. This is important because differences in the accumulation of human capital can explain persistent differences in the growth paths of locations.

The details of these mechanisms are complex and whether or not growth in an integrated economy of several regions actually diverges depends on the assumptions of factor mobility and knowledge diffusion. Provided that positive external effects of human capital and capital on factor productivity exist agglomerations are likely to develop (Martin, Reiner 1998: 28). This, however, means that regional growth paths can permanently diverge depending on whether a region was lucky enough to have a headstart in the race for human capital or production clusters. Only these regions will be able to develop a dynamic comparative advantage in high-tech, high-value-added goods. If the effect of knowledge accumulation on growth is purely global, each new idea has the same effect on aggregate output at each location. Convergence is then obtained with the mechanism generating convergence being the same as in Solow's model (Bröcker 1995: 23).

New growth theory points to the same forms of regional policy interventions as the exogenously determined "technological gap perspective" mentioned above. Public policy interventions can target the technological potential of problem regions, e.g., by improving technology transfers from more advanced to lagging regions or by investing in better education. As a matter of fact, these two approaches are the cornerstones of European regional policy (*Inforegio Newsletter* 1999: 61).

### 3.2.4    New Location Theory

Location theory classically stressed the importance of transport costs for the location of economic activity. As far as more recent contributions to location theory or "economic geography" are concerned, Krugman (1991a: 96f; 1991b: 484-486; 1995: 90f) presents a model with one large and one small region and an industrial sector characterised by increasing returns of scale. He finds that agglomerations emerge from the interaction between increasing returns at the level of the individual production, facility transportation costs and factor mobility. It is advantageous to concentrate the production of each good at a few locations because of increasing returns. Because of transportation costs, the best locations are those with good access to markets (backward linkage) and suppliers (forward linkage). Access to markets and suppliers will be best precisely at those points at which producers have concentrated, and hence drawn mobile factors of production to their vicinity. However, not all factors are mobile and the presence of immobile factors provides the centrifugal force that works against agglomeration, e.g. there is the incentive to set up new production facilities in the periphery to serve a dispersed agricultural hinterland.

Empirical investigation of the relative importance of different factors for locational decisions are frequently based on business surveys (European Commission 1990b: 9). As it turns out, the factor quoted most frequently – proximity to markets – cannot be influenced by public policies. Nearly all the other determinants, such as the endowment with infrastructure and financial assistance, can be influenced by public policies although for most of them not in the short run. This in turn opens up the debate on locational competition and attempts by the state to influence the spatial pattern of economic activity.

### 3.2.5    Locational Competition and Governmental Intervention

Kotler (1994: 13) defines locational competition as the competition among immobile factors of production for mobile factors, mainly capital. It is useful to look at indicators of competitiveness in order to find out how attractive locations are for mobile factors of production. The European Commission (1990b: 28) points out that the key issues of locations are the ability to provide the conditions for private enterprises to be competitive and the flexibility with which regions deal with the continuous changes taking place at the micro-level. This, in turn, depends heavily on the effectiveness and adaptability of their institutions (Martin, Reiner 1998: 30; see also Chapter 6.1.2).

What can regions do to influence their relative competitiveness? Most economists argue in favour of pro-market interventions with deregulation being the most preferable kind of intervention (Frey and Kirchgässner 1994: 139). They work in tandem with the market and are cost-neutral. It is easy to imagine examples of over-regulation, which can have detrimental effects on the economic situation in particular locations. The introduction of European statutory minimum wages that are out of line with productivity levels in lagging regions, for instance, would drive peripheral industries out of the market (Martin, Reiner 1998: 31). Nevertheless, the discussion about the spatial effects of economic integration have shown that over-regulation cannot be made solely responsible for regional differences in economic performance and income levels (see Chapter 2.1.2). The option for other cost-free pro-market measures is limited. Governments can also try to improve the general business climate in their location. This, however, is a vague concept with limited applicability because of the importance of long-standing traditions (North 1994: 15; Putnam 1993: 184).

What are the costly pro-market interventions that public authorities can pursue in order to improve the competitiveness of their location? First of all, they can try to improve the physical infrastructure. Secondly, they can try to enhance the quality of the regional workforce and the region's overall human capital endowment. The rationales for these measures have been implicitly provided above. Improvements in physical infrastructure reduce transport costs, which can be a disadvantage for enterprises, especially in peripheral locations. Investments in human capital not only help in the short run, but also lead to positive external effects which in turn might have a beneficial effect on the endogenous growth performance of a region.

### 3.2.6    Sectoral Structure

This section looks at the sectoral structure of regional economies, which can be taken as an indicator for differences in economic development and competitiveness. It is usually differed between three sectors: agriculture (primary sector), industry (secondary sector) and services (tertiary sector). The argumentation of the effects of sectoral structure rests on the assumption that the prospects for productivity growth are better in "modern" sectors than in "traditional" sectors (Verspagen and Fagerberg 1996: 438). In peripheral areas agricultural activity is predominant and as it is normally capital extensive it constitutes a low value-added activity (Molle *et al.* 1980: 123). Unlike agriculture a relatively high share of the industrial and service sector can be interpreted as an indicator for a more advanced, diversified and dynamic regional economy (Schmidt 1997: 127), for industry and services have been the most expansive of the three basic economic sectors during the last decade. The growing number of jobs in services has not only absorbed the relative decline of employment in the southern European agriculture and industry, but it has even created net gains in employment (European Commission 1994c: 73). One would therefore expect a positive link between the size of the industry/service sector and cohesion. Convergence of productivity will be the result, as poor economies put relatively more resources in sectors with a higher productivity than developed economies (Schmidt 1997: 128).

## 3.3    *Structural Transfers and Convergence*

Economic integration does not guarantee an equal distribution of welfare gains as was elaborated earlier (see Chapter 2.2). The argument for European regional policy can thus be built on four rationales: equity, efficiency, adjustment costs and external effects. According to the cohesion goal and the concentration principle of European regional policy, poor economies should receive structural transfers which help them to catch-up with the developed ones.

**Figure 3-1: Economic Development and the Role of Compensation**

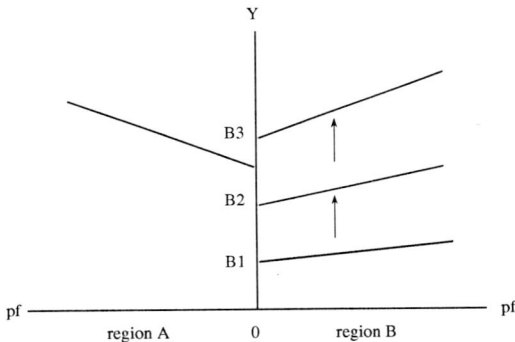

*Source: Molle 1990a: 164.*

Molle (1990a: 163-165) presents a graphical illustration of financial compensation raising the level of productivity in less developed regions (see Figure 3-1). Suppose income growth (*Y*) is determined completely by increases in the production factor availability and productivity, together called *pf*. Suppose further that region B is not only a slow-growth (*$OB_1$*) but also a low-level-income region, while region A is a fast-growth (*0A*), but also a high-level-income region. To make income levels converge, the curve of region B has to move upwards, with the intercept moving from point *$OB_1$* through *$OB_2$* to *$OB_3$*, beyond point *0A*, equalling the structural growth in region A. This can be reached only through financial transfers, raising the level of income and improving the capacity of production factors in region B.

The following hypothesis can thus be stated. Financial transfers have a positive influence on economic development and, in the case where poor regions are supported, cohesion will be achieved. If we find a significant positive relation between European financial transfers and convergence we can, thus, say that the regional policy is successful. According to divergence theories development assistance should be invested in projects that improve the physical infrastructure, promote technology transfer and develop human capital.

## *3.4 Synopsis*

A summary of the foregoing review of economic theories that bear on the convergence versus divergence debate leaves one with predictions that are diametrically opposed to each other. According to the neo-classical school of economic thinking, economic integration is not only likely to increase the aggregate welfare of the participating locations, but it also leads to an equalisation of factor returns within the integration area provided there are sufficiently strong adjustment mechanisms (namely goods or factor movements) among the integrated locations. The neo-classical theory allowed us to derive two convergence hypotheses: absolute and conditional β-convergence, of which the latter rectifies for individual steady-states of different economies. The search for variables influencing convergence was guided both by pragmatic thoughts of data availability and different divergence theories. Divergence approaches predict an increasingly uneven spatial distribution of economic activity due to economic phenomena such as technology, external agglomeration effects and transport costs. According to divergence theory, regional policy efforts should point to investments in human capital, either in the form of general education or support for R&D. The divergence theory also stresses the importance of transport costs for economic activity. The overlap between geographical peripherality and below average income within the EU supports this point of view and stresses the importance of investments in infrastructure. The above-stated hypotheses are summarised in Figure 3-2.

**Figure 3-2: Model of Hypotheses**

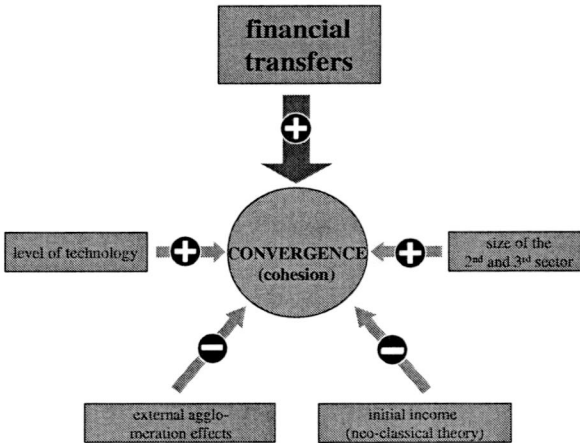

*Source: own figure.*

# 4 METHODOLOGICAL ASPECTS OF THE CONVERGENCE MODEL

In the preceding chapter, a convergence model was developed that allows us to measure the impact of European structural transfers. The following section will now elaborate the technical and methodological aspects of this model. In the first section, I discuss the advantages and disadvantages of the macro-quantitative research strategy. Secondly, I present empirical convergence concepts, which help to analyse the general cohesion pattern in southern Europe. I focus, on the one hand, on those empirical concepts that can be derived from the neo-classical convergence theory, that is absolute β-convergence and conditional β-convergence. On the other hand, I present σ-convergence. Finally, pooling of data and estimators, indicators and research units are discussed. This includes data reliability and validity.

## 4.1 Strengths and Weaknesses of Quantitative Analysis

Quantitatively oriented social scientists seek to understand probabilistic relationships between variables by conceptualising, measuring and analysing information about the real world by means of numerical data. The strength of quantitative analysis is the fact that it is incapacitated by a large number of cases and therefore invites a generalisation of results in other areas (Ragin 1989: 69). Data is analysed by statistical procedures to compare a large number of cross-sectional or longitudinal observations with the aim of identifying potentially strong, non-random correlations between independent variables (IV) and dependent variables (DV) (Mitchell and Bernauer 1997: 2). In the case of 40 southern European regions a quantitative research strategy is adapted for assessing probabilistic relationships between cohesion and European financial transfers.

There are two main weaknesses of quantitative research strategy. On the one hand, there is its tendency towards abstract, and sometimes vacuous, generalisations (Lijphart 1971: 683f). On the other hand, it has problems in determining causality, which is essential in capturing the structures that generate convergence and economic development. For quantitative explanations do not seek to identify the mechanisms through which specified outcomes occur, when they do (Molle 1988: 16). Rather they seek to locate the conditions under which specified outcomes will occur (Dessler 1991: 342).[32] Lastly, econometric estimations are sometimes constrained by data availability which is likely to occur in the case of southern European regions (European Commission 1998: 101). The methodological design of this study aims to overcome

---

[32] Quantitative research can gain causal explanation from theoretical reasoning. However, it hardly ever empirically tests those mechanisms.

the first two problems by combining quantitative and qualitative research strategy. Data availability, on the contrary, can be influenced only to a limited degree.

## *4.2   Empirical Convergence Concepts*

### 4.2.1   Absolute and Conditional β-Convergence

As noted above (see Chapter 3.1.2), there is *absolute β-convergence* in a cross-section of economies if we find a negative relation between the economic growth rate of income per capita and the initial level of per capita income. The regression equation is[33]

$$log\,(y_{i,t+T}\,/\,y_{i,t})\,/\,T = \alpha - \beta\,log\,y_{i,t} + \varepsilon_{i,t+T}. \qquad (2)$$

A set of economies displays *conditional β-convergence* if the partial correlation between economic growth and initial income is negative. In other words, if we run a cross-sectional regression of growth on initial income, holding constant a number of additional variables, and we find that the coefficient of initial income is negative, then we say that the economies in the data set display conditional β-convergence.[34] In this case the regression equation is, with $X$ replacing additional variables

$$log\,(y_{i,t+T}\,/\,y_{i,t})\,/\,T \qquad\qquad\qquad\qquad (3)$$

$$= \alpha - \beta\,log\,y_{i,t} + \psi X_{(i,t+T)} + \varepsilon_{i,t+T}.$$

Both absolute and conditional β-convergence analyse whether, on the one hand, economies converge towards their own steady-states and, on the other hand, whether there is convergence among the sample in the sense that the poorer economies grow faster than the richer ones.

An interesting alternative of equation (3) is the analysis of a single economy in relation to the European average. The regression equation is

---

[33]  The notation is standard: $y_{i,t}$ is the per capita output of economy $i$ at $t$, and $T$ is the number of years observed. As one can see the growth of output in equation (2) is written in logarithms which results in the hypothesis of relative convergence of the productivity levels. A very strong form of convergence is postulated by using absolute numbers, that is convergence of real productivity levels. Convergence of real (per capita) income would mean that poor economies register bigger increases of income (expressed in output or currency units!) than rich ones. The following example shows the effect of using log instead of absolute figures. Doubling the output per capita in a rich region (e.g. from Euro 50'000 to Euro 100'000 p.a.) and trebling the output per capita in a poor region (from Euro 20'000 to 60'000) shows convergence (in log) although the absolute distance between those two regions (from Euro 30'000 to 40'000) has increased. The variance of the log income per capita would have decreased because the poor region grew faster than the rich one.

[34]  Another way of holding constant the steady-state is to restrict the convergence study to sets of economies for which the assumptions of similar steady-states is not unrealistic.

$$log \ (y_{i,t+T} / y_{i,t}) / T - log \ ( \ \bar{y}_{t+T} / \ \bar{y}_t ) / T \qquad (4)$$

$$= \alpha - \beta \ (log \ y_{i,t} - log \ \bar{y}_t) + \psi (X_{i,t+T} / \bar{X}_{t+T}) + \varepsilon_{i,t+T} \ .$$

In this case we test the hypothesis if southern European economies converge towards the European average which is interesting from a political point of view. Compared to the concepts of absolute and conditional β-convergence which predict the narrowing of disparities, the test allows us to analyse the convergence process to a politically accepted reference point. The reason for choosing the European per capita average is on the one hand that weighting and country-specific issues matter less in this case. Furthermore, the European average per capita income is a politically accepted point of reference.

### 4.2.2   Critique of β-Convergence

Although absolute and conditional β-convergence are two established concepts of convergence, there is a three-fold criticism of them. First of all, critics doubt the *robustness* of the results of existing studies of conditional β-convergence. The most important contribution to this problem comes from Levine and Renelt (1992: 942) who found all fifty variables (in order to correct for different steady-states) included in Barro and Sala-i-Martin's study (1991) as non-significant.[35] They identify only two positive, robust correlations between growth and the share of international trade to GDP and growth and gross fixed capital. Some researchers interpret this result to mean that one should not pay much attention to cross-sectional growth and disparity analysis since any variable can be made to look significant if looked at hard enough.

However, there is a different reading of Levine and Renelt. If one keeps trying combinations of explanatory variables, one is destined to find a set that will change the sign on the coefficient. This suggests, firstly, that the extreme-bounds test may be too strong. Secondly, and perhaps more important, Levine and Renelt always find some group of policy variables that matter. The problem is that since policies are so highly correlated with each other, the data cannot always tell them apart (Sala-i-Martin 1994: 742). For example, countries with high inflation rates tend also to have very distorted trade regimes and repressed financial sectors. They are also countries that tend to be politically and socially unstable. None of the variables is a perfect measure of the

---

[35]   Levine and Renelt use a variant of Edward E. Leamer's extreme-bounds test which can be described as follows:

$$\gamma_{i,t, \ t-T} = \beta_x X_{i,t-T} + \beta_m M_{i,t-T} + \beta_z Z_{i,t-T} + \varepsilon_{i,t},$$

where $\gamma_{i,t, \ t-T}$ is again the growth rate, $X$ is a set of base variables always included in the regression, $M$ is the policy variable of interest, and $Z$ is the set of up to three additional variables. The extreme-bounds test involves changing variables until one finds a set of $Z$ for which the coefficient $\beta_m$ changes sign or becomes insignificant. When this happens, the variable M is labelled "fragile"; otherwise it is "robust".

phenomenon that matters: a government in disarray affects the nation's growth adversely. Hence, the main message from the Levine and Renelt study is not that nothing matters but that policy matters. The data, however, cannot really tell exactly which policy is good or bad.

Secondly, there is methodological criticism of *interpreting the coefficients,* which cannot be viewed as structural parameters. They do not say how much growth is changing (e.g., if policies are changing) because the coefficients do not refer to a single economy but to the average of economies. This is true in theory, though the coefficients can give at least an idea of which policy measures support convergence (Schmidt 1997: 160f).

Thirdly, there is a serious problem of systematic shift towards convergence due to *measurement errors* (Quah 1993: 427). This can happen because data of earlier growth phases is less accurate and less complete. Economies that are already relatively highly developed are less vulnerable to this problem. Exogenous shocks (e.g., shock of terms of trade, war, etc.) or extreme points of the business cycle at the beginning or the end of the observed period are also a cause of distortions. However, there are ways to cope with these distortions. On the one hand, the beginning and the end of a period can be computed from the average of different periods. On the other hand, pooling of data allows us to use the mean of an indicator for a period of time. Pooling also brings about more cases for the same unit. The latter method will be applied in this analysis.

### 4.2.3   σ-Convergence

The concept of β-convergence (absolute and conditional) is often confused with an alternative definition of convergence where the dispersion of real per capita income across groups of economies tends to decrease over time. If the standard deviation of the GDP growth of the observed regions tends to fall over time, we talk about σ-convergence.

This is a strong form of convergence for it means the catching-up of poorer economies in terms of currency units. A less rigorous form of convergence is the use of the standard deviation of logarithmic figures, or to normalise the standard deviation of the sample with the arithmetic mean (= variation coefficient *VC*). Both methods result in relative convergence and are in practice very similar (Schmidt 1997: 136).[36] The standard deviation of log $y$ is

$$\sigma_t = \quad 1/n \; \Sigma (log \; y_{i,t} - log \; \bar{y}_t)^2 \; , \qquad\qquad (5)$$

where log $y_t$ is the arithmetic mean of all log $y_{i,t}$. The definition of σ-convergence is:

---

[36]   In my empirical analysis, the standard deviation is computed with log figures.

$$d\sigma_t / dt < 0 \qquad (6)$$

The variance coefficient (*VC*) is

$$VC_t = \quad 1/n \, \Sigma (y_{i,t} - \bar{y}_t)^2 / \bar{y}_t \qquad (7)$$

Here again, we talk about σ-convergence if

$$dVC_t / dt < 0 \qquad (8)$$

## 4.2.4　σ-Convergence versus β-Convergence

Although the concepts of σ and β-convergence are different, they are related to each other. In fact, the existence of β-convergence is a necessary condition for the existence of σ-convergence (Sala-i-Martin 1996b: 1329).[37] It is natural to think that when an initially poor economy grows faster than a rich one, then the levels of GDP per capita of the two economies will become more similar over time. In other words, the existence of β-convergence will tend to generate σ-convergence.

Figure 4-1a is an example where β-convergence exists and is associated with σ-convergence. Figure 4-1b provides an example where the lack of β-convergence (the initially rich economy grows faster) is associated with the lack of σ-convergence (the distance between the economies increases over time).

Hence, it would appear that the two concepts are identical. However, at least theoretically, it is possible for initially poor economies to grow faster than initially rich ones, without observing that the cross-sectional dispersions fall over time. We could find β-convergence without finding σ-convergence. This is the situation in Figure 4-1c. The figures illustrate that the two concepts both examine interesting phenomena, which are conceptually different. In summary, β-convergence studies how the

---

[37]　Quah (1993: 429) criticises the concept of β-convergence and finds it irrelevant. According to him, the only thing of interest is whether the distribution of income becomes equitable over time. The following illustrating example shall underline the importance of β-convergence: Consider the ordinal rankings of the World Cup over time. The dispersion of rankings is constant by definition. Sports analysts, soccer fanatics and national presidents are interested in questions such as "how quickly the great teams revert to mediocrity" and "how long do dynasties of national soccer teams last". For example how long did it take for the great Uruguayan team of the 1950s and 1960s to become an average team? How long will it take for the Swiss national team to be promoted again to the World Cup?
We could ask what the mechanisms are that allow for this outcome (for instance, in Switzerland the salary of the national coach is less than that of a Nationalliga coach and the soccer soul of a Swiss man never gets as hot as that of an Uruguayan. Once we identify these mechanisms, one can think about ways to increase the competitiveness of the Swiss national team. All of these examples refer to β-convergence, not to σ-convergence. In fact, reducing the cross-sectional variance in the World Cup would probably not make any sense. Consider how interesting the World Cup would be if all teams tied for first place every four years! (Idea from Sala-i-Martin 1996b: 1327).

distribution of income evolves over time and σ-convergence analyses the mobility of income within the same distribution (Sala-i-Martin 1996a: 1022).

**Figure 4-1: The Relation Between σ- and β-Convergence**

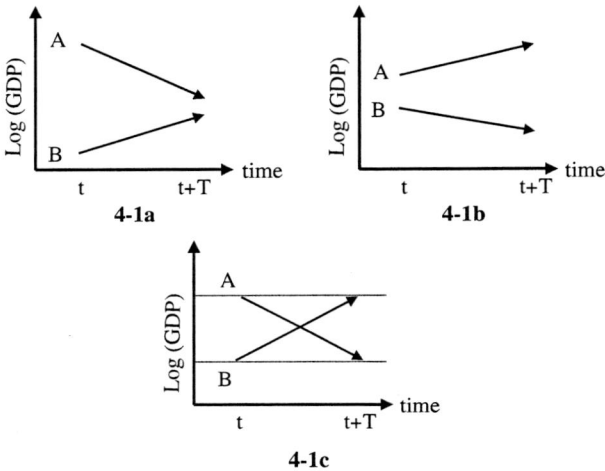

4-1a                                        4-1b

4-1c

*Source: Sala-i-Martin (1996a: 1021).*

## 4.3     Method

### 4.3.1     Pooling of Data

A lot of empirical studies work with simple cross-sectional data. This method assumes the exclusion of permanent differences of the production function (Sayrs 1989: 24f). However, this assumption is not realistic since there are specific regional factors that influence economic growth (e.g. climate, topography, etc.). The use of panel analysis (instead of pure cross-sectional analysis) enables a more accurate and more consistent study of convergence. Panel analysis has different positive aspects. The main advantage of combining cross-sections and time series is to capture variation across different units in space (Markus 1979: 5) as well as variation that emerges over time (Sayrs 1989: 7).[38] Another advantage of panel analysis are the additional degrees of freedom which allows one to take account of more exogenous variables (Berry and Feldmann 1997: 11).

---

[38]   This sort of time series analysis is different from (traditional) stochastic times series techniques such as ARIMA and others. Due to non-availability of long-term statistics, ARIMA is not applicable with the existing data set.

A panel can be generated by pooling data, that divides the entire (observed) period into shorter sub-periods (Bohley 1992: 516). The shortest possible time span between two sub-periods would be one year (because European regional data is collected each year). However, this pooling approach would be of little help in determining the long-term effects of underlying factors on convergence because short-term effects (e.g., extremes of business cycles) would be given too much attention. The economic literature suggests intervals of at least three to seven years, which reduces the influence of cyclical effects (Schmidt 1997: 166). This analysis uses three- and four-year pooling intervals.

## 4.3.2 Estimators

Ordinary least square (OLS) models – the most often used model for the analysis of pooled data – are a natural starting point in a review of estimators for panel designs. For OLS to be the optimal estimator, it is necessary to assume that all error processes have the same variance (homoscedasticity) and that all error processes are independent of each other. The latter assumption can be broken down into the assumption that errors for one unit are unrelated to errors for that unit at all other times (no serial auto-correlation) and that the errors for one unit are unrelated to the errors for every other unit (no spatial auto-correlation). Under these assumptions panel designs should be estimated by OLS (Pindyck and Rubinfeld 1997: 147).[39]

Some analysts are not willing to accept these assumptions as two particular violations are likely to accompany stacked pooled data (Beck and Katz 1995: 636; Stimson 1985: 919f). Firstly, a particular form of heteroscedasticity is inherent in pooled data. Some units are inherently more variable than others at all times. Such differential variability is usually of modest concern in unpooled data because it affects only a single case at a time. In pooled data it is likely to affect whole sets (e.g., all years for one region) and form a potential for mischief. The cases, secondly, are not independent along the time dimension within units. We expect serial auto-correlation in such data. In the case of cross-sectional dominance $n > t$ (as it is the case in this study) the least square with dummy variables (LSDV) method would be an accurate estimator for panel analysis

---

[39] According to Beck and Katz (1995: 646) the various panel errors assumptions can be stated symbolically as:

*Panel heteroscedasticity:* $E(\varepsilon^2_{i,t}) \neq E(\varepsilon^2_{j,t})$, but $E(\varepsilon^2_{i,t}) = E(\varepsilon^2_{j,t'})$, so one can write $E(\varepsilon^2_{i,t}) \neq \sigma^2$.

*Contemporaneously correlated errors:* $E(\varepsilon_{i,t}\varepsilon_{j,t}) = E(\varepsilon_{i,t'}\varepsilon_{j,t'}) \neq 0$, but $E(\varepsilon_{i,t}\varepsilon_{j,t'}) = 0$, so one can write $E(\varepsilon_{i,t}\varepsilon_{j,t}) = \sigma_{ij}$, with all other covariances being zero.

*Unit-specific serially correlated errors:* $\varepsilon_{i,t} = \rho_i\varepsilon_{i,t,t-1} + v_{i,t}$, where the $v$ are incoming "shocks" that are *temporally* independent, identically distributed, zero-mean random variables.

*Common serially correlated errors:* $\varepsilon_{i,t} = \rho\varepsilon_{i,t,t-1} + v_{i,t}$, where the $v_{i,t}$ are incoming "shocks".

(Sayrs 1989: 26; Schmidt 1997: 172; Stimson 1985: 929).[40] As the number of regions is much bigger than the points of time in my work (n>>t), the degrees of freedom become too small in order to estimate the equation with dummy variables for each region. I therefore compute the regressions with OLS. I vary the starting points[41] of the intervals in order to test the robustness of the model against serial auto-correlation. I also execute a hard test by adding the dependent variable with a negative time lag of one period (t-1) as an independent variable. The cases where heteroscedasticity could be a problem are mentioned in the text.

## 4.4 Unit of Observation, Data and Indicators

### 4.4.1 The Region as Unit of Observation

The unit of observation is defined according to the official European NUTS classification (Nomenclature of Units for Territorial Statistics). The NUTS regions which provide the spatial basis of European regional and competition policy are defined on three levels: NUTS 1 regions, NUTS 2 regions and NUTS 3 regions. The national level is sometimes called NUTS 0 (Eurostat 1996b: X). The link between the NUTS regions of southern European member states and national spatial entities are shown in Table 4-1.

**Table 4-1: Nomenclature of Units for Territorial Statistics (NUTS)**

| Country | NUTS 1 | NUTS 2 | NUTS 3 |
|---------|--------|--------|--------|
| Greece | NUTS 2 groupings | Development regions | Nomoi |
| Italy | NUTS 2 groupings | Regioni | Provincie |
| Portugal | NUTS 2 groupings | NUTS 3 groupings | Grouping of concelhos |
| Spain | NUTS 2 groupings | Comunidades | Provincias |

*Source: Eurostat (1996b: X).*

The definition of NUTS regions often reflects certain historical and institutional processes which, although they might have produced some degree of spatial cohesion, do not necessarily accord with what one might view as appropriate for economic scrutiny (McDonald and Dearden 1992: 101). The main problem that goes with this is

---

[40]  The LSDV method allows us to abolish the restriction of having the same estimated parameter for all units. It is, thus, possible to take account of specific (fixed) effects of a single economy with individual parameters. The LSDV model is also called Fixed Effect Model (FEM) because it aims at fixing the covariation. This stands in contrast to the General Least Square method (GLS) that rather assumes the covariation to vary as a random variable (the GLS method is also called Random Effect Model; REM). The REM assumes that individual specific effects are randomly distributed over the sample (that is non-existence of covariation between specific effects and independent variables; Schmidt 1997: 170). For a detailed description and explanation of those methods see Beck and Katz (1995); Berry and Feldman (1985); Pyndick and Rubinfeld (1997); Sayrs (1989); Stimson (1985).

[41]  The models are tested with 7 data sets with different starting points (3 starting points for 4-year averages and 4 starting points for 3-year averages).

the varying sizes of administrative units at different levels. Fortunately, in the case of Greek, Italian, Portuguese and Spanish regions the differences between the biggest and smallest regions (in terms of population and surface) are modest. Except for Greece, the regions of this work belong all to the *NUTS 2 level*.[42] In the case of the Greek regions, I had to merge the 13 existing NUTS 2 regions into the seven administrative regions that are used for the EU structural transfer payments. All together, the sample consists of 40 southern European regions.[43]

## 4.4.2    Data and Indicators

Complete data on financial transfers are available from 1989. They are processed and published by the Directorate General XVI (of the European Commission), which is responsible for the management of structural funds.[44] Data for all other indicators is from the REGIO database, which is collected and processed by Eurostat (the statistical office of the EU). The first fully comparable regional data on major indicators was published in 1971. However, for southern European member states a complete data set is only available from 1982 on. Data of R&D expenses and patent application rates is available since 1985 and 1989 respectively. Precious as these data are for describing the regional situation in southern European member states, these statistics also have deficiencies. A major one is that EU statistics depend entirely on the willingness of national statistical offices to produce the data according to the European standard specifications (Molle *et al.* 1980: 9). This has a negative effect on the reliability of data, which is more serious in the case of the four observed countries than it would be in the case of core European countries because the services of national statistical offices are less developed. This aspect becomes less of a problem with the progress of time and the development of administrative mechanisms directed at greater accuracy (McDonald and Dearden 1992: 102).

The standard indicator of *welfare* and *economic growth* is GDP per capita (Gillis 1992: 79).[45] Inequalities in regional GDP per capita can be measured in two ways (Dunford 1993: 729). Measurement in Euro indicates the international value of the output of regional economies. The money value of regional output shows, first, what the output of the exposed sector can be sold for and can command on the home market. Measurement in purchasing power standards (PPS), which is used in this study, makes

---

[42]   The reason for NUTS 2 regions as units of observation lies in the quality and completeness of available data.

[43]   Appendix A1 lists all regions.

[44]   Appendix A3 gives details on the indicators.

[45]   Some analysts object to using income as the measure of welfare. They focus more on social indicators and basic human needs (such as infant mortality rate, life expectancy, access to health care, etc.). However, even those critics admit that as a rule improvement in social indicators goes hand in hand with a rise in per capita income (Gillis 1992: 80).

allowances for differences in the prices of goods and services in different areas. The quantity of goods and services that a given sum in Euro will exchange for is greater in a low-cost than in a high-cost region.[46] The PPS measure is, in other words, an indication of differences in living standards. There are also some noteworthy deficiencies of the GDP indicator (Pintarits 1996: 120). The income that results from regional production does not necessarily accrue to a region's inhabitants. When the inhabitants of other regions have property rights in a region there is an outflow of income. The same is true when human capital of other regions is used locally. The distribution of original income is also biased by redistributive transfers, that result from government taxation, benefits and social security expenditures. A major problem with GDP figures in southern European countries are the informal and hidden economic activities, which obviously are excluded from official statistical figures.[47] However, there is no data available that corrects this bias. As mentioned above, I use a three-, or respectively four-year average growth rate of regional GDP per capita. All GDP figures are computed at 1995 prices. European average data EU(12) are computed from the sums of national figures in relation to the total European population (respectively total employment for some indicators). Another common indicator of welfare is the unemployment rate. Additional to the GDP indicator unemployment rates often provide important information of possible social tensions. For the analysis a three- (four-) year average is computed.

*Regional policy* is measured by the total flow of financial transfers that is delivered to regions out of the structural funds (ESF, ERDF, EAGGF and FIFG) and the Cohesion Fund. The reader should be aware that other national transfer systems, including direct (through the tax and benefits system or fiscal federalism) and other indirect compensation (which are often used to comply with the European co-financing requirements) are not taken into consideration. These transfers are not taken into consideration in the analysis because there is no such data available for the observed regions.[48] Effective (not committed) payments are used as this study aims at assessing *ex post* the convergence effect of structural investments.[49] Since the Directorate General 16 of the European Commission provides no regional breakdown of financial implementation before 1994, I classed the major projects to regions (where this was

---

[46]   The theory of PPS is based upon the idea that an identical basket of goods and services should cost the same in all regions (Bohley 1992: 21; *The Economist*, January 3rd 1998: 98).

[47]   There are only "guestimates" on the extent of hidden economic activities in southern Europe. According to those figures, the hidden economic activity is estimated at between 10 and 25 per cent of the GDP with southern Italy as the worst case (European Parliament 1993: 25f; *Neue Zürcher Zeitung*, 69/1999: 83).

[48]   This is not too big a disadvantage in the case of southern Europe because European transfers are more important in terms of volume than other indirect national compensation schemes (European Commission 1998: XV).

[49]   Due to technical problems which caused time lags in the beginning of the programmes, there is a substantial difference between effective and planned payments.

possible). The rest of the structural transfers was divided equally among the regions.[50] The effects of specific investment categories, such as physical infrastructure or R&D, are not traceable because of a lack of data on the regional level.

Patent applications and R&D expenditures stand for the *technology* factor. These two measures are commonly accepted as indicators of innovative activity (Guerrero and Seró 1996: 382; Verspagen 1996: 438). Patent applications are studied as a reflection of the production of innovation.[51] A basic assumption is that a patent will have its economic effects in the region where the application was made. In spite of the usefulness of those indicators, the reader should be warned that patents and R&D expenditures have certain shortcomings. The problem is that all innovations are not necessarily patented and there is a difference between process and production innovation.[52] For the analysis a three (four) average is computed. Data on those two indicators are available since 1985 (respectively 1989). An analysis of R&D expenses relative to the EU average is not possible because data on EU(12) are not available for this indicator.

*External agglomeration effects* are proxied by the level of urban agglomeration, which is measured by a three- (four)-year average of population density. The indicator of *sectoral structure* is the percentage (three/four year averages) of the employment in the 2nd and 3rd sector (in relation to total employment). The sectors are defined in line with Eurostat (Eurostat 1996a: 208f). The primary sector (agriculture) comprises agriculture, fishing and forestry. The secondary sector (industry) includes mining and quarrying, manufacturing and repair, construction and public utilities. The tertiary sector (services), finally, consists of commerce, transport, business and personal, social, medical, recreational services and public administration.

## *4.5  Synopsis*

The empirical concepts of analysing cohesion are absolute and conditional $\beta$-convergence and $\sigma$-convergence. An interesting variant of $\sigma$-convergence and $\beta$-convergence is the analysis of a single economy in relation to the European average. This shows, additionally to an economy *i*'s convergence towards its own steady-state, whether a sample is converging to a politically accepted point of reference. Depending on whether convergence is measured in absolute or relative figures, and on whether it

---

[50]  About 45 per cent of the annual transfers could be classed to a region unequivocally.

[51]  Other indicators (e.g., percentage of employment that work in R&D departments) would also be possible but are not available on the NUTS 2 level.

[52]  Rossi (1995: 161-167) points out that production and process innovation have different effects on regional growth. Product innovation is more common in core areas where skilled researchers and engineers are available. Once products are invented, they are likely to be produced in the periphery where labour is cheaper.

is correcting for different steady-states or not, there exist different forms of convergence. Table 4-2 summarises these theoretical concepts.

Data is pooled so that the panel consists of forty NUTS 2 regions of Greece, Portugal, southern Italy and Spain. The pooling interval of three (four) years reduces the influence of cyclical effects and possible auto-correlation of the term of error. The estimators are computed with OLS because the LSDV method is not applicable due to limited degrees of freedom. The dependent variables are growth of regional *per capita* GDP (in PPS) and the unemployment rate. Financial transfers, patent applications, R&D expenditures, population density and employment by sectors are indicators of the independent variables. Proxy variables for country specific effects are also included.

## Table 4-2: Convergence Concepts

| 1 Convergence of Absolute Figures | 2 Convergence of Relative (log) Figures |
|---|---|
| **1.1  Real $\beta$-Convergence**<br><br>• Real adjustment of $y_{poor}$ to $y_{rich}$<br><br>• $(y_{poor} - y_{rich}) \rightarrow 0$ (for $t \rightarrow \infty$); the gap between rich and poor economies diminishes<br><br>• Standard deviation of $y_i$ is decreasing | **2.1  Absolute $\beta$-Convergence**<br><br>• Relative adjustment of $y_{poor}$ to $y_{rich}$; $(y_{rich} / y_{poor}) \rightarrow 1$ (for $t \rightarrow \infty$)<br><br>• Poor economies grow faster than rich ones (up to the steady-state)<br><br>• Convergence of log $y_t$<br><br>• Standard deviation of log $y_i$ is decreasing |
| **1.2  Real conditional $\beta$-Convergence**<br>• 1.1 with control of structural and technology parameters | **2.2  Conditional $\beta$-Convergence**<br>• 2.1 with control of structural and technology parameters |

*Source: Schmidt (1997: 72)*

# 5 EMPIRICAL RESULTS: CONVERGENCE OF SOUTHERN EUROPEAN REGIONS

This chapter presents the empirical results of the macro-quantitative analysis. It provides first an analysis of the cohesion pattern within the sample of forty southern European regions, both in terms of *per capita* income and unemployment ($\sigma$-convergence). The impact of the initial income on regional growth is analysed in the second section (absolute $\beta$-convergence). The third section tests the impact of European structural transfers on growth and unemployment. A multivariate approach, in the fourth section, analyses the impact of structural and policy variables on economic development and unemployment (conditional $\beta$-convergence). I finally discuss the commonly stated criticism that EU transfers are a side-payment to the poorer member states for not blocking deeper economic integration.

## 5.1  $\sigma$-Convergence

### 5.1.1  Disparities of Regional GDP Income

#### 5.1.1.1  Analysis of 40 Southern European Regions

Figure 5-1 shows the standard deviation $(\sigma_i)$ of regional income (not growth rates) within the forty observed southern European regions. The overall pattern (1980-1996) shows only a very small decline in the standard deviation of the log of regional GDP *per capita*. We can neither find substantially increased disparities nor is there a clear convergence process between 1980 and 1996. However, this is only half of what the figures display. Examining closer the evolution of disparities reveals an increase of the standard deviation until 1987 (respectively 1991). This suggests that adjustment costs of both the accession of the three southern European economies and the preparation for the SEM were considerable. There was a rise of $\sigma$-convergence since the costs of integration were spatially unequally distributed. On the contrary, a substantial decrease in disparities occurred since the introduction of the SEM in 1992. This could be, on the one hand, the result of an equalisation of competitivity among the forty regions. On the other hand, smaller disparities might be due to structural transfers. This explanation is interesting since effective payments really took off in 1991, exactly the year before the decrease in  disparities. The following sections will have to enlighten the impact of financial transfers.

Because of the lack of data, one cannot draw a clear conclusion on the cohesion trend before 1983. However, my results coincide with long-term research (1960-1990) on Italian and Spanish regional income which found a convergence process that is strongest in the beginning and evens out with time (Barro and Sala-i-Martin 1995: 401).

**Figure 5-1: σ-Convergence of Real Regional GDP Income per capita (40 Southern European Regions at 1995 Prices; Logged)**

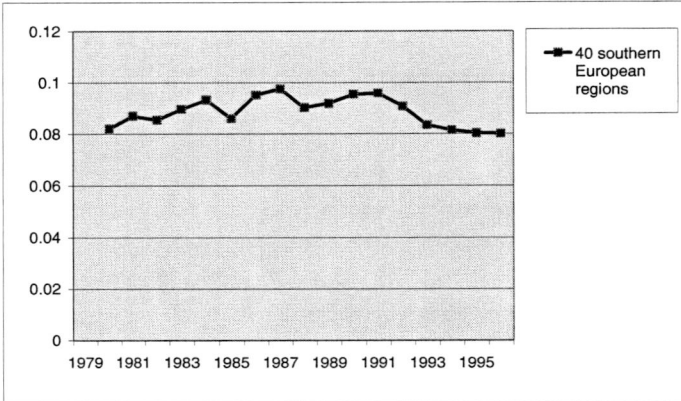

Source: own calculation, data from Eurostat.

### 5.1.1.2 Analysis by Country

The development of regional welfare differences within the four countries follows a convergence pattern. In *southern Italy* the disparities have been more or less stable in the observed period of time with a slightly upward trend since 1986. The fact that disparities are only about half of the extent of the three other countries owes much to inter-personal transfers of the Italian redistributive system. In *Portugal* and *Spain* intra-regional disparities were diminishing, but they were still fifty per cent higher than in the case of the Greek and Italian regions. In both countries this was due to strong growth in the poorest regions. The evolution of disparities suggests that structural transfers indeed supported the development of the very backward regions since a substantial part of the decrease occurred after 1988. Other reasons for the success in Spain and Portugal lie in sound macro-economic policies and substantial restructuring efforts. The impending accession to the EU in 1986 acted both as a convenient excuse and a catalyst for an unpopular package of measures. Some of the results were quickly evident: inflation fell rapidly (it started picking up again in 1989), and profits rose steadily which had a positive effect on investment (Tsoulakis 1991: 229f). However, the price paid in terms of job losses between 1986 and 1988 was heavy (see Chapter 5.1.2). The steep increase in disparities in Portugal between 1987 and 1991 owes much to the fact that the European recession hit the Portuguese regions by more than the EU average.

**Figure 5-2: σ-Convergence of Real Regional GDP per capita (By Country at 1995 Prices; Logged)**

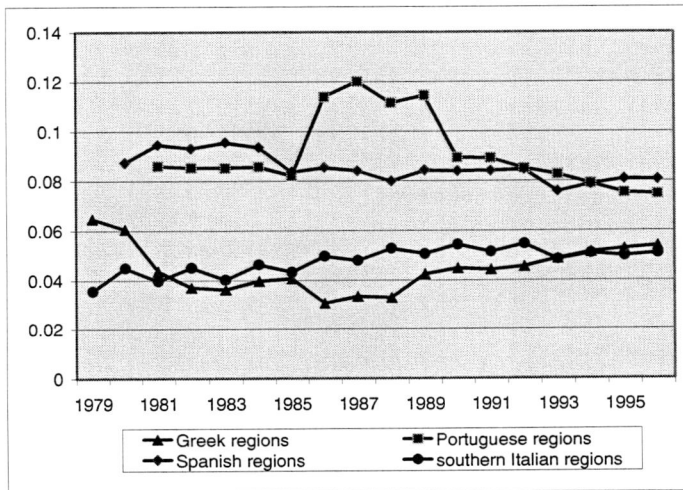

Source: own calculation, data from Eurostat.

A special case is *Greece* where the disparities have been growing since 1986. In fact, the Greek inter-regional disparities are today the same as before the European membership. Given that Greece has been a member of the EU since 1981 and that it has been the recipient of major funding programmes, the question remains as to why the poorest regions have not responded to massive structural transfers? Looking for the reason for the low Greek performance in the 1980s three factors seem to be decisive. Firstly, Greece joined the Community at the start of a general European-wide recession. Thus the poorest parts of the Greek economy were not able to take advantage of the expanding European market and the greater availability of resources (Tridimas 1996: 69).

Secondly, Greek macro-economic policy was guided mainly by myopic principles. The authorities' growth strategy relied on expansionary fiscal and income policies while policies in the rest of the EU generally aimed at deinflation and fiscal consolidation (Sarris 1992: 162). Throughout the 1980s the announced inflation and budget targets were consistently exceeded. Overall, expansionary financial policies did not elicit a sustained output response. On the contrary, they crowded out private investment, with the result that GDP growth in the 1980s slowed considerably, especially in the lagging Greek regions (Tsoulakis 1991: 226f). Thirdly, Greece's inadequate institutional infrastructure at the regional level served to retard growth in poor regions. Centralisation has severely constrained the development of networks linking private and public actors.

Striking the balance of the impact of European regional policy on cohesion, there is evidence of structural funds being successful in Spain and Portugal where the increased structural transfers had a considerable effect on the decrease in disparities. An exceptional case is Greece where disparities have grown to a level of above the first years of European membership. In southern Italy where regional disparities are not as striking as in the three southern cohesion countries, European regional policy has not brought an evident decline in disparities.

### 5.1.2    Disparities of Regional Unemployment Rates

#### 5.1.2.1  Analysis of 40 Southern European Regions

The standard deviation of the second welfare indicator is shown in Figure 5-3. The unemployment disparities among the forty southern European regions were in 1996 about the same as 15 years ago with a slight downward trend in sight at the time being. The reduction of disparities in unemployment in the second half of the 1980s reflects the economic boom in this period of time, which allowed backward regions to reduce their high unemployment rates. The positive trend came rapidly to an end when recession hit the southern European economies in the early 1990s. The increase of disparities between 1992 and 1994 was also fuelled by the preparation for the EMU. The latest downward trend is, on the one hand, connected to the recovery of the European economy. On the other hand, the figures seem to reflect the European Commission's efforts to fight unemployment in the most backward regions.

**Figure 5-3: σ-Convergence of Regional Unemployment Rates (Southern European Regions in Relation to the EU Average)**

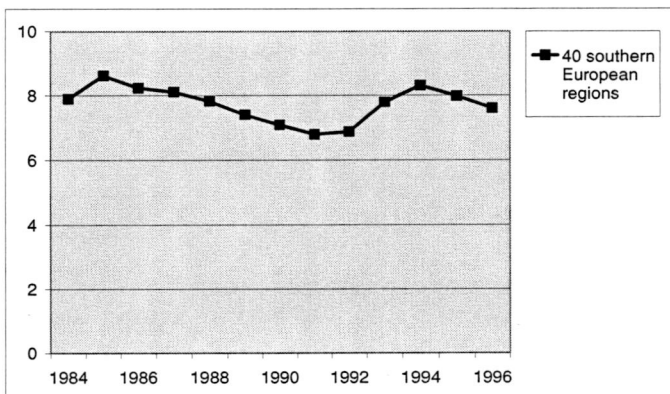

*Source: own calculation, data from Eurostat.*

## 5.1.2.2 Analysis by Country

There is no homogenous picture in terms of unemployment disparities. The European financial transfers did not bring a substantial reduction in unemployment disparities with the exception of Portugal. *Spain* paid the price for accession to the EU with very high unemployment rates in some regions due to major stabilisation programmes. Structural funds seemed to lower the costs for the SEM and EMU. *Southern Italy's* unemployment disparities have increased since 1991. Contrary to relatively low disparities of GDP income, Italy faced big differences of interregional unemployment rates. In the *Portuguese* case, there was an astonishing decline in unemployment since accession to the EU, which correlates with the positive development in terms of GDP disparities. However, only little improvement took place since the increased European structural funds. The case of *Greece* is striking for intra-regional disparities are small. However, disparities have been growing since 1991.

**Figure 5-4: σ-Convergence of Regional Unemployment Rates (By Country In Relation to the EU Average)**

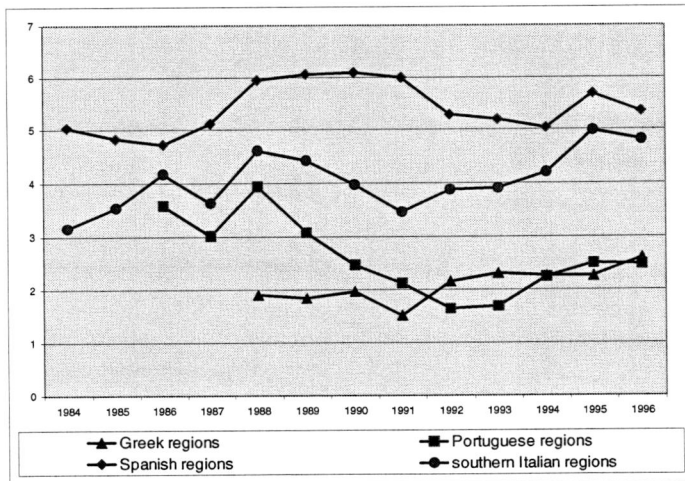

*Source: own calculation, data from Eurostat.*

## 5.2 Absolute β-Convergence: Impact of Initial Income on Regional GDP Growth

Column 2 and 4 of Table 5-1 show the beta-coefficients for the period and sub-periods from 1982 to 1995.[53] The regressions confirm the hypothesis of absolute β-convergence. All results show a negative relation between the initial level of income and growth rates. However, only the β-coefficients of the regression in relation to the European average are significant at conventional levels (95% confidence interval) with a β of -0.15 (for both the 3 and 4 year average).[54]

**Table 5-1: Absolute β-Convergence of Regional GDP per capita Across Southern European Regions**

| Period | Southern European Economies | | | | Southern European Economies in Relation to the European Average | | | |
| --- | --- | --- | --- | --- | --- | --- | --- | --- |
| | Simple Regression | | Multiple Regression | | Simple Regression | | Multiple Regression | |
| | $\beta$ | $R^2$ | $\beta$ | $R^2$ | $\beta$ | $R^2$ | $\beta$ | $R^2$ |
| 3 year average (n = 194/73/194/73) | -0.094 (t=-1.581) | 0. 009 | -0.057 (t=-0.910) | 0.201 | -0.148 ** (t=-2.073) | 0.022 | -0.169 * (t=-2.050) | 0.213 |
| 4 year average (n = 154/69/154/69) | -0.122 (t=-1.503) | 0.015 | -0.110 (t=-1.80) | 0.192 | -0.138 ** (t=-2.071) | 0.019 | -0.168 * (t=-1.951) | 0.191 |
| 1982-1995 (n = 36/36) | -0.281 ** (t=-2.323) | 0.078 | n too small | | -0.483 *** (t=-2.837) | 0.233 | n too small | |

*Note: *: significant at 90% level. **:significant at 95% level. ***: significant at 99% level.*

*Source: own calculations, data from Eurostat.*

The $R^2$ of the various three- (four-) year average regressions is rather low. Additional national dummies do not have substantial explanatory power for either model and are insignificant. Regional dummies could not be included because the number of degrees of freedom was limited. The results over the entire period from 1982 to 1995 indicate a possible reason for the low $R^2$ of the three- (four-) year average regression: the pooling period might be too short with business cycles causing bias effects.

Figure 5-5 shows for 40 regions the relation of the regional growth rate of *per capita* GDP from 1982 to 1995 to the log of *per capita* GDP at the beginning of the period. The correlation between the growth rate and the log of initial *per capita* GDP is -0.48. Since the underlying numbers are expressed relative to the EU mean, the relation

---

[53]  Statistical calculations and plots are enlisted in Appendix A4. The starting point of the 3-year (4-year) average regressions of growth on the initial level of GDP is 1982. The other five regressions with different starting points produced almost identical outcomes (with slightly different levels of significance). Appendix A.3 provides a list and description of all indicators.

[54]  The ongoing discussion of the results refers therefore from now on only to the equation in relation to the EU average.

pertains to β-convergence within the European Union. This result again rejects the hypothesis of the southern European regions being systematically discriminated against the European economic integration.

**Figure 5-5: Growth Rates (1982-1995) versus Initial GDP per capita (1982) of 40 Southern European Regions**

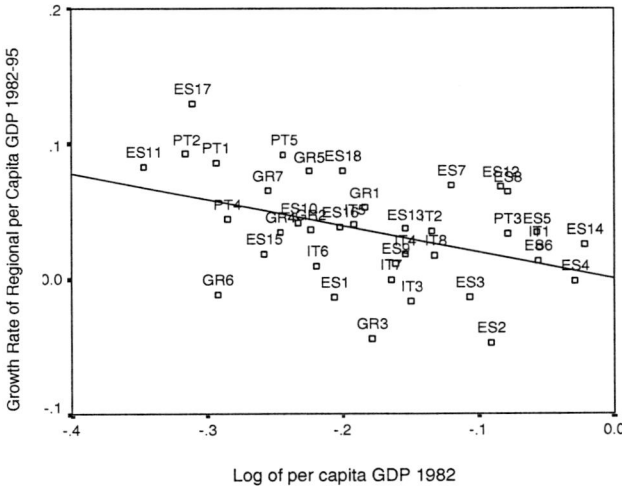

Source: own calculation, data from Eurostat.

## 5.3 The Impact of European Structural Transfers on Cohesion

### 5.3.1 Impact of European Structural Transfers on Regional GDP Growth

The simple regression of EU structural transfers on regional GDP growth reveals a strong positive relation between transfers and economic growth (see Table 5-2 and Figure 5-6). An increase of structural funds of one percentage point raises regional GDP growth of about 0.5 points. The results confirm, thus, the first evidence of the analysis of β-convergence in southern Europe.

**Figure 5-6: European Structural Transfers versus Regional per capita GDP Growth (Logged)**

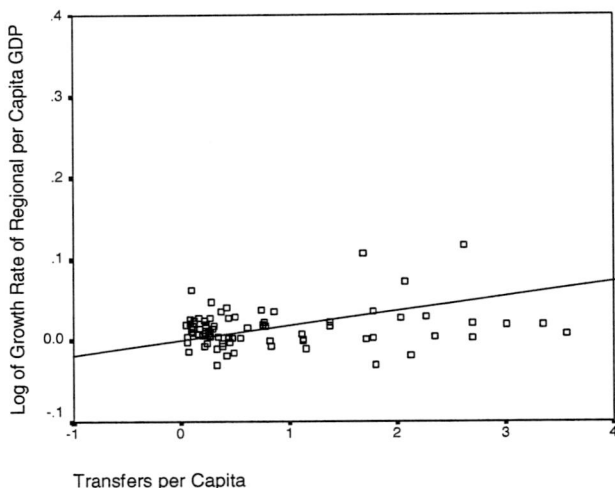

Transfers per Capita

*Source: own calculation, data from Eurostat.*

The results stand, firstly, in contrast to the neo-classical growth theory which predicted that transfers are hampering convergence. Secondly, the positive convergence effect of structural transfers supports the hypothesis stated above: the decrease of GDP income disparities since 1992 has owed a substantial part to EU regional policy.

**Table 5-2: Regression of European Structural Transfers on Regional GDP Growth**

| Period | Southern European Economies | | Southern European Economies in Relation to the European Average | |
|---|---|---|---|---|
| | $\beta$ | $R^2$ | $\beta$ | $R^2$ |
| 3 year average (n = 80/80) | 0.402 *** (t=3.877) | 0.162 | 0.491 *** (t=4.107) | 0.168 |
| 4 year average (n = 80/80) | 0.398 *** (t=3.212) | 0.171 | 0.423 *** (t=3.330) | 0.177 |

*Note:  *: significant at 90% level.  **:significant at 95% level.  ***: significant at 99% level.*

*Source: own calculations, data from Eurostat.*

## 5.3.2    Impact of European Structural Transfers on Regional Unemployment Rates

European regional policy has had also a positive impact on cohesion in terms of unemployment. The higher the transfers for a poor region the lower is its unemployment rate. The coefficient of all regressions is again highly significant with strong t-values (see Table 5-3). $R^2$ is not extraordinarily high but the univariate regression still explains thirty per cent of the variance in unemployment rates across southern European regions, which is remarkable for a factor that critics of European regional policy consider as ineffective.

**Table 5-3: Regression of European Structural Transfers on Regional Unemployment Rates**

| Period | Southern European Economies | | Southern European Economies in Relation to the European Average | |
|---|---|---|---|---|
| | $\beta$ | $R^2$ | $\beta$ | $R^2$ |
| 3 year average (n = 73/73) | -0.459 *** (t=-4.358) | 0. 211 | -0.461 *** (t=-4.211) | 0.277 |
| 4 year average (n = 73/73) | -0.398 *** (t=-3.857) | 0.232 | -0.399 *** (t=-3.932) | 0.296 |

*Note: \*: significant at 90% level. \*\*:significant at 95% level. \*\*\*: significant at 99% level.*

*Source: own calculations, data from Eurostat.*

Two points should be mentioned for the interpretation of these results. Firstly, the effect is not due to female workers leaving the labour market without applying for unemployment compensation. In the observed period, unemployment developed similar for male and female workers (European Commission 1999k: 131f, 135, 139). The second aspect concerns early retirement. The logic behind the argument is the following. Public enterprises laid off the workers who were over 55 years old in order to become more competitive for the SEM and EMU. These workers did not appear any longer in labour market statistics since they received severance pay. Consequently, unemployment rates sank. According to labour market experts, this mechanisms seemed to be present in most of the observed regions, although, it is hard to come by from a methodological point of view since no data on this social phenomenon is available.

## 5.4 A Multivariate Approach (Conditional β-Convergence)

### 5.4.1 Impact of European Structural Transfers on Regional GDP Growth

The two multiple regressions included the following independent variables: European financial transfers *per capita*, population density, employment of the 2nd sector, patent applications *per capita* and GDP *per capita* at the starting point of the period. Employment of the 3rd sector is omitted as it correlated heavily with employment of the 2nd sector. These variables are as close as one can get with the present data for the NUTS2 regions to measuring structural differences between economies. National dummies were all insignificant.

**Table 5-4: Coefficients and t-Values of Multiple Regression (Y = GDP Growth)**

| | Southern European Economies in Relation to the European Average | |
|---|---|---|
| | $\beta$-coefficient | *t*-values |
| constant | -0.007 | -1.099 |
| financial transfers per capita | 0.215 * | 1.641 |
| population density | -0.200 * | -1.891 |
| employment 2nd sector | 0.274 ** | 2.131 |
| patent application per capita | 0.035 | 0.222 |
| GDP starting point | -0.169 * | -1.88 |

*Note: *: significant at 90% level. **:significant at 95% level. ***: significant at 99% level.*

*Source: own calculations, data from Eurostat.*

All the variables are significant and behave as expected, although sometimes with low *t*-values (see Table 5-4). The relation between financial transfers and economic growth is still positive and significant. The estimate of the $\beta$-coefficient of initial income is now -0.17. The insignificance of the variable "patent applications" could probably be avoided with R&D expenses *per capita* figures which showed a significant indicator in the regressions of southern European regions only (not in relation to the EU average). Unfortunately, no European average on this technology indicator is available.

### 5.4.2    Impact of European Structural Transfers on Regional Unemployment Rates

The multiple regression with unemployment as dependent variable display better results for southern European regions in relation to the EU mean, especially in terms of partial coefficients. The independent variables explain 32 per cent (respectively 22 per cent) of the variance of the dependent variable (see Table 5-5). Additional national dummies do not have substantial explanatory power for either model and are insignificant. They are thus omitted. Regional dummies cannot be included because the number of degrees of freedom is limited.

**Table 5-5: Convergence of Unemployment Rates Across Southern European Regions**

| Period | Southern European Economies | | | Southern European Economies in Relation to the European Average | | |
|---|---|---|---|---|---|---|
| | $R^2$ | F | Sig. | $R^2$ | F | Sig. |
| 3 year average (n = 71/71) | 0. 222 | 4.762 | 0.002 | 0.323 | 6.210 | 0.000 |
| 4 year average (n = 69/69) | 0.209 | 5.026 | 0.002 | 0.236 | 4.903 | 0.002 |

*Source: own calculations, data from Eurostat.*

Table 5-6 shows the results for the independent variables that are included in the regression. European regional policy has a positive effect on cohesion as the relationship between financial transfers and the unemployment rate is significantly negative. Population density is also significant. Employment of the $3^{rd}$ sector is again omitted as it correlates strongly with the employment of the $2^{nd}$ sector which itself is insignificant. The technology variables and the GDP starting point are also insignificant, or show different signs in the two regression.[55]

**Table 5-6: Coefficients and t-Values of Multiple Regression (Y = Unemployment)**

|  | Southern European Economies in Relation to the European Average | |
|---|---|---|
|  | $\beta$-coefficient | *t*-values |
| Constant | 26.673 *** | 3.737 |
| financial transfers per capita | -0.401*** | -3.398 |
| population density | 0.471 *** | 3.746 |
| employment 2nd sector | -0.098 | -0.802 |
| patent application per capita | -0.088 | -0.634 |
| GDP starting point | 0.199 | 1.535 |

*Note: *: significant at 90% level. **:significant at 95% level. ***: significant at 99% level.*

*Source: own calculations, data from Eurostat.*

## 5.5 Are European Structural Transfers Side-Payments?

The positive cohesion effect of European financial transfers does not support those critics who categorically deny that structural funds foster cohesion. They interpret European financial transfers as a side payment to the less developed countries within the Community for not blocking market integration and the creation of the EMU. Aside from never being explicit about what the concept of a side payment really means and how it can be operationalised for testing, those critics usually adhere to the centre-periphery approach towards regional disparities. According to them, little can be done to alleviate conditions of underemployment (Tsoukalis 1993: 27). The theoretical expectation is that the massive structural transfers of the EU will not stimulate positive economic growth but will instead be used to pay for the social support of the unemployed and underemployed. Financial transfers are not expected to lead to increases in local production and convergence of regional GDP. Summing up, financial transfers have mainly a redistributive and not an allocative character (Hudson and Lewis 1985: 122).

My results, however, reveal that these negative expectations are not at all a reflection of what is actually happening within the regional and national economies in objective 1 areas. Financial transfers have indeed a positive influence on convergence. Nanetti

---

[55] Note that the GDP *per capita* at the starting point has no theoretically stated behaviour as in the case of the GDP growth.

(1996: 66) comes to the same conclusion by analysing fund allocation broken down by objectives. The side-payment types of policies predicted by the centre-periphery analyses are specifically represented by the two horizontal objectives 3 and 4 (youth and long-term unemployment). These objectives have always had a national focus and are administered exclusively by national governments. However, in the 1994-1999 structural fund package, objectives 3 and 4 represented only 11 per cent while in the 1989-1994 period it was 12 per cent of overall CSF allocations. Moreover, most of these funds were earmarked for the countries not receiving objective 1 support.[56] In the case of the CF allocations with their national focus, the amount of transfers involved is also small – some Euro 15 billion over five years (1994-1999) – compared to the Euro 141 billion flowing through the structural funds in the same period (European Commission 1995a: 17).

In contrast, the other structural fund objectives (1, 2 and 5b), which use the bulk of financial means, have a predominantly regional focus. They are not targeted towards the simple alleviation of unemployment. Rather, they are specifically designed to support investment programmes to build infrastructure and capital equipment, tourism facilities and engage in agricultural restructuring – that is, to tackle the specific causes of underdevelopment identified in the past by the economics and regional planning literature. All in all, the following conclusion can be drawn: contrary to the widespread opinion that the European Union  squanders structural funds, European structural transfers have had a positive impact on cohesion.

## 5.6    Synopsis

This chapter analysed European regional policy and its impact on the cohesion pattern of southern European regions. The most important finding is the strong evidence for the hypothesis that European financial transfers have a significant positive influence on cohesion. The results are significant for simple and multiple regressions, both in terms of unemployment and economic growth. I also found evidence for the neo-classical convergence theory. The negative relation between initial income and GDP growth suggests that market forces and economic integration indeed fostered cohesion. The results on external agglomeration effects, the level of technology and the size of the $2^{nd}$ sector behave according to the theoretical predictions. They are, however, not always significant. I come to the following conclusions in terms of $\sigma$-convergence. The reduction of GDP disparities within the forty regions over the entire period of time

---

[56]    This fact suggests a possible interesting twist to the concept of side payments: objectives 3 and 4 constitute side payments for formerly developed countries undergoing decline so that they will not complain about the use of regional funds to spur growth in traditionally underdeveloped (southern) areas. 11 to 12 per cent of the structural funds are used as side payments while the remainder can be used for regional development (Nanetti 1996: 87).

is a small one. A closer look at the figures revealed that adjustment costs for both the accession and the preparation for SEM were considerable whereas the decrease in disparities since 1992 confirms the hypothesis of European financial transfers being successful. In the case of unemployment, the overall figures of forty southern European regions display no improvement. However, there is a decline of unemployment disparities since 1994, which coincides with increasing structural transfers of the Union.

# 6  A MODEL OF INSTITUTIONAL PERFORMANCE (MICRO-LEVEL)

The macro-quantitative analysis looked at the general cohesion pattern in southern Europe and the convergence effects of European structural transfers. We found that financial transfers worked for cohesion both in terms of economic growth and unemployment. However, the quantitative analysis has helped little in understanding how the European funds led to economic development once they had arrived in the beneficiary regions. By focusing on two particular cases – Andalusia in Spain and Algarve in Portugal – the following chapters will analyse at the micro-level the role of institutions and actors involved in regional development. How did regional administrations prepare the structural policies that were co-financed by the EU funds? What investment priorities did they have? How did the implementation of planned interventions work? In which ways was the private sector in the policy process involved? Questions like these are addressed in order to assess the functioning of the institutions concerned with structural policy and, of course, to find out how the European regional policy reform of 1988 affected the performance of these institutions.[57] In order to analyse regional and local actors a model of eight regional roles in development is elaborated. The aim of this analytical framework is to assess institutional functions for economic development. In detecting core growth functions, I was guided by the following methodical principle. The theoretical framework should not be exclusive, being able to capture a wide range of institutional activities. From this starting point, empirical evidence guided the search for institutional functions where the partnership principle had the greatest performance impact. The chapter is structured as follows. In the beginning, I look at the reasons why regional institutions became important in European regional policy and also at the implications of the more decentralised approach of this policy. I then explain the relationship between regional institutions and regional development. Finally, a model of eight regional roles in development is presented whose application allows us to fine tune the results of the macro-quantitative analysis.

---

[57]  Remember that institutional performance was defined as the capacity to respond to the demand of the public and private environments.

## 6.1    The Role of Regional Government in the Context of Deeper European Integration

### 6.1.1    The Rise of Regional Institutions and SMEs

As already elaborated Europe has been undergoing a significant but silent transformation in its political institutions, economy and social structure. In the preparation and adjustment process for the SEM and EMU an important role has been allocated to the regional level of government which had been excluded from direct participation in the process of European integration in earlier times due to the dominant position of national governments (Leonardi and Nanetti 1990: 1). The involvement of regional institutions in the European regional planning process has been the most prominent example. Knodt (1998b: 98), Kohler-Koch (1998: 23f) and Marks (1998: 335) have all shown that European regional policy is promoting the devolution of institutional power by directly involving the regions into different phases of the political process.[58]

In the economic field it has been argued by Leonardi (1995: 212) that, all over Europe, one of the consequences of European integration and the opening up of national markets has been the loss of power of the nation-state in regulating the national economy in favour of "national champions". The need to be competitive placed into crisis large non-competitive national firms and opened up greater possibilities for smaller firms operating at the regional and local levels (Europäische Kommission 1994b: 10-12). Accordingly the role of large firms in accounting for employment across Europe has declined and employment in SMEs has steadily increased. Today, SMEs are viewed as the backbone of economic development (despite the fact that multi-national blue chip firms usually make headlines in newspapers; Europäische Kommission 1993: 29-31; 135-137; European Commission 1999c: 14f).

### 6.1.2    Regional Business Needs Regional Institutions

Becattini Becattini (1994: 243) showed that increased competition through the Single European Market and the Monetary Union has forced SMEs to externalise a number of functions which before had been integral parts of the company. The functions which no longer remain exclusively within the firm range from keeping track of salaries, invoices, and sub-contracting agreements to marketing, searching for partners, experimentation with new technology or recruiting workers. The current form of industrial organisation needs, thus, to create economies of scale external to the plant in the production process in such a manner that each producer survives as long as he is a specialist in one phase or subphase of the overall production process. Each producer must draw from external networks in the form of interacting with professional

---

[58]    "Decentralisation" and "regionalisation" are used as synonyms for devolution.

associations and governmental institutions to gain access to a series of social and business services, which can no longer be internalised within the firm for reasons of cost and expertise (McDonald and Dearden 1992: 111).

The micro-management of services to regional SMEs is beyond the capabilities of national governments, but it is well within the activity range of regional institutions, especially those with a strong capacity to interact with sub-regional levels of government and with representative sectoral associations. The strength of regional institutions in interacting with SMEs are the following (Frey 1997: 37-39). Firstly, their geographical size allows them to operate at the area-wide level and make use of a variety of resources and institutional functions. Secondly, they can achieve a critical mass of administrative and technical expertise in interacting with relatively small production units scattered across a region's territory. Thirdly, regions manage significant amounts of financial resources in providing incentives to small local producers and can fine tune these incentives in collaboration with sectoral associations. Fourth, depending on the territorial system, they have legislative powers in matters related to industrial parks, loans to entrepreneurs, infrastructure planning, environmental control, vocational education, social service planning and provision, business services and transfer of technology to local firms. Finally, regions can define intersectoral policies to serve a broad range of economic and social interests which are territorially based and functionally interconnected within the region.[59]

The European Commission learnt its first lesson of regional advantages in responding to the needs of decentralised production during the industrial crisis of the late 1970s and in the 1980s when the traditional industrial model based on big, capital-intensive and vertically organised firms proved to be inefficient (Eissel 1994: 46). Similar problems occurred during the years of IMPs (post-1985). In view of the challenges of economic transformation to the SEM and EMU, these considerations were not without political consequences in the 1988 reform of the structural funds. The role of the region was no longer one of a spectator, but it became an active participant in the development process. The mandate for regions was to act as development planners and promoters (European Commission 1999c: 3; Garofoli 1992: 72; Nanetti 1996: 73).

---

[59] Critics of strong regional institutions argue that decentralisation prevents the exploitation of economies of scale and causes both high co-ordination costs and negative spill-overs. However, their argument neglects the fact that centralisation has also its price (such as the tendency to bureaucracy, neglecting the preferences of individuals, etc). For a review of the centralisation versus decentralisation debate see Frey and Kirchgässner (1994: 59-67).

### 6.1.3    Regional Government Within the Model of Multi-Level Governance

The 1988 reform of European regional policy was not the only step in the devolutionary process of power to the regions. The last twenty years have seen the emergence throughout the EU of regional public and private actors (Wishlade 1996: 385). The trend towards new increased regionalisation owes less to any particular swing in political reformation, but more to the pragmatic approach of how best to accommodate through concerted action the principal economic and social actors. Regionalisation in southern Europe has taken place mainly in Italy where elected regional institutions were created in 1970. Spain adopted a regional governmental structure in 1982. The devolutionary process brought a shared decision-making and administration devolved to regional governmental units that are partially self-financing (Hooghe 1996a: 121). In Portugal and Greece there is still a highly centralised relationship between national and sub-national units of government without the opportunity for regional institutions to finance themselves. Decision-making is centralised and administrative action is carried out through the national administrative machinery (Featherstone and Yannopoulos 1995: 260-264). The functions of regional institutions in countries with decentralised governments have expanded to cover most sectors in development planning. In southern Italy, the regions have primary legislative responsibility for agriculture, tourism, health, urban and territorial planning and vocational training, and they are to acquire limited fiscal autonomy (Maresso 1996: 24). In Spain, autonomous regions cover similar policy areas, that is urban planning, housing, public works and environment, in addition to social services, culture, and economic policy (Morata 1992: 116-118).

The revival of the regions altered the existing pattern of governance. Leonardi and Nanetti (1990: 8) demonstrated on an empirical basis that the traditional model used in studying regional government within a national juridical and institutional context had become obsolete. Regional government no longer had solely the role of an intermediate, interacting with national government on the one hand and local government on the other. The regional level exercised fundamental power with regard to the delivery of social services and regional development – and these activities could no longer be conceived of as atypical or temporary. The two above-mentioned authors suggested therefore an alternative model of regional government.

Figure 6-1 illustrates a model which takes into account the institutional change implicit in the reform of European regional policy and the SEM. National boundaries are limited and governmental linkage networks no longer have to operate on a vertical (top-down) dimension only, but can now effectively operate horizontally in an inter-regional and transregional dimension. Furthermore, the regional and the European level interact more directly, sometimes even without the interference of the national level. The opportunity of regional units to operate on the horizontal dimension, as well as directly interacting with the European level, has significantly changed their ability to respond to and absorb the demands of the environment, which proved to be vital for economic development (Dollar and Pritchett 1998: 3). It would be premature to finally judge the value of the multi-level government approach. In the scientific community, however, it is widely accepted that the role of regional institutions, both in states with a centralised or decentralised political and administrative system, has become more important through the new institutional relations invoked by the European regional policy reform and the SEM (Grote 1996: 236; Hooghe 1996: 121).

**Figure 6-1: Model of Multi-Level Government Before and After the Reform of EU Regional Policy (1988) and the Creation of the SEM (1992)**

Pre-1988/92 Model: Vertical Linkages Dominated by National Governments

Post-1988/92 Model: Horizontal Linkages Added to the Vertical Ones

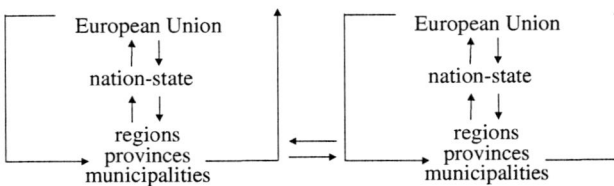

*Source: Leonardi and Nanetti 1990: 11.*

## 6.2 The Relationship Between Institutions and Development

So far, the functional advantages of regions interacting with a decentralised form of production have been discussed. The question now is: how do these functional advantages of regional institutions lead to regional economic development? Theoretical research on the relationship between institutional factors and regional development has been conducted mainly in the context of *new institutionalism*.

New institutionalism[60] builds on the assumption that institutions form a part of the incentive system of a society. The rules and standard operating procedures make institutions leave their imprint on political outcomes (e.g. economic development) by structuring political behaviour (North 1994: 359; Ostrom 1990: 47). For institutions act as restrictions of individual and collective action that structure human interaction. Institutions influence, thus, political outcomes because they shape the actors' identities, power and strategies (North 1990: 15; 1992: 480; Putnam 1993: 7). In a non-neo-classical world with frictions between market participants institutions minimise transaction costs (information, search and opportunity costs). They do this by reducing uncertainty: institutions define an environment within which exchange and production processes can develop. The minimisation of transaction costs results in a maximisation of economic efficiency.

**Figure 6-2: Model of Institutional Factors of Development**

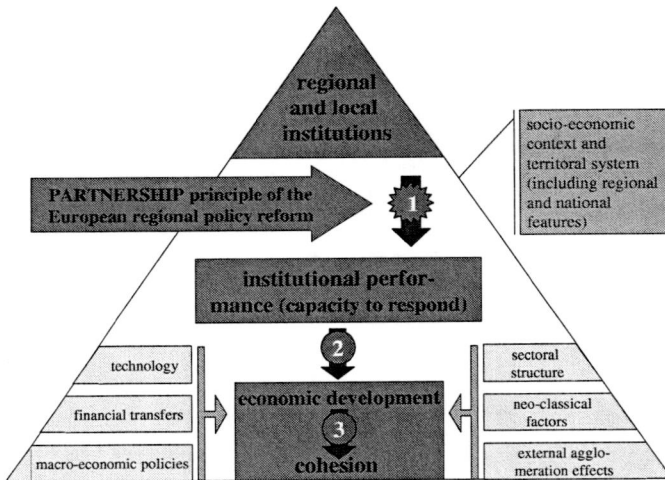

*Source: own figure.*

Figure 6-2 presents the conceptualisation of the relationship between institutions and economic development. Within the socio-economic and historical context of an area, the model proposes that institutions shape institutional performance and economic development. Relation number 1 means that the rules of institutions determine institutional performance defined as the capacity of a region to respond to the demands of the public and private (entrepreneurial) environment. The case studies of European

---

60  New institutionalism is an amalgam of various theoretical approaches. The theory of property rights, and the theory of collective action are central in the context of *new institutionalism* (Frey and Kirchgässner 1994: 28-31; Obinger 1999: 11).

regional policy in Andalusia and Algarve aim to explore this relation. Taking institutions as an independent variable, I explore how the partnership approach of European regional policy affected the performance of regional institutions. Partnership involves "close collaboration between the Commission and all the relevant authorities at national, regional or local level appointed by each member state, at all stages in the programming" (European Commission 1993a: 19).

Theoretical and empirical literature predict an improvement of institutional performance in the case of institutional decentralisation. *The more regional institutions are involved in the process of European regional policy* – planning, negotiation, formulation, implementation and monitoring – *the better will be the institutional performance* (Frey and Kirchgässner 1994: 57, 59-62; Nanetti 1996: 72, 75). The causal pathway of the positive performance effect is that a region can better articulate its needs (to both the EU and the nation state) for responding to the demands of its environment if it is directly involved in the European regional planning process through the partnership principle, than in the case where national and European authorities decided structural interventions on their own. The degree of partnership and the competencies in regional development depend both on the system of territorial relations which is nationally defined. The revised structural funds regulations of 1994 made this point clear: "... partnership will be conducted in full compliance with the respective institutional and legal powers of each of the partners" (European Commission 1993a: 19). The hypothesis is thus: the involvement of regional institutions in the European regional policy process should boost institutional performance. This effect should be stronger in regions with a high degree of autonomy than in the case of less autonomous regions.

The second relation shows that regional development is the consequence of an appropriate response to the demands of the environment. The better regional institutions perform, the more a region develops economically (Dollar and Pritchett 1998: 135-137; Feld and Savioz 1996: 7, 18).[61] According to relation number 3 cohesion will occur if regional development is translated into relatively high gains for

---

[61] One could argue that the relationship between institutional decentralisation and institutional performance is not an important one because the only point of interest is regional development, the consequence of high institutional performance. However, measuring institutional performance helps us to understand what is happening on the ground at regional level, as well as to pinpoint various critical areas of a successful European regional policy. Further reasons for analysing institutional performance stem from a methodological point of view, since it is uncertain that institutional decentralisation has an immediate influence on regional development. On the one hand, regional development is a complex process including a variety of explanatory factors that might heavily influence growth (Marks 1998: 335). On the other hand, economic development takes time, e.g. time lags are likely to occur (Rodríguez 1998: 224). Both effects could cover the impact of institutional performance which does not make institutional performance unimportant, though.

the disadvantaged regions of the Union without halting or reversing the growth of the more developed regions (European Commission 1999g: 31f, 35). In the preceding chapters, it was elaborated that other variables (such as sectoral structure or macro-economic policies) also influence the convergence process. These variables can be seen as a part of the socio-economic and historical context in which institutions perform.

## 6.3 A Model of Eight Regional Roles in Development

Exploring institutional performance requires us to develop a framework with the ability to capture the region's capacity in responding to the exigencies placed on them by economic integration and the political demand for economic development and employment. As a first step, we have to know what regions should do in order to achieve economic development. Following the mandate for regions to act as development planners and promoters raises the following questions: How could the role of a development planner and promoter be articulated for regional institutions? What are regions attempting to do in response to the demand that they should be the principal institutional partners in development? Proceeding from an analytical framework which answers these questions, empirical investigation shall detect the most important institutional functions for regional development in a second step.

There is a range of analytical approaches to institutional activities (European Commission 1993c; Dasgupta 1997; Hall and Jones 1998; Ioakimidis 1996; Opello 1993; Paraskevopoulos 1998). The drawback of these frameworks is that they are either not comprehensive enough in their understanding of institutions or that they aim at testing a specific development theory. The most comprehensive analytical framework was presented by Nanetti (1996; see Figure 6-3), building on the work of Leonardi (1993), Leonardi and Nanetti (1990) and Nanetti (1987). There are eight roles that regions play as development planners and promoters.[62] Four roles relate to the interplay between institutions that lie within its own boundaries. The model identifies these as intra-regional roles:

- *Facilitator:* Involving the private sector in the regional policy process is important in order to understand better the demands of those actors. Activating private actors allows the inclusion of those who profit from public development interventions.

---

[62]    As mentioned above, the search for the most important functions is guided by empirical research. From a theoretical point of view, it is not possible to weigh the importance of the eight roles because the intensity of a region's activity in the different functional areas varies over time depending on the phase of the European regional process and on the funds involved. One should remember that regions are involved only in the European policy-making which consists of the following sub-phases: planning, negotiation, formulation, implementation and monitoring of development programs. There is no or only negligible participation in the other two phases, that is the creation of the budgetary envelope of European regional policy and the design of institutions (Marks 1998: 390).

The main facilitators are entrepreneurial associations and unions, but all other enterprises and private actors at both the regional and local level are also included. Semi-public and public enterprises do not belong to the group of private actors.

- *Stimulator:* Introducing new planning procedures mobilises unused or underused resources. Planning procedures produce coherent development strategies instead of a multitude of single projects, match available resources with development priorities and manage funds according to development plans.

- *Monitor:* The controlling of structural interventions through Monitoring Committees as well as *ex ante*, ongoing and *ex post* evaluations improve the short-term and long-term quality of European regional policy.[63] They can also increase the learning capacity of institutions through the systematic analysis of interventions undertaken.

- *Experimenter:* Promoting and carrying out experimental projects helps to find new ways to overcome structural deficits. Experiments assist regional planners in overcoming both their preference for infrastructure projects and risk aversion from innovative projects.

**Figure 6-3: Regions as Development Planners and Promoters**

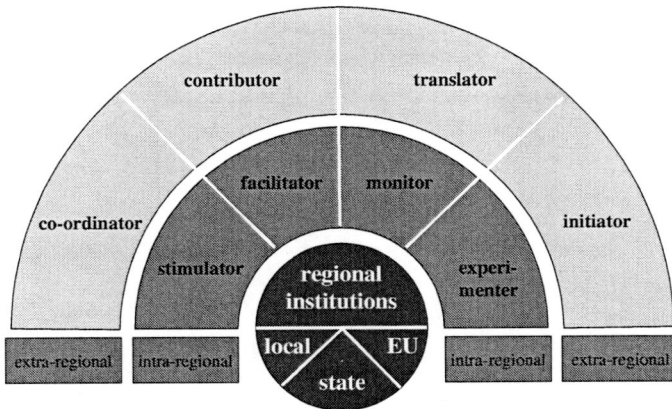

*Source: Nanetti (1996: 74).*

---

[63]  "Evaluations" should be understood as classical impact assessments of specific policies. They do not include the assessment of institutions.

The other four roles define the region's initiatives outside its own boundaries. Extra-regional roles include both what a region does within the boundaries of its own nation-state (inter-regional) and the actions which a region develops in other member states (transregional) or the European Commission.

- *Contributor*: Preparing and being involved in the planning and negotiation of CSFs (Community Support Framework) together with national proponents and the European Commission best allows regions to articulate their preferences. The contributor role is performed by political and administrative actors only.

- *Translator*: Preparing and executing OPs (Operational Programmes) at the regional level best allows regional authorities and public enterprises to integrate their knowledge in the planning and implementation of structural interventions.[64]

- *Co-ordinator*: Horizontally co-ordinating vis-à-vis various governmental institutions of other regions raises the efficiency of regional development work and allows the familiarisation of the best practices in regional policy.

- *Initiator*: Undertaking transregional co-operation establishes horizontal and vertical networks. This helps to learn from the best practices and to organise political pressure in areas of common (regional) interest.

Applying the framework of eight regional roles has a range of advantages. First of all, the model initially proposed by Nanetti (1987) proved to be an efficient tool in the empirical analyses of institutions (Leonardi 1993; Leonardi and Nanetti 1990; Nanetti 1996; Opello 1993; Trigilia 1989). Other analytical approaches are less comprehensive in their understanding of regional institutions (European Commission 1993c; Paraskevopoulos 1998) or focus on slightly different things than institutional performance (Grote 1998; Ioakimidis 1996). Secondly, the framework is not based on a single growth theory, but includes a wide range of variables identified by various development theories ranging from development theories of the Third World (Dollar and Pritchett 1998) and the theory of locational factors (Kotler 1994) to new institutionalism which lays emphasis on factors such as social capital[65] (Dasgupta 1997; Hall and Jones 1998; Paraskevopoulos 1998) or horizontal and vertical

---

[64]   Private actors do also implement parts of OPs. Their involvement, however, is analysed in the facilitator role.

[65]   Social capital refers to "features of social organisation such as trust, norms and networks that can improve the efficiency of a society by facilitating co-ordinated action" (Putnam 1993: 167); or to "internalised norms which stress the acceptance on the part of citizens of the positive role played by collective action in pursuing collective goods related to economic growth and social protection" (Leonardi 1995: 169). Trust constitutes the most important form of social capital. It is closely linked to the volatility and hence uncertainty of modern economic and institutional settings and is seen as the crucial conceptual mechanism

networking[66] (Grote 1998). Thirdly, the framework captures a broad spectrum of institutional activities which allows us, on the one hand, to evaluate institutional performance in a comprehensive way and, on the other, to understand what is happening at the regional, national and European levels.

## 6.4 Synopsis

Regional institutions have become more important in the economic development of the EU. The rise of the regions is, on the one hand, due to the fact that regional institutions can best respond to the demands of SMEs, which are under pressure to stay competitive in the SEM and EMU. On the other hand, the European Commission promoted the devolutionary process of institutional power by directly involving the regions into different phases of the European regional policy process. From a theoretical point of view, new institutionalism predicts institutional performance in the case of a high degree of partnership between regional, national and European actors. The more regional institutions are involved in the process of European regional policy-making – planning, negotiation, formulation, implementation and monitoring –, the better will be the institutional performance, which eventually leads to economic development. The degree of partnership and the competencies in regional development depend both on the system of territorial relations which is nationally defined. A framework of eight regional roles in development was presented in order to explore institutional performance. Four roles relate to the interplay between regions, the other four define the region's initiatives outside its own boundaries. The advantage of the framework is its capacity to capture a broad spectrum of regional activities and the fact that it has been successfully applied in empirical research.

---

to resolve this uncertainty by shaping the relations between partners and facilitating collective action" (Paraskevopoulos 1998: 34f).

[66]    Institutional networks can be defined as "systems of interactions involving both public and private institutional actors which are linked around a certain policy domain or territory and hence bounded by it". By definition, a network should not be seen merely as a corporate body but as a "new quality completely different from the total of the features of the involved organisations" (Paraskevopoulos 1998: 36).

# 7 METHODOLOGICAL ASPECTS OF ANALYSING INSTITUTIONAL PERFORMANCE

This chapter provides insight in the methodological aspects of analysing institutional performance. I first discuss the advantages and disadvantages of case study research strategy. The second section explains methodical aspects to be considered for the application of the analytical framework, which was presented in the last chapter. I proceed with the case selection of Andalusia and Algarve. The chapter closes with a discussion of the unit of observation and of data sources.

## 7.1    Strengths and Weaknesses of the Case Studies

A case study is defined as an observational study based on qualitative and quantitative information, few (or only one) cases, and non-statistical procedures for analysing information (van Evera 1997: 52). Qualitative methods prove useful when the empirical focus of interest is associated with difficulties in quantifying the major variables of interest (Ragin 1991: 2). Case studies allow the researcher to develop a richer, more detailed understanding of the variables and how they influence each other, that is, to explore causal explanation between facts of the social world (Miles and Huberman 1994: 4). This means, on the other hand, giving up the idea that variables have to be operationalised in the same strict and detailed way as quantitative analysis demands (Mitchell and Bernauer 1997: 3).

The principal problems of case studies are many variables and a small number of cases. Critics have long considered case studies the weakest method, compared to experimentation and observation using large-n analysis (Lijphart 1971: 685). In their view experiments are the best method, because the investigator eliminates the possible effects of omitted variables by exposing the group to only one stimulus, while holding the others constant. Large-n analysis is second-best, because the investigator can run partial correlations to control the effect of specific omitted variables. He can also rely on the randomising effect of examining many cases to reduce the effects of other omitted variables. Studies of one or a few cases are worst, because data is unrandomised and partial correlations are unfeasible since the data points are too few. However, this criticism of case studies is unfair and false. Case studies offer several methods of controlling the impact of omitted variables, such as the "controlled comparison method", "congruence procedures" or the "process tracing method" (van Evera 1997: 55-65). A second criticism of case studies – that "case study results cannot be generalised to other cases" – has more merit, but applies mainly to single-case studies. Finally, one has to be aware of the following tempting but dangerous fallacy in the interpretation of case study results, the fallacy of attaching too much significance to negative findings. Deviant cases weaken a probabilistic hypothesis, but they can only invalidate it if they turn up in sufficient numbers to make the hypothesised relationship disappear altogether (Ragin 1989: 52).

## 7.2   Method

It is good medicine for researchers to make their preferences clear. I think of myself as a "realist" which has come to mean many things. Realists think that "social phenomena exist not only in the mind but also in the objective world – and that some lawful and reasonably stable relationships are to be found among them" (Miles and Huberman 1994: 4). In order to test the correlations predicted by the model as well as to uncover causal explanations and regularities in day-to-day situations of European regional policy, the analytical approach of this book was based on successive observation and interviews. Through the process of "deep attentiveness and empathetic (mutual) understanding of the perceptions of local actors" (Silverman 1997: 12), I tried to gain a holistic (systematic and integrated) overview of the context. This position assumes that people create and maintain meaningful worlds. In accordance with the *interactivist position* (Miller and Glassner 1997: 100, 105), I argue not only for the existence of this world, but also for the "ability as researcher to capture elements of these worlds".[67]

There are two critical areas of this approach. Firstly, the relation between the dependent variable (institutional performance) and the independent variable (decentralisation of European regional policy) is not likely to be mono-causal. Other variables, e.g. economic and cultural factors, might provide a more plausible explanation for the variation of institutional performance. Careful case selection reduces this problem (see Chapter 7.3). The second issue is about time since the more decentralised approach of European regional policy was not expected to instantly raise institutional performance. The solution to this problem is a longitudinal study at three different points of time, where a number of paired observations of values on the independent and dependent variable were taken across a range of circumstances within the case (see Chapter 7.4.1). It is then assessed whether these values co-vary in accordance with the theoretical predictions. The drawback of the within-case comparison approach is that the longitudinal approach is hampered by the conflict between internal and external validity. The method of holding the value of certain

---

[67]   According to the interactivist position, research cannot provide the mirror reflection of the social world that *positivists* strive for. However, it may provide access to the meanings people attribute to their experiences and social worlds. On the other hand, interactivists do not follow radical social constructionism which suggests that no knowledge about reality can be obtained from interviews, because the interview is obviously and exclusively an interaction between the interviewer and the interview subject in which both participants create and construct narrative versions of the social world. In summary, interactivists believe that "while the interview is itself a symbolic interaction, this does not discount the possibility that knowledge of the social world beyond the interaction can be obtained" (Miller and Glassner 1997: 100).

variables constant increases internal validity, but it simultaneously limits the range of cases to which one can validly generalise. Holding variables constant across cases prevents conclusions about whether the independent variable would influence the dependent variable in the same way if these control variables had different values (Mitchell and Bernauer 1997: 29f). I mitigate this problem to a certain extent by conducting case studies on two regions, so that control variables are not exactly identical. However, one should take notice of this restriction in the interpretation of the results.

## 7.3 Case Selection

Case studies are carried out on the following two regions: Andalusia in Spain and Algarve in Portugal. Both are objective 1 regions, which are poorly developed compared to the respective national average and, of course, in relation to the European average.[68] Besides personal interest in the two regions, the cases were chosen on the basis of the following criteria. (1) The economic structure of the regions, with SMEs and micro-enterprises responsible for most of the output, meet theoretical requirements. (2) Interviews with executives of SMEs and entrepreneurial associations revealed that the pressure for externalisation exists in both regions. (3) Different values in terms of the dependent variable (institutional performance). In Andalusia a variety of active institutions (such as governmental bodies, universities, monitoring committees, entrepreneurial associations) are occupied with regional development whereas in the region of Algarve a deficit of institutional bodies concerned with regional planning can be observed. (4) A large between-case variation of the independent variable (degree of devolution within the territorial system). Andalusia is an autonomous region, where the regional government exercises substantial power. Institutions in Algarve, on the contrary, work in a highly centralised environment with a strong role of the national government. In neither region the system of territorial relations was constitutionally changed during the period of observation which means that within-case variation of this explanatory variable is small. (5) Other potentially explanatory variables exhibit only little or no between-case variance, namely the amount of structural transfers *per capita*, the sectoral structure of the economy, geographical exposure on the Iberian Peninsula (both Andalusia and Algarve are neighbouring the sea) and the cultural background. (6) Wealth of data. Finally (7), Andalusia and Algarve are both border regions, which allows us to analyse

---

[68] Andalusia is the second poorest region in Spain and the sixth poorest in the EU. Algarve ranks as the third poorest region both in national and European comparison. Regional development in other types of regions – such as objective 2 regions suffering from de-industrialisation – was not studied. Given the limits which the study had to adopt, it was felt that the investigation of objective 1 regions best suited the purpose of the study because of the broad-based development mandate and more complex responsibilities which the regional level is called to fulfil in comparison with other types of regions.

transregional co-operation established within the Community Initiative "Interreg".[69] The biggest differences between the two regions concerns the size of the surface, population and economic output.

No southern Italian region was chosen because there exist already empirical studies on the institutional performance of this area. A further study on southern Italy might have added to and confirmed earlier research but would have neglected Spain and Portugal, two areas where the evaluation of institutional performance has been nonexistent. Language problems prevented a case study on a Greek region.

## 7.4    Unit of Observation and Data

### 7.4.1    The Community Support Framework as Unit of Observation

The case studies were conducted in summer and winter of 1999, which was at the end of the second planning period. At that time, information on the evaluation phase of the 1994-1999 CSFs and on the preparation of the third CSF round (2000-2006) was gathered by interviews and the analysis of documents. The situation both in the beginning of the first planning period (1989-1993), as well as in the beginning of the second planning period (1994-1999), was reconstructed in order to obtain further points of observation. This was done by studying documents and by asking the interviewees about the conditions at that time. The units of observation are thus the three CSFs in each region at the beginning of the planning period. I also analysed how Andalusia and Algarve were involved in Community Initiatives and in projects funded by the CF, in order to complete the picture of European regional policy.

The assumption of this approach is, on the one hand, that information gathered in interviews from members of the elite (executives and experts) reflects the behaviour (respectively output) of an institution.[70] The validity of interviews was tested by comparing various statements of different actors on the same question. On the other hand, I assume that the retro-perspectives of interviewees truly reflects the past. Cross-checking of statements with official documents showed that this assumption is reasonable. Furthermore, interviewees had the opportunity to review the transcription of their statements.

### 7.4.2    Data Sources

For the case studies I relied on data from the following sources:

---

[69]    The "Interreg" Community Initiative, which was adopted in 1990, intended to prepare border areas for a EU without internal frontiers.

[70]    This assumption causes methodological problems in so far as different levels of analysis are mixed (the individual and the institution). Two reasons justify my approach: (1) Although an institution is not exactly the sum of individual actions, it can be assumed that institutional action is formed by the decisions of

(1) Interviews with representatives of public and private institutions who deal with regional development.[71] The survey includes a total of 34 interviews which were conducted between August and October 1999.[72] The interviewed persons were chosen from (a) the regional elite, including proponents of regional governmental bodies, development institutions or monitoring boards, sectoral associations, and entrepreneurial associations; (b) the national elite, including experts of regional policy planning units and contact partners of the European Commission; (c) the Directorate General 16 of the European Commission, where experts of the Spanish and Portuguese ERDF, ESF and Cohesion Fund country desks were interviewed. The interviews included a mixture of structured and open questions.[73]

(2) Quantitative data from various statistical offices and publications.

(3) Review of primary literature and documents.

(4) Review of secondary literature and documents, including a variety of economic, social, political and cultural analyses.

## 7.5   Synopsis

The case studies on Andalusia (Spain) and Algarve (Portugal) allow us to develop a detailed understanding of the relation between the institutional performance (dependent variable) and the decentralised European regional policy approach (independent variable). There are many  reasons for conducting case studies on Andalusia and Algarve, the most important being between and within-case variation of the dependent variable, largely between-case variation of the independent variable, wealth of data, and little variation of other explanatory variables, especially in terms of European structural transfers and sectoral structure of the economy. The method applied in the case studies is a mixture of longitudinal within-case analysis and between-case comparison. The investigation includes a number of paired observations of values on the independent and dependent variable across a range of circumstances within the case in the former, and between the cases of Andalusia and Algarve in the latter. The units of observation are the three CSFs (1989-1993, 1994-1999, 2000-2006), including as well aspects of the region's activity with the Cohesion Fund and Community Initiatives. Data was collected during the summer and winter of 1999

---

individuals, especially in the case of executives. (2) Limited resources prevented the author from interviewing several proponents of the same institution.

[71]   Appendix A.5 lists the interview partners.

[72]   The main actors of structural policy in Andalusia were chosen on the basis of Newton's (1997) detailed analysis of Spanish institutions and Grote's (1998) analysis of policy networks. Interviewees in the case of Algarve were chosen from similar institutions as in the case of Andalusia. A survey among experts of Portuguese regional policy completed the list of main actors.

[73]   Appendix A.6 shows an example of an interview protocol.

when interviews with 34 proponents of European regional policy were undertaken (at the regional, national and European levels). Additional information was gathered from official documents, secondary literature and various statistical publications.

# 8 ANDALUSIA: LEARNING THAT EUROPEAN FUNDS ARE MORE THAN MONEY

This chapter is the first case study on institutional performance and European regional policy. The complexity of the structural policy in Andalusia, including a variety of public and private actors, makes it necessary to introduce the reader into the case. The first section of the chapter reviews the physical environment and demographic trends of Andalusia, the evolution and structure of its economy as well as the basic principles of territorial politics. The second section presents regional policy interventions that are co-financed by European structural funds. The institutions that are involved in regional development are discussed in the third section. Finally, institutional performance in each of the eight roles identified by our analytical framework is analysed.

## 8.1 Portrait of the Region

### 8.1.1 Physical Environment

Spanish speaking Andalusia is the second-most southerly region in the Community. The region is endowed with a range of sceneries, its climate, rich natural resources (farmland, sea, minerals and forests), a largely intact environment and a rich historical heritage, which is based on the superimposition of different periods and cultures. Andalusia is also one of the most extensive European regions with a surface of 87'268 square kilometres (17.3 per cent of Spain). The eight provinces extend over five hundred kilometres from the border with Portugal in the west to the eastern coast of Spain. The relief of Andalusia shows four distinct topographical zones. The only sparsely populated massif of the Sierra Morena makes up the natural border to the central Meseta in the north. The Baetic basin is formed by the Guadalquivir, the longest river of Andalusia, and is a corridor for easy communications across the region and access to other parts of Spain. The west of the basin is characterised by extensive lowlands where the mouth of the Guadalquivir has played an important role in stimulating development by offering sites for settlement, ports and opportunities for agricultural and industrial development, e.g. Seville (the capital of Andalusia), Cordoba, Huelva and Cadiz.

The Baetic mountains, extending in a series of ranges from Cadiz to Almeria and culminating in the peak of Mulhacen (3481m) in the Sierra Nevada, present a sharp backdrop to the Mediterranean coast. Within the imposing mountainous areas there are numerous basins and river valleys offering opportunities for the development of agriculture and industry. Finally, the coastline of Andalusia has developed as a dynamic zone of population growth and economic activities. Parts of the coast have been sites of intensive tourist development, most notably along the Costa del Sol. Yet despite its reputation as an international tourist playground, the Mediterranean coastline has also been the site of intensive agriculture and important new industrial development, which along with the growth of tourism and the service industry, have attracted an ever-growing population. The coastline also contains sites of important ecological value such as the Doñana National Park, the last great European wetlands reserve, or the volcanic landscapes and marine park of Cabo de Gata. The equable character of the climate in this zone, as well as its role as a transport hub to Africa, have added to the attraction as a place to live and work (Eurostat and European Commission 1993: 132; Salmon 1992: 17-20).

**Figure 8-1: The Region of Andalusia**

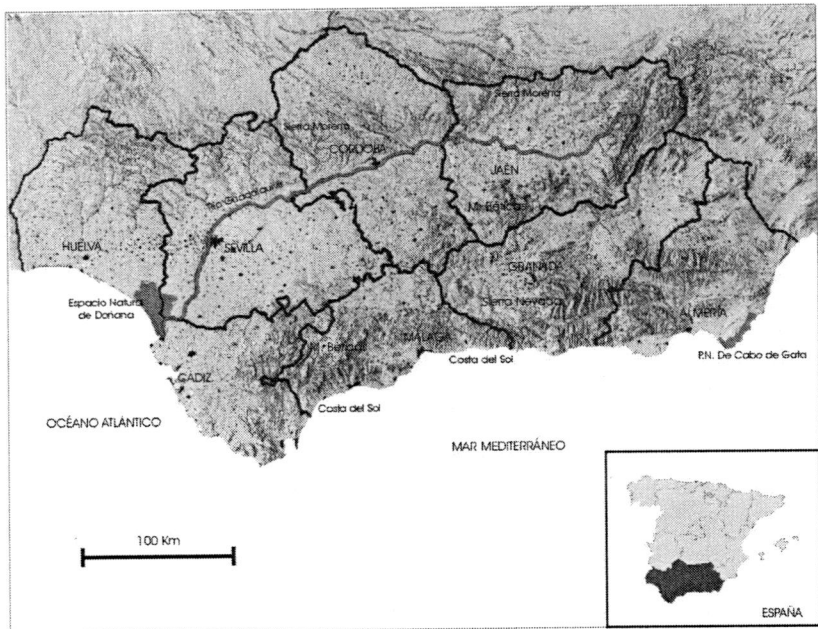

*Source: own map.*

## 8.1.2  Demographic Characteristics

In 1996 the legally resident population was recorded in the census at about seven million, some 18 per cent of the total population of Spain (see Figure 8-2). In relation to the surface area this results in a relatively low population density of eighty-three inhabitants per square kilometre. However, the population is unevenly distributed across the region. Some 55 per cent of the population are concentrated in urban and coastal areas, which account for only 14 per cent of the total surface area, whereas there has been a depopulation of the mountainous areas in the last twenty years. The trend of urbanisation is likely to continue due to a positive migration balance and a young population. There remains, moreover, a substantial reservoir of people currently dependent on agriculture to nourish the growing population of the cities (IEA 1998b; JdA, CEH 1999b: 58-60).

During the second half of the twentieth century all the regions of Andalusia completed their passage through the demographic transition, common to industrialised countries, from high to low birth and death rates, so that the natural growth rate of today is around 0.5 per cent, compared to the national average of 0.25 per cent. Contrary to the development of the natural growth rate, migration has varied in volume, direction and composition. The extremely high rate of out-migration in the twentieth century with 1.7 million persons leaving the region between 1900 and 1970 sharply decreased with the recession following the first oil shock in the early 1970s. Net migration loss began to turn to net migration gain in the late 1970s and these gains have continued until the end of the 1990s (IEA 1998a).

**Figure 8-2: Demographic Data of Andalusia**

| Provinces | Population | Area | Density | Growth Rate | Population by Age (in 1000) |
|---|---|---|---|---|---|
| Almeria | 501'761 | 8'774 | 57.2 | 1.2 | |
| Cadiz | 1'105'762 | 7'385 | 149.7 | 0.7 | |
| Cordoba | 761'401 | 13'718 | 55.5 | 0.4 | |
| Granada | 808'053 | 12'531 | 64.5 | 0.4 | |
| Huelva | 454'735 | 10'085 | 45.1 | 0.5 | |
| Jaen | 648'551 | 13'498 | 48.0 | 0.1 | |
| Malaga | 1'249'290 | 7'276 | 171.7 | 1.2 | |
| Seville | 1'705'320 | 14'001 | 121.8 | 0.9 | |
| Andalusia | 7'234'873 | 87'268 | 82.9 | 0.7 | |
| Spain | 39'669'394 | 504'790 | 78.6 | 0.3 | |

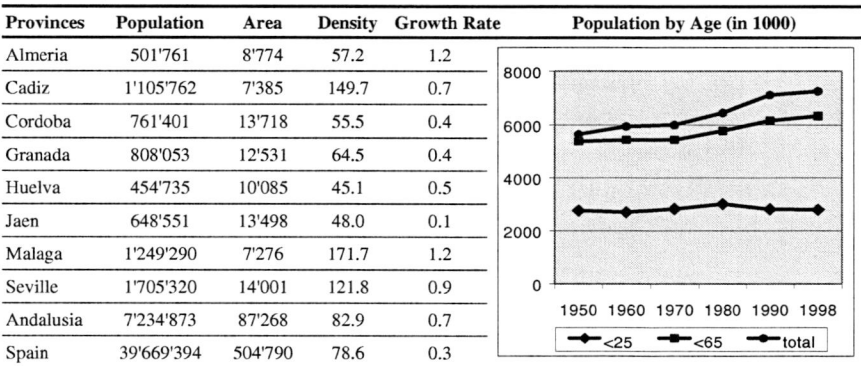

*Note: All figures are for 1996. Population figures are based on resident population; density figures are persons per square kilometre; growth rates are annual average rates in per cent (1981-1996); area in square kilometres.*

*Source: Eurostat; IEA 1998b.*

The product of the decline in birth rates and the migration balance turning positive has been one of the most youthful and fastest growing populations of Europe, with an annual average growth rate of 0.73 per cent (1981-1996) which is 0.4 per cent above the national figure. The present age structure of the Andalusian population highlights the high proportion of young people: more than 40 per cent are aged under twenty-five, while the population over sixty-five accounts only for 12 per cent (JdA, CEH 1999a: 3). The youthful structure has crucial implications for the composition of demand, the labour market, education and the provision of other services. An expanding population of working age puts pressure on employment which is likely to restrain rises in wages, thus maintaining the region as one of relatively low labour costs, especially in the unskilled segment of the labour market. This reduces the possibility that GDP *per capita* will rise fast to average European levels. In education, pressure of student numbers will require that further resources be allocated to this area, especially for higher education (Salmon 1992: 26).

### 8.1.3    Evolution and Characteristics of the Economy (1980s and 1990s)

Throughout the twentieth century the economy of Andalusia has been progressively integrating into the world economy, especially into the western European economic system. Its evolution has been closely linked to changes in the structure and organisation of the national and European economy, while simultaneously being shaped by its own unique characteristics. In the beginning of the 1980s the Andalusian economy was dominated by the national economic crisis, which was on the one hand nourished by rising oil prices that threw the international economy into recession (Alshuth 1994: 125; Economist Intelligence Unit 1999c: 21). On the other hand, an economic slow down was the result of the political and social upheavals invoked by the transition from dictatorship to democracy following the death of General Franco in 1975 (Nohlen and Hildenbrand 1992: 29-31). The consequent integration of a regional economy, formerly operating within a protected national economic system, into the international economy revealed the limited degree of competitivity of the Andalusian economy with its many public enterprises. Preparations for entry into the European Community intensified this problem (Alshuth 1994: 127f). Agriculture entered a new phase of crisis associated with rigid product prices and increasing production costs (especially energy, fertilisers and labour costs). Many mines in Huelva and Seville were facing closure. The manufacturing industry was also severely affected, being squeezed between increased competition from newly industrialised countries and the decline in demand for products, which left surplus capacities in many sectors (namely in the oil refining, shipbuilding and textile industries). Even in services there was little expansion with tourism collapsing and the construction business in recession (Salmon 1992: 39f). The economic crisis in Andalusia was clearly demonstrated by unemployment rates of over thirty per cent (see Figure 8-3). Unemployment rose not only owing to a tide of job losses, but also because of an expanding population of working age, a changing migration pattern and an increased economic activity of women, who traditionally had not participated in the labour force (Eurostat and European Commission 1993: 135).

**Figure 8-3: Unemployment and Growth Rate of Regional GDP in Andalusia (1983-1998; in per cent)**

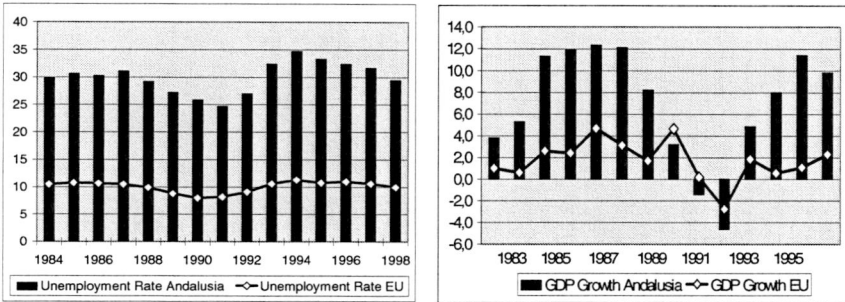

*Note: GDP growth rates are based on BIP figures at factor prices, inflation adjusted (at 1986 prices).*

*Source: Data from European Commission 1999k; Eurostat; Fundación BBV 1998: 322f.*

From the second half of the 1980s (until the early 1990s) the economy of Andalusia began a process of recovery, responding rapidly to the new wave of expansion of the national and international economy (Lawlor and Rigby 1998: 103f; Liebermann 1995: 290-293). Economic growth rose at one of the fastest rates in Europe and employment increased from 1.46 million in 1985 to 1.76 million in 1989. Unfortunately the rate of unemployment declined very slowly due to an ever-increasing labour force. The dynamism exhibited by the economy of Andalusia predominantly reflected the greater reliance on services and the accompanying growth of construction, both related to tourism (Salmon 1992: 42).

At the turn of the decade, the continent fell into recession again. Contrary to the European, but similar to the Spanish economy, Andalusia continued to grow in the early 1990s although growth rates had slowed from 1989 on (Scobie 1998: 5; Liebermann 1995: 340f). As part of this deceleration in growth, there was a notable decrease in private investment. It is suggested that German reunification and the opening up of eastern Europe increased the severity of the downturn, by diverting foreign direct investment away from Spain to these new areas of development (Lawlor and Rigby 1998: 104). An analysis of the sectoral growth pattern reveals, furthermore, that the buoyancy of the early 1990s was maintained essentially through the large volume of public investments for the preparation of the Expo 1992 in Seville, of which the construction industry profited most (Salmon 1992: 45). Once this public consumption came to a halt, all the Andalusian sectors found themselves in deep recession with a negative growth rate of half a per cent (1992 and 1993) and a rise of unemployment of up to 27 per cent (1992). However, the downturn was mitigated to a certain degree by a turnaround of the external sector, when the 1992 devaluation of the peseta fuelled exportation and provoked a reduction in import growth (Economist Intelligence Unit 1999c: 22).

By 1994 a strong tourism and export recovery had pulled the Andalusian economy out of the recession and a new era of growth was initiated which has continued up to now (JdA, CEH 1997: 39f). The service sector was again the primary driving force for this development with employment increases in nearly all sub-sectors, except in financial services. The tourism subsector achieved record highs and two trends that have been observed in the preceding years continued their consolidation: a less seasonal nature in traveller influxes and the creation of new alternatives to the usual "sun-and-beach" tourism, leading to significant higher overnight hotel stays in the inland areas (JdA, CEH 1997a: 44). Agriculture added to this positive trend, especially in 1996 and 1997, when the sector greatly benefited from the end of a drought that had lasted since 1992 (Economist Intelligence Unit 1999: 25). The performance of the industrial sector from 1996 on was moderate but in line with national and international standards. Despite the positive economic performance, unemployment continued to be the Achilles' heel with rates of above thirty per cent between 1993 and 1997.

One of the main reasons for Andalusia's high unemployment is the lack of skilled labour (Eurostat and European Commission 1993: 134; JdA, CEH 1997: 111-113; JdA, CEH 1999a: 142-148). Over 40 per cent of the total population over 10 years of age had no school qualifications in 1997. Among those with school qualifications (and part of the working population) higher vocational training and university graduates were still rare although some progress has been made in the last few years (see Figure 8-4). Another feature of the labour market is the high proportion of temporary employment, which has always been well above the national average. The reasons for this are rigidities in the labour market and the seasonal nature of tourism and agricultural activities (JdA, CEH 1997: 110f).

**Figure 8-4: Educational Level of the Working Population in Andalusia**

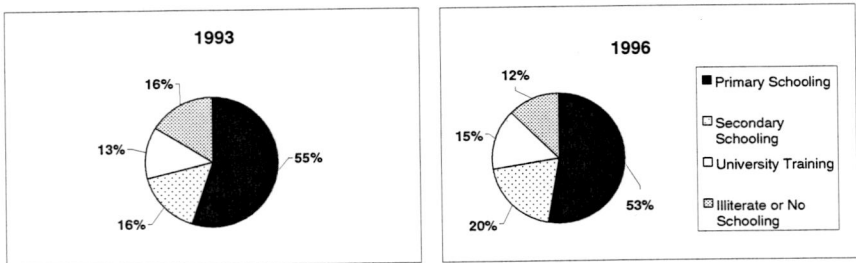

*Source: Eurostat and European Commission 1993: 134; IEA (www.iea.junta-andalucia.es); JdA, CEH 1997: 112; JdA, CEH 1999a: 144.*

In common with other western European regions, the transformation of the Andalusian economy has been a remarkable development, with the agricultural sector gradually declining in importance and the service sector rising to dominate the economy (Pérez 1998: 228f; Salmon 1992: 44f). The concentration of economic activity in the tertiary sector can be seen in the following figures (IEA 1998b; IFA 1999: 77-82). In 1985 about 54 per cent of the regional GDP came from services, by 1996 this figure had grown to 59 per cent. In contrast, the importance of the agriculture sector continued to dwindle from over 13 per cent of regional GDP and 22 per cent of the occupied population in 1985 to about 3 per cent of GDP and 12 per cent of employment in 1996. The contribution of industry (including mining, gas, electricity and water) to the GDP increased from 18 per cent in 1985 to 23 per cent in 1996. However, the size of the Andalusian industrial sector is relatively small compared to the European average. The regional industrial system has not been able to satisfy the total regional demand for industrial goods, which translated into an important avenue of income leakage from the region (Pérez 1998: 232). The productivity levels of the industrial sector is slightly above the national average, whereas that of the service sector is considerably lower than that of the rest of Spain. The productivity level of the agricultural sector, for its part, is nearly 30 per cent higher than the national figure. This reflects the major gains in productivity of this sector through the continuing modernisation of agricultural structures in order to exploit the advantages of Andalusia's climate and natural conditions. The key problem of agricultural production remains the irregular precipitation, but not a general shortage of water (Nohlen and Hildenbrand 1992: 99).

**Figure 8-5: Welfare Indicators for Andalusia**

| Welfare (per 1000 hab.; 1991) | Andalusia | EU-12 | GDP Income |
|---|---|---|---|
| doctors | 3.6 | 3.1 | |
| beds in hospitals | 3.2 | 8.0 | |
| dentists | 0.2 | 0.7 | |
| electricity consumption (kwh/hab) | 203 | 1'527 | |
| televisions | 264 | 419 | |
| **Infrastructure (km per 1000 km²; 1991)** | | | |
| highways | 2.0 | 15.0 | |
| railway | 23.1 | 54.1 | |

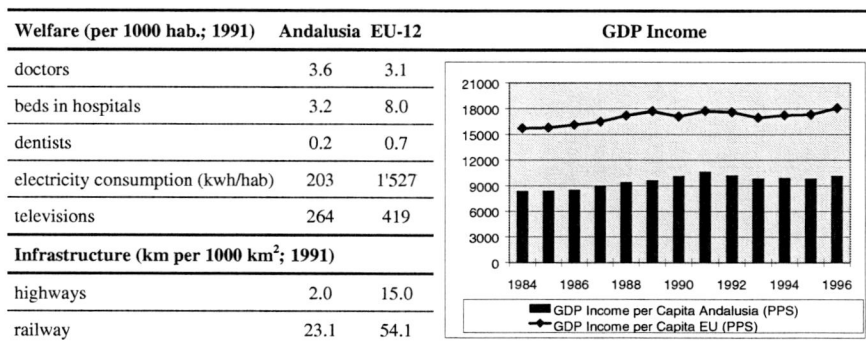

GDP Income per Capita Andalusia (PPS)
GDP Income per Capita EU (PPS)

*Source: Eurostat; IEA (www.iea.junta-andalucia.es); JdA, CEH 1996c: 13.*

The modernisation of the economy has led to the creation of employment and a substantial improvement in the living and income situation of Andalusia. Nevertheless, Andalusia is still a poor European region where the situation of basic infrastructure, e.g. roads, railways and sanitary installations, has been improved only in the last 20

years (see Figure 8-5). Regional GDP *per capita* was only 53 (57) per cent of the
European Community average in 1986 (1996). Moreover, economic development has
been both structurally and spatially selective. Some companies and sectors in the
regional economy display all the features of modern industry as elsewhere in Europe
(e.g., the electronics factories in Malaga or the dairy food company Uniasa). Others
remain bogged down in traditional practices and old technologies (e.g., small rural
food processing and clothing plants; IFA 1999: 159-164). Similarly, some areas of the
region have a well developed and diversified economy (namely Seville), whereas other
areas are less favoured and display features of rural and urban poverty, an unskilled
population, frequently unemployed at least for part of the year and often dependent on
marginal agriculture or part-time construction work. This uneven structure has been
the reason for significant intra-regional disparities, so that the provinces of Granada
and Jaen have a regional *per capita* GDP nearly 40 per cent lower than in Huelva and
Cadiz where much of the industrial activity is concentrated (IEA 1998a; Martín and
Lizarragea 1994: 223f).

Striking the balance in potentials and drawbacks, Andalusia displays an intact potential
for future development due to its natural resources, the favourable climate, a rich
historical and artistic heritage, a largely intact environment and a demographic
dynamism, including a young workforce. Nevertheless, there are a number of obstacles
to the exploitation of this potential. The low level of qualifications in the work force
hampers a rise in productivity and competitivity, which is the reason for very high
youth unemployment. Further investments in basic infrastructure are necessary
(namely railway, roads and communications). Moreover, an underdeveloped industrial
sector – with the exception of food processing – has few links between branches or
with other sectors of the economy. Finally, the lack of diversification makes the
economy of Andalusia vulnerable against business cycles and external shocks.

### 8.1.4    Regional Government and Administration

The regional government and administration of Andalusia (*Junta de Andalucía*; JdA),
based in Seville, came into being in 1982, following a referendum in the region and
approval of its statute of autonomy by the central government. The government of
Andalusia is, thus, subject not only to the Constitution, but also to its own statute of
autonomy, which together cover all aspects of political life in the region and build a
hybrid system of government, which is neither unitary nor federal, but based on the
"unity of the Spanish nation" and the "autonomy of the nationalities and regions which
constitute it" (Heywood 1995: 143). The Constitution establishes that each
autonomous region shall have a government headed by a president, a high court of
justice and a legislative assembly (parliament) elected by universal suffrage every four
years (Morata 1995: 116). Andalusia has the statute of an autonomous region of the
special category, which enables the region to organise its own institutions of self-

government and to establish the parameters of the relationship with central authorities (Newton 1997: 140).[74] Since the formation of the region, the centre-left Spanish Socialist Worker's Party (PSOE, *Partido Socialista Obrero Español*) has dominated the political scene throughout the 1980s and 1990s. Until 1996 the Andalusian government could count on the PSOE majority at the national level. In the 1996 general election, however, the centre-right Popular Party (PP, *Partido Popular*) emerged as the largest parliamentary force which has caused a series of political clashes between the Andalusian and national governments.

The regional government of Andalusia has gained considerable power through the transfer of responsibilities (*competencias*), material, human and financial resources from the peripheral administration of the Spanish state to the JdA (Newton 1997: 143f; Salmon 1992: 32). Among the exclusive powers of Andalusia are regional development, industrial policy, public works, communications and transport, environment, banking and credit, agriculture and fisheries, tourism, housing and urban planning. As a region with full autonomy Andalusia has also taken the responsibility for education, health, local administration and police. However, in addition to traditional federal functions such as foreign policy, defence, monetary policy and general communications, the central state is empowered to lay down basic legislation or principles in any policy area. The complex and ambiguous division of power produced a lack of clarity and has been a source of constant political and judicial controversy. In general, however, regional authorities considered their competencies in the field of regional development as sufficient and did not ask for more competencies.

The administrative body of the Andalusian government consists of thirteen departments (*consejerías*) to whom a range of autonomous bodies and public sector enterprises are attached (JdA 1999b).[75] In each of the eight provinces the consejerias are represented by delegations (*delegaciones*), usually mirror-imaging the structure of the JdA. The delegaciones have no legislative or executive powers, but are purely administrative agencies which serve to carry out regional (not only structural) policies at the provincial level on the basis of budgets delegated to them. At the provincial level exist, furthermore, county councils (*diputaciónes*) which the central government formerly used to administrate and control the local level. The councils are still linked

---

[74] Unlike federal systems, Spanish regional autonomy is settled on a heterogeneous basis according to political and institutional considerations. Broadly speaking, statutes of autonomy fall into two main categories: special and general. The first one covers the three national minorities (the Basque Country, Catalonia, and Galicia) and Andalusia which all have "full" autonomous status. The general statute, applying to eleven regions, was intended to be transitional since the regional authorities could request more powers. The gap between both categories has been considerably reduced since 1993 (Economist Intelligence Unit 1999: 7; Martínez-Pujalte López 1998: 206f; Morata and Munoz 1996: 198).

[75] Chapter 8.3 contains further details on the structure of the administrative body where I focus on the actors involved in regional development.

to the central government. Their position, however, is not strong anymore and it includes functions such as the provision and co-ordination of municipal services and legal, economic and technical assistance, particularly to smaller municipalities. Provincial activities are financed by regional and national grants and taxes levied on the municipal business tax (Newton 1997: 135).

The second tier of local administration (besides the provinces) is built by a dense patchwork of 766 municipalities that have also administrative bodies, differing in form and function depending on the size of the municipality. Additionally to a minimum catalogue of duties, the municipalities can be executors of regional and national competencies. Municipalities often organise themselves in *mancomunidades* or *comarcas*, which are functional associations of a few municipalities with joint juridical responsibilities, in order to provide better public services. These territorial units between the provincial and municipal level are especially popular with small municipalities. The municipalities have their financial resources from regional and national grants as well as from their own tax incomes. Contrary to the conflictive relationship between the regional and central government, competencies between the regional and local level are more clearly defined. In fact, the local level has almost no competencies under the terms of the Constitution and it is largely under the control of the regional government, which has often been reluctant to cede powers to local governments (Heywood 1995: 157).

Political autonomy of the regions must be underpinned by financial autonomy for it to be effective. There are four sources of revenues for the region of Andalusia (Held 1994: 207f; Heywood 1995: 150-154; Hildenbrand 1998: 122f). The single largest source of income comes from budget transfers of the state, which are calculated on the basis of a series of parameters, which include population, surface area, migration, relative poverty and relative tax revenues. The formula, which provoked controversy over the relative weight given to each factor, has been subject to revision every five years since its introduction in 1985. Andalusia, secondly, receives income from the Interterritorial Compensation Fund (FCI; *Fondo de Compensación Interterritorial*), whose purpose is the transfer of resources from the richer to the poorer regions. Thirdly, Andalusia is one of the regions, which benefits most from European structural funds. Finally, income is raised through taxes ceded to the region by the state (e.g., inheritance tax), local levies, income from property owned by the region and money borrowed on the capital markets (which has led to an alarming level of debt; Newton 1997: 127).

It should be stressed that proper regional resources constitute still a small percentage of total revenue, which is indeed one of the main deficits of the current system, as it does not respect the principle of fiscal equivalence. Andalusia welcomes the grateful role of spending money, but does leave the unthankful job of tax collection to the central government (Hildenbrand 1998: 125). Regional financial responsibility has been increased through a transfer of tax collection rights in recent times (*Neue Zürcher Zeitung,* 101/1996: 25; *Neue Zürcher Zeitung,* 223/1996: 23). This transfer should also have a positive effect on the scale of corruption, since it raises the demand for transparency in public spending. The existence of corruption is a fact (*Frankfurter Allgemeine Zeitung,* December 12th 1995: 16) but its exact extent is impossible to measure. According to Della Porta and Mény (1997: 81-83) the most prominent form of corruption has been client and nepotist relationships, which led to politically biased investment decisions. Several interviewees confirmed this type of corruption, especially for interventions financed by global grants.[76] However, the degree of political corruption in Andalusia should neither be exaggerated nor put on an equal footing with the endemic kind of corruption existing in Italy (Mauro 1995: 710). The EU, moreover, has devoted quite formidable resources to the task of ensuring that structural expenditures are legitimate. A specific European institution, the Court of Auditors, is complemented within the Commission by a financial control service (DG-20), while monitoring committees perform *ex post*, ongoing and *ex ante* evaluations (Kearney 1997: 314).

## 8.2    European Regional Policy Interventions

In order to analyse the performance of regional institutions in economic development it is necessary to understand how European regional policy interventions were organised. The following pages review, therefore, the size, form and axes of European regional policy interventions.

Andalusia receives the biggest share of structural transfers of all the European regions. The funds have grown in absolute figures with each CSF, but they diminished in relative terms (see Table 8-1). Adding co-financing of the central and regional administration to the EU funds, public spending for regional policy in Andalusia came up to around Euro 5'200 million in the CSF 1989-1993.[77] In the CSF 1994-1999, public spending amounted to Euro 9'150 million. Provisional financial plans estimate public investment for the CSF 2000-2006 in the range of Euro 8'200 million (Comisión Europea 1996: 71, 91, 215; JdA, CEH 1996a: 40; www.inforegio.org). The financial resources dedicated to the region of Andalusia were only partially under the control of the JdA (and other regional institutions), since the Spanish structural

---

[76] As an example stands the *Sevilla Siglo XXI,* a public enterprise responsible for the creation and maintenance of employment in the province of Seville. This institution was founded in 1993 and since then has constantly distributed national and European funds without any impact on employment. The reason for failure were changing investment priorities and political instrumentalisation of the institution.

[77] Public spending includes structural payments and co-financing of the central and regional administration, but neglects private investments. The figures include interventions financed by the ERDF, ESF, FIFG and EAGGF.

interventions differed between regional and pluri-regional investments. The former resources were planned within the regional sub-CSF Andalusia and was under the competence of the Andalusian government. This part made up about 36 per cent of public expenses in each of the three CSFs (Comisión Europea 1996: 71, 91, 215; JdA, CEH 1994: 14-16). The latter was written down in the (Spanish) CSF for objective 1 regions and was managed by the central government.[78]

**Table 8-1: Interventions of Structural Funds in Andalusia (1989-2006)**

|           | CSF 1989-1993 | | CSF 1994-1999 | | CSF 2000-2006 | |
|-----------|-----------|------------|-----------|------------|-----------|------------|
|           | Mio Euro | % of Spain | Mio Euro | % of Spain | Mio Euro | % of Spain |
| Andalusia | 2'749    | 29.3       | 6'870    | 26.1       | 10'772   | 25.0       |
| Spain     | 9'393    | 100.0      | 26'300   | 100.0      | 43'087   | 100.0      |

*Source: Comisión Europea 1990: 18, 25, 91; Comisión Europea 1996: 71, 91, 215; JdA, CEH 1996a: 40; Nohlen and Hildenbrand 1992: 97f; www.inforegio.org.*

The regional and pluri-regional investments were targeted on seven (eight) axes of development (see Figure 8-6). The distribution among the axes was more or less similar for the first two CSFs.[79] In the second CSF, additional structural transfers were allocated in the second axis (development of an economic network), the fifth axis (basic development for economic activities) and the sixth axis (qualification of human resources) due to a substantial increase of funds. This was in line with the strategic goal of strengthening the regional competitivity through endogenous development. The latest draft of the CSF 2000-2006 (there were not yet official figures available) gave about the same weight to the axes of interventions as the second one. An analysis of the allocation of structural funds reveals an unequal effort of the JdA in order to overcome the main deficits of regional development (see Chapter 8.1.3). There has been a tendency to invest in infrastructure projects, whereas the development of intangibles (qualification of human resources, R&D capacity) has been neglected. This was the case especially in the first CSF, but also in the other two CSFs. The CF reinforced this tendency as this fund financed only investments in the field of transport and environment (JdA, CEH 1996a: 45).

---

[78]  Besides the regional sub-CSF for Andalusia and the pluri-regional CSF for objective 1 regions, there were two pluri-regional CSFs each for objective 2 and 5b regions, as well as a multitude of other regional sub-CSFs.

[79]  The calculations are based on data of the regional sub-CSF (but exclude projects financed by the CF) because of the MEH's refusal to regionalise its own funds and those allocated to the local governments.

## Figure 8-6: Axes of Structural Interventions in Andalusia (1989-2006)

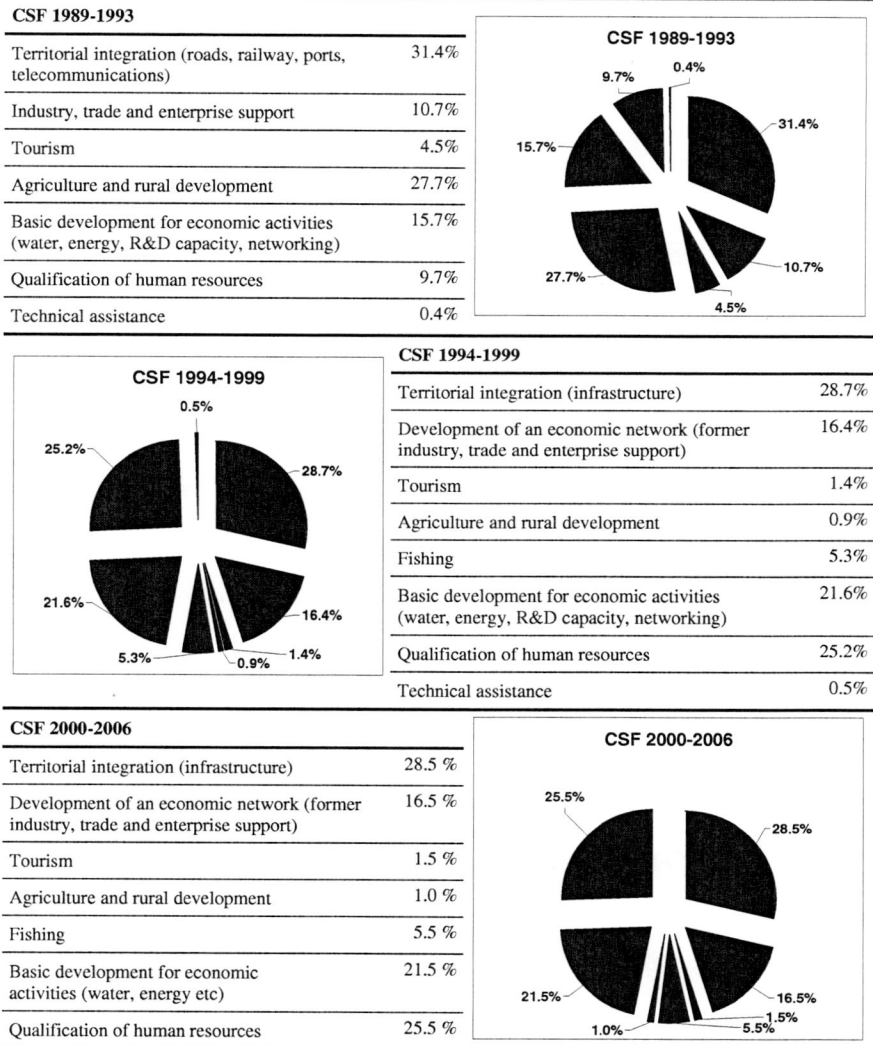

| CSF 1989-1993 | |
|---|---|
| Territorial integration (roads, railway, ports, telecommunications) | 31.4% |
| Industry, trade and enterprise support | 10.7% |
| Tourism | 4.5% |
| Agriculture and rural development | 27.7% |
| Basic development for economic activities (water, energy, R&D capacity, networking) | 15.7% |
| Qualification of human resources | 9.7% |
| Technical assistance | 0.4% |

| CSF 1994-1999 | |
|---|---|
| Territorial integration (infrastructure) | 28.7% |
| Development of an economic network (former industry, trade and enterprise support) | 16.4% |
| Tourism | 1.4% |
| Agriculture and rural development | 0.9% |
| Fishing | 5.3% |
| Basic development for economic activities (water, energy, R&D capacity, networking) | 21.6% |
| Qualification of human resources | 25.2% |
| Technical assistance | 0.5% |

| CSF 2000-2006 | |
|---|---|
| Territorial integration (infrastructure) | 28.5 % |
| Development of an economic network (former industry, trade and enterprise support) | 16.5 % |
| Tourism | 1.5 % |
| Agriculture and rural development | 1.0 % |
| Fishing | 5.5 % |
| Basic development for economic activities (water, energy etc) | 21.5 % |
| Qualification of human resources | 25.5 % |

*Note: Calculations are based on the regional sub-CSF (without CF).*

*Source: JdA, CEH 1994e: 26, 34-37; JdA, CEH 1996a: 34-37; JdA, CEH 1999a: 26-35; Mancha Navarro and Cuadrado Roura 1996: 356; Pajuela 1994: 16, 20.*

## Table 8-2: Structure of Structural Interventions in Andalusia (1989-2006)

**CSF 1989-1993**

6 territorial OPs:

- Almeria-Levante
- Malaga
- Jaen-Granada
- Northern Huelva
- Bajo Guadalquivir
- National Park Doñana

7 sectoral OPs:

- Forestall plan for Andalusia
- Improvement of agricultural infrastructure
- National highway program of regional interest
- Local OP
- Regional incentives
- Improvement of scientific infrastructure
- Environment and water resources

global grants[23]

around 100 individual projects

CIs:

- Interreg (transregional co-operation)
- Leader (stimulation of rural development)
- Envireg (protection of environment)
- Stride (development of R&D capacity)
- Prisma (services to businesses in connection with SEM)
- Retex (diversification and modernisation of the textile sector)
- Telematica (development of telecommunication services)

**CSF 1994-1999**

1 regional OP Andalusia

global grants

OP Doñana (2nd Phase)

CIs:

- Interreg II
- Leader II
- SME (strengthening of competitivity)
- Konver (economic diversification)
- Rechar (economic conversion of coal-mining industry)
- Urban (regeneration of crisis-struck areas in medium-sized and large towns)

**CSF 2000-2006**

1 regional OP Andalusia

global grants

OP National Park Doñana (3rd Phase)

CIs:

- Interreg III
- Leader III
- Equal (former Employment and Adapt)

*Source: European Commission 1994a; 1999i: 2; Guerrero 1997: 242, 249, 252; Inforegio (www.inforegio.cec.eu); JdA, CEH 1994e: 26, 34-37; JdA, CEH 1996a: 24; Pajuela 1994: 16, 22f.*

The form of interventions changed much between the first and the second period, mainly because the European Commission demanded a reduction of the complexity of structural interventions. The first CSF was characterised by a large number of individual projects and territorial and sectoral OPs, whereas the second CSF reduced the number of managing units so that the "OP Andalusia" was responsible for about 83 per cent of all investments under regional competence (see Table 8-2). The CF worked contrary to the trend of reducing complexity since it financed a variety of projects but did not bundle them into a coherent programme. The CSF 2000-2006 is going to have the same structure as the preceding one, but the CIs are simplified once again.

## 8.3 Institutions Concerned with Regional Development

A variety of actors have been involved in regional policy in Andalusia, ranging from public and semi-public to private institutions at the European, national, regional and local level. The interests of these actors have been diverse and the internal balance of power depended more often on political negotiation and intergovernmental co-operation than on constitutional interpretation (Morata 1995: 121). In order to get to know the institutions involved in regional development, it is helpful to analyse the process of European regional policy in Andalusia. Similar to the standard participation of European regions (see Chapter 2.5.4), Andalusia was almost not present in the first two main phases: the creation of the budgetary envelope of European regional policy and the design of the institutional context. The central authorities, jealous of their competencies, excluded the region from these negotiations. Andalusia, on the other hand, wanted to participate in them, since they were responsible for the implementation of a substantial number of structural policies. In a trial to settle this dispute, the central government and the JdA (plus other autonomous regions) agreed in October 1988 to institutionalise regional participation in Community affairs through the Conference of European Affairs (*Confederación para Asuntos Relacionados con las Comunidades Europeas*). This conference has dealt with various issues, such as the development of the European integration process, regional institutional participation in Community matters and the encouragement and monitoring of regional participation in each Community policy through the sectoral conferences already existing (Morata and Munoz 1996: 202). However, the role of Andalusia in these matters is still very limited and the conference does not go far beyond an information meeting.

Contrary to the first two phases, regional actors have been involved in the policy-making (see Figure 8-7). This phase consists of the following sub-phases: planning of the CSF; negotiation of the CSF with the European Commission; formulation of OPs; and finally the implementation and monitoring of planned development actions. For the formulation of the CSF (first phase), the Department of Planning (*DG de Planificación*) of the JdA presented a regional development plan (RDP) to the central administration, including all investment demands for the planning period, regardless of whether they were under regional or national competence.[80] The Ministry of Economy and Finance (*Ministerío de Economia y Hacienda;* MEH) in Madrid divided the investments into regional and pluri-regional, in an attempt to harmonise the regional demands with the competencies of each tier of government. The JdA checked the draft of the national development plan and discussed it with the regional social partners, which were the UGT (*Unión General de Trabajadores*), the CCOO (*Confederación Sindical de Comisiones Obreras*) and the CEA (*Confederación de Empresarios de Andalucía*).

**Figure 8-7: Actors of European Regional Policy in Andalusia**

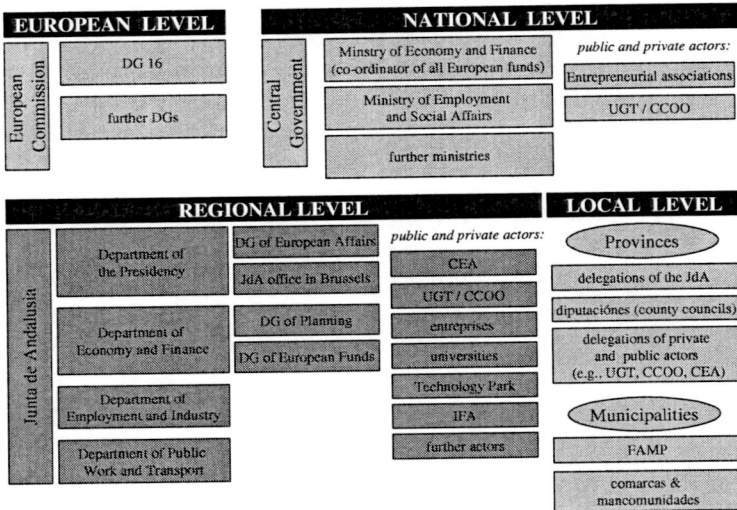

*Source: own figure.*

The JdA then negotiated investment decisions with the central authorities in the Public Investment Committee, a co-ordination body of the central government and the regions concerned. Conflicts usually arose about the pluri-regional investments on the territory of Andalusia, which the JdA tried to maximise. Once a compromise on the pluri-regional CSF for objective region number 1 was reached, the national development plan was forwarded to the European Commission, who forged the plan into a binding CSF (second phase). This step was characterised by negotiations on the axes of intervention (e.g., infrastructure, qualification of human resources or enterprise

---

[80]    The RDP document is a planning instrument known already during the dictatorship, which formulates regional development strategies based on the analysis of the regional strengths and deficits.

support). The key players of the second sub-phase were authorities of the MEH and representatives of the DG-16 of the European Commission, which is responsible for European regional policy.

The formulation and implementation of the regional OPs (third and fourth phases) saw more involvement of the JdA. The responsible departments (DG of Planning and DG of European Funds) were responsible for the preparation and management of regional OPs and related funds. On the one hand, the two DGs relied on inputs from other consejerias and provincial delegations of the JdA (such as the department of agriculture and fishing, culture, education and science, public works and transport or health). On the other hand, local actors (diputaciónes, mancomunidades and comarcas, municipalities and their representing body FAMP[81] (*Federación Andaluza de Municipios y Provincias*; Federation of Andalusian Municipalities and Provinces), entrepreneurial associations, unions, universities, semi-public and public enterprises could propose and realise development actions. In the case of pluri-regional OPs, the central government also relied on the proposals and actions by regional and local actors, but the regional level had no influence on the final decisions.

## *8.4 Analysis of Institutional Performance*

### 8.4.1 Contributor

In all three planning periods, the role of the JdA as a contributor was limited to the preparation of CSFs and even this function was restricted to the regional sub-CSF since the JdA had no influence on the pluri-regional parts of the Spanish CSF. The negotiation of national CSF propositions with the European Commission took place without those regional authorities that were involved in this step.

In the first CSF (1989-1993), the Andalusian Department of Planning (a part of the regional Ministry of Economy and Finance; CEH, *Consejería de Economía y Hacienda*) delivered a RDP to the MEH in Madrid (JdA, CEH 1989a). Under the co-ordination of several central ministries (namely the MEH, the Ministry of Labour and the Ministry of Agriculture and Fisheries), the CEH was responsible for fixing budget lines for the regional sub-CSF with respect to the priorities formulated in the RDP. Overall, the RDP was of mediocre quality, consisting of a pure analysis of development deficits (especially in terms of territorial problems), sometimes contradicting development strategies of different consejerias and a weak *ex ante* evaluation. The reason for the low quality of the plan was partially the novelty and the

---

[81] The FAMP is the representing body of the Andalusian local level for all public organisations, mainly the JdA. The federation provides basic services to all municipalities and provinces as well as being responsible for the economic promotion of the Andalusian municipalities. The FAMP's network of local development (RADEL: *Red Andaluz de Desarrollo Local*) is an important institution for the JdA since the regional government itself lacks an administrative link to citizens.

complexity of long-term programming imposed by the European Commission. On the other hand, there was an obvious lack of both the involvement of the local level (provincial delegations, diputaciónes, municipalities, mancomunidades and comarcas) and the co-ordination between the consejerias of the Andalusia administration. However, the JdA delivered its input on time and was not responsible for the delay of the Spanish CSFs. There existed only the limited influence of the JdA on the formulation of the pluri-regional Spanish CSF for objective 1 regions. The procedure did permit regional input, though, but it contradicted the partnership principle, since the pluri-regional CSF allowed Madrid to decide on the territorial and sectoral allocation of resources without regional interference. Despite Community pressures the Spanish government did not renounce its position on this issue, since the closing down of a pluri-regional CSF would have limited the operational margin of the national authorities. The JdA was involved in national investment decisions only through the Public Investment Committee where it had no word on the final priorities.

In the second CSF (1994-1999), the JdA again participated only in the formulation of the regional sub-CSF as the Spanish authorities successfully insisted on the pluri-regional CSF being under their own control. The RDP (JdA, CEH 1994c) had the same shortcomings as in the previous period but Andalusian authorities were not willing to align their regional sub-CSF with the Commission's expectations. This proved to be a handicap when the JdA applied for reprogramming[82] in 1996. In order to convince the Commission of the necessary changes, the JdA had to draw up a new OP (JdA, CEH 1996c; 1996d) which replaced the insufficient parts of the RDP of 1994 in hindsight. These changes significantly improved the coherence of development strategies and the co-ordination among administrative departments. Local actors were still excluded from the planning process, except for some provincial delegations that had been asked for input on provincial development problems by their respective partner consejerias in Seville. The weakest point of the second planning phase was still the axis "qualification of human resources" which did not contain handy measures to fight the urgent problem of unemployment in Andalusia.

The formulation of the third CSF (2000-2006) worked according to the same logic as the previous CSFs with the almost nonexistent involvement of the JdA in the pluri-regional CSF. The third RDP (JdA, CEH 1999a) followed the scheme of the improved version of the OP of 1996. Improvements were made in interventions for the qualification of human resources, which have been based on a clear identification of problems. Local actors were still excluded from the planning of the regional sub-CSF.

---

[82]   Reprogramming means a reallocation of financial resources from one axe (sub-axe) of intervention to another.

The involvement of the JdA in the planning and negotiation of the CF interventions, of which Andalusia has benefited since 1994, was small. For the logic of the fund has been a national one. The national government felt free to decide both how these funds were to be distributed across the country and who would be in charge of their effective management. The JdA did not question investments in the field of transport as these were under the national competence. However, conflicts arose around investment decisions for environmental projects where responsibilities were shared between all levels of government, but regional authorities played the most relevant role since they implemented and managed environmental policies. By the end of 1995, Madrid had invited the regional authorities to contribute to the planning of environmental measures because the national authorities found it hard to present enough projects in order to absorb the funds available.

The fact that Madrid excluded Andalusia from the pluri-regional CSFs (and the CF) has been a constant source of conflict between the two tiers of government. During the first CSF formulation the JdA was still absorbed by the complexity of multi-level European regional policy. The Andalusian government, however, tenaciously fought for a higher share of pluri-regional investments on its territory in the next two CSFs. The JdA used three strategies in order to maximise the Andalusian part of which the first two were not directly connected to European regional policy. Firstly, the JdA was demanding the transfer of new competencies to the regional level, which was not a successful strategy. Secondly, the JdA insisted on the criteria of splitting pluri-regional investments among the Spanish regions. There is evidence that national authorities tried to influence the distribution of European structural funds according to their own interests.[83] However, the final allocation was biased only in a minor way according to various interviewees, because the national government depended on the consensus of all the autonomous regions in order to approve the Spanish RDP, before it could be presented to the European Commission. Andalusian complaints that the region did not get its "fair" share of pluri-regional investments in the second CSF owed a lot to partisan behaviour, for different parties were in power in Madrid and Seville since the 1996 general election.

Thirdly, the JdA established regular, informal contacts with institutions in Brussels in order to influence Community decisions despite the formal opposition of the central authorities (Martínez-Pujalte López 1998: 84-87). The direct involvement in the application and management of European policies since 1988 indeed made it inevitable that Andalusia should be in contact with interested Commission officials,

---

[83]   One interviewee reported that the JdA successfully intervened when the central authorities tried to finance roads in Catalunya with resources out of the pluri-regional CSF for objective 1 regions. Catalunya is not eligible for these transfers since the region belongs to the objective 2 and 5b regions. However, the Catalans were the coalition partner of the conservative party in Madrid.

for their part, in following structural policies in the region which profited most from European transfers. The most prominent step was the establishment of an office of the JdA in Brussels in 1990. During the first CSF the JdA tried to cover their lobbying activities and the office worked as a representation of the Institute for Regional Promotion (*Instituto de Fomento de Andalucía*; IFA). The IFA was set up in 1987, with EU financial assistance, to promote the region's productive resources, industrial competitiveness, technological progress and access to financial markets. The office enabled constant contacts with the main decision-making centres as well as channelled the demands of Andalusian interest groups. Setting up the office provoked the central government to lodge a "conflict of competencies" case, as a result of which the Andalusian government officially obtained the right to establish direct contacts with the European Union for some policy fields, usually those under exclusive regional competence (Martínez-Pujalte López 1998: 215-217; Newton 1997: 335). The verdict of the Constitutional Court had a significant symbolic value and the Andalusian representative in Brussels became more active in the second CSF. Nevertheless, the lobbying activities were not very powerful. As one interviewee put it: "The office in Brussels is mainly an information lobby". The JdA experienced this in the first CSF when the Commission showed little interest in thoroughly discussing the Andalusian RDP, but tried to impose its own views on the effective allocation of the subsidies for the regional sub-CSF according to "Community priorities".

### 8.4.2 Translator

Following the organisation of CSFs, there were regional and pluri-regional OPs. The JdA was the key player in the translation of regional sub-CSFs into Andalusian OPs, a process, which consisted in the planning and implementation of operative programmes according to the priorities and axes of intervention outlined in the CSFs. For pluri-regional OPs the JdA was partially responsible for the implementation of national plans.

The translation of the first period was characterised by a variety of regional (sectoral and territorial) OPs (JdA, CEH 1992c; 1992d; 1993c; 1993d; JdA, CTAS 1991a; 1991b). The preparation of the OPs was done by the Andalusian DG of Planning, which collected development projects from various consejerias, public enterprises and private actors. The territorial OPs lacked concise development goals owing to the inconsistent development strategies of the regional sub-CSF. The advantage of the territorial OPs, on the contrary, was that provincial delegations could put forward their views on local development via the partner consejerias of the JdA. However, the planning process lacked a real bottom-up approach since the involvement of the municipal government was small. The JdA included the municipalities – the FAMP had a co-ordination role – mainly in the implementation of planned actions. Investments were undertaken mainly in infrastructure because Andalusia showed a huge gap in this field. However, the demand side explains only half of the truth. On the supply side, the JdA showed severe problems in setting up consistent programmes for the dynamisation of the industrial base or the qualification of human resources. Another reason for the high share of infrastructure projects was that these investments delivered fast and visible results. The often heard argument that the high percentage of infrastructure projects was a result of the European Commission following the northern European construction lobby (which views southern Europe as an important market) is not convincing, because it seems highly improbable that national and regional Spanish authorities would accept such an influence.

In the 1994-1999 period, the high number of OPs was drastically reduced to one OP Andalusia including both sectoral and territorial development measures. The European Commission, which heavily criticised the document (IDR 1996; JdA, CEH 1994d) for incoherent objectives, had to accept the OP since the democratically elected government of Andalusia did not want to change their plans. However, the JdA had to alter their position and drew an entirely new OP in 1996, replacing the insufficient parts of the first one, since the JdA wanted to reallocate structural funds. The reprogramming, which included most departments of the JdA, induced intense debates on development strategies – it was decided to focus on the development of endogenous potential – and the goal of European and regional structural policies. The result of the significant efforts was on the one hand the improvement of the coherence of the Andalusian OP and the presentation of better and more diversified projects co-financed by the European Union. The second Andalusian OP was apparently one of the best OPs presented to the European Commission from a technical point of view. Interviewees also stated that the dialogue between actors of structural policy became more dynamic after the reprogramming. On the other hand, the JdA experienced a learning process, which induced a change in the way of viewing European structural funds. The funds were still an additional source of income, but authorities understood that the funds included also a certain way of carrying out public policies, including strategic regional development planning, according to which resources should be allocated (not necessarily in the politically most convenient way). It was also accepted that all public policies co-financed by European structural funds were subject to *ex ante*, ongoing and *ex post* evaluations. At the time of editing this manuscript, work on the regional 2000-2006 OP was still ongoing. Statements of policy makers revealed that the regional OP should reach the same quality as the previous (improved) one.

The implementation of the OPs in the first two periods was characterised by co-operation and good relations between the regional authorities and the European Commission. Overall, the regional authorities would have liked more competencies. They questioned the eligibility criteria with regard to all programme areas, ranging from the definition of geographical boundaries to the decision of what categories of workers were eligible for training purposes. Another point of criticism concerned pluri-regional actions where the JdA wanted to have more influence on the choice of projects. Lobbying efforts in Brussels were fruitless but lead to tensions with the central authorities. As a consequence Madrid tried to overcome the demands of the JdA by bypassing the regional level. This was done by putting the local level (municipalities and the FAMP) in charge of the implementation of pluri-regional programmes instead of regional actors. The second period saw also a reorganisation of the departments involved in European funds. In order to improve the communication with European and national authorities, the management of the Andalusian OP and the related funds was separated from the DG of Planning. The newly established DG of European Funds took over this task and was responsible for the co-ordination both of different funds and consejerias.

### 8.4.3    Monitor

For the Spanish CSF of objective 1 regions there was a Monitoring Committee, chaired by the General Secretary of Programming and Budgeting (a part of the MEH), in which Andalusian representatives participated. Andalusia had only a small influence in that Monitoring Committee. There were also Monitoring Committees for regional OPs and sub-programmes. In these committees, which were chaired by the JdA, regional actors had more influence. The committees included the following duties: co-ordination of structural interventions, proposing the allocation of the resources annually generated by deflector application and the monitoring/evaluation of OPs on the basis of financial, physical and impact indicators. The composition varied between different programmes, but the committees usually contained representatives of the involved regional departments (consejerias), the central government, social partners, the IFA, municipalities and provincial delegations.

Regional authorities were also responsible for three types (*ex ante*, ongoing and *ex post*) of evaluation.[84] During the first round of CSF plans, the debate at the regional level was mainly about how to conduct impact assessment. The Commission was not able to reinforce evaluations as time pressure to develop the plan proposals and the complexity of regulations had, in fact, limited the work on evaluations. Therefore, the learning effects within the CSF 1989-1993 period were small. The first trials of *ex ante* evaluations took place only in 1991. The analysis remained superficial and vague qualitative indicators were used because of the Junta's reluctance to quantify the expected impact of structural measures. There was no intermediate evaluation in the first CSF. In the field of *ex post* assessment, evaluations were done for global grants

---

[84]    Evaluations of the pluri-regional OPs were performed by the central government. Actions financed by the CF were evaluated *ex ante* by Madrid, *ex post* impact assessment was done by the European Commission.

and for all OPs together (JdA, CTAS 1994a). The evaluations focused on the global impact of the OPs and did not separate the impact of territorial and sectoral OPs.[85]

Monitoring substantially improved during the second CSF period when the European Commission insisted on the enforcement of EU regulations. *Ex ante* evaluations were carried out for all Andalusian interventions (Comisión Europea 1996; JdA, CEH 1994c; 1994d). Some quantitative indicators had been introduced, but models and data bases for estimating macro-economic effects were still missing. The Andalusian authorities welcomed the introduction of intermediate evaluations (Arenal Grupo Consultor 1998; IDR 1997a; ; 1998; Idom 1998; 1999), not just for re-allocation decisions but also to reflect their own interventions and to plan any re-formulation of policy approaches from one programming period to another, for the inevitable time lags before *ex post* conclusions could be drawn proved to be too big to evaluate the best practices. *Ex post* evaluations of the second period were being carried out at the time of editing this manuscript. The significant progress of intermediate evaluations from a qualitative and quantitative point of view raises expectations that *ex post* evaluations will be of adequate quality. Nevertheless, their results will come too late to be considered for the planning of the regional sub-CSF 2000-2006. The absorption of evaluation results in the planning department seemed to be a general problem since the DG of Planning considered insights from evaluations not as valuable. The same was true in the case of ESF actions where those responsible did not even read through evaluation reports, since they did not expect them to contain any new insights. The *ex ante* evaluation of regional effects has been improved in the preparation for the third planning period. Special focus has been attached to the impact assessment of socio-economic and environmental effects and the equality of women and men.

The requirement of evaluating OPs according to the outlines of the European Commission met with the resistance of the Andalusian authorities because of several reasons (IDR 1997b). There was widespread dissatisfaction with the emphasis on quantitative indicators required by the Commission, in particular, when assessment was related to training and other ESF-supported activities. Quantitative indicators restricted the manoeuvring room of the administration, which was interpreted as an interference in the sovereignty of the administration. The Andalusian authorities also heavily criticised the weight of external consultants in independent mid-term evaluations. The recommendations of the experts were viewed as technocratic analyses without adequate consideration of the political aspects.

Monitoring of the OPs raised the problem of personnel. Especially in the first CSF period there were not enough qualified people to carry out impact assessments. The

---

[85]   An exception to this was the evaluation of the territorial OP Almeria.

internal shortage forced regional administrations to rely on large numbers of external consultants. The regional administration felt abandoned by the Commission, which did not deliver support for the evaluations it was asking for. As a consequence of this criticism (which came not only from Andalusia, but from many other European regions), Andalusia profited from training programmes which were co-financed within the axis of technical assistance in the second CSF. Another point of concern arose about the scope of policies under the EU evaluation regulations. The regional authorities blamed Brussels for imposing evaluations for all the Andalusian structural policies, although EU co-financing was below twenty per cent in some cases. Despite the critical attitude of the regional authorities, by the end of the second CSF period the JdA considered evaluations as a normal step in the policy process. The Commission's insistence on evaluating all projects co-financed by European funds led to the spread of an evaluation culture in the entire JdA, including not only the DG of European Funds (IDR 1997b).

### 8.4.4   Facilitator

Many private actors have been involved in European regional policy. However, most of them took part in the implementation phase and were only benefiters of structural payments. The involvement of private sector agents in other phases of the regional policy process was small, which had to do with the long-standing tradition of the public sector's dominance in Andalusia. Private key actors were the regional social partners (all having their own provincial representations): the two unions UGT and CCOO and the entrepreneurial association CEA. The former two represented the Andalusian labour force while the latter defended the interests of the private and entrepreneurial sector.

The involvement of the key actors in the preparation phase of the CSFs and OPs changed substantially between the first and second planning periods. In the 1989-1993 CSF, the JdA presented to the social partners the national draft of the Spanish RDP (including the regional CSF for Andalusia) and then negotiated bilaterally with each of them on issues concerning regional interventions. In the second and third CSF, the JdA and the social partners deepened their co-operation through the social contract (since 1993; JdA, CP 1999), which had contributed much to the social stability in a region with one of the highest unemployment rates in Europe. According to the social contract, each line of the RDP Andalusia was thoroughly discussed. The social partners reported that they felt much better informed about the possibilities of profiting from structural funds with the new approach.

Private actors were most involved in the implementation phase. This happened, on the one hand, when regional consejerias and provincial delegations instructed private enterprises to realise planned development projects. This was not very often the case (in all three CSFs) since the Andalusian economy has been penetrated by public enterprises, which were responsible for most of the implementation work. However, the private sector could apply for projects financed by pluri-regional OPs through regional and provincial organisations of the social partners. In general, OPs and sub-programmes that focused primarily on infrastructure or productive investment were relatively more successful in involving private sector partners than development actions focusing on soft projects. On the other hand, private actors were benefiters of structural funds, especially in the case of the development of an economic network. The IFA, which was the key responsible for this axis of intervention, typically supported projects such as ISO certification of SMEs, the modernisation of production plants or technology parks (IFA 1998a; 1998b; 1998c; w.y.). The unions implemented mainly projects for the qualification of human resources and the re-integration of unemployed workers into the labour market. The CEA provided no direct financial support to their members, but profited from EU funds with which the CEA installed an information centre for their members. The centre collected and distributed all the available information on structural funds in order to maximise the absorption of funds by their members (CEA w.y.b). By the end of the first CSF period, the JdA contacted the CEA to inform their members that they could benefit from enterprise support. The reason behind the Junta's approach was the low absorption rate of global grants, since the IFA demonstrated problems in establishing contacts with the private sector in the first CSF. Nothing similar happened in the second CSF (which can be explained by the better functioning of the IFA).

Regional private actors participated in the Monitoring Committee of regional CSF/OPs, which was highly welcomed by interviewees. There was no representation in Monitoring Committees of pluri-regional CSF/OPs, although this would have been possible within the EU regulations. For the MEH, the chairman of the national committee, has always been reluctant with respect to such a participation. Thus, the knowledge about pluri-regional OPs among private and social partners was small and information was provided only on an informal basis.

### 8.4.5 Stimulator

Regional Andalusian authorities were already familiar with regional planning prior to the reform of the structural funds (JdA, CEH 1984; 1987; MEH, DGAPP 1993-1998). However, these plans used short-term, project-based techniques and lacked the co-ordination of different development goals. That is why an overwhelming majority of participants regarded the planning phase of the CSFs/OPs as extremely valuable and a new experience. Thinking in terms of integrated programmes, engaging in analysis and projections of levels of needs over a five-year cycle, and relating them to the available resources, was universally praised (IDR 1997b), even though the regional authorities complained in the first CSF that the European and national administrations were unclear in what they really wanted. Regional and local bureaucracies also sometimes lacked the resources and knowledge to plan according to the European regulations. The axis of technical assistance in the second CSF helped to overcome these problems so that no more surprises were expected in the third CSF. Another effect of the European planning techniques was the adaptation of the administrative structure to the European system such as the creation of the DG of European Funds. Overall, technical and methodological problems were hardly ever the main reason for failure or delay of structural interventions. If this was the case it was usually because of a lack of political will behind these measures.

### 8.4.6 Experimenter

"We do not like new things in the Junta very much", as one interviewee put it. This position stands for the general attitude of most of the policy makers, and it has not altered much since the 1988 reform. Policy planners and implementers universally agreed that they would have preferred investments in infrastructure instead of soft projects. The reason for this is that development actions with an experimental character were time and resource consuming without guaranteeing the success of the project. The analysis of the allocation of structural funds revealed that the tendency towards infrastructure investments was indeed strong (see Chapter 8.2). Contrary to this position stood the opinion of the European Commission, which favoured a higher relative share of experimental projects. It is not surprising that what has been done in this area was financed within the framework of CIs which were under the competence of the Commission. Overall, the available funds for experimental projects were small in each of the three CSFs.

In the first CSF, very little was done to promote experimental projects so that the available funds were not entirely absorbed. The number of soft projects increased due to the pressure of regional politicians who did not want to lose again eligible funds during the second CSF. Innovative measures of that period included projects such as the development of an electronic booking and reservation system for hotels in Andalusia or locally rooted formations of farmers in order to promote their products. The absorption was higher, but still below the European average. There was a definite relationship between overall performance in the OP's implementation and the novel versus traditional characteristics of sub-programmes, measures and projects. The more innovative sub-programmes had a slower start and implementation, while the more traditional ones had an easier time. Delays in planning and implementation were often due to weak project management. Those responsible reported problems in finding reliable implementation partners with public enterprises not being used to these kinds of projects and the private sector not developed enough to take over.

### 8.4.7   Co-ordinator

In all three CSF periods the Andalusian authorities were rarely able to play a co-ordinating role vis-à-vis other regions. The reason for this was that there existed no multi-regional projects financed by regional OPs because the JdA showed no interest in spending their own funds on another territory. In terms of pluri-regional OPs, the co-ordination was the national ministries' duty. Informal work contacts among programme operatives of regional OPs, however, occurred frequently, since Andalusia as an autonomous region operated freely. Furthermore, the Forum of Economy and Regional Politics (*Foros de Economia y Politica Regional*), a national meeting concerned with the implementation of pluri-regional OPs, allowed an institutionalised exchange of ideas around European regional policy for policy makers twice a year. So did "sectoral tables" (*mesa sectoral*) which brought national and regional authorities together in order to exchange information on specific sectors. Members of the JdA reported that they had been contacted quite often by other regions because of the improved (second) version of the regional OP Andalusia. Overall, the interest in interregional co-operation was limited and regional authorities would not have valued a deeper collaboration.

### 8.4.8   Initiator

Transregional co-operation has not been on the top of the policy makers' priority list and the interest of regional authorities was ambiguous. Some representatives highly welcomed the experience of transregional co-operation. Others viewed it as a waste of time and resources, which did not help at all to overcome structural deficits for development. Projects in this field had an explicit experimental character since transregional actions had hardly been known before. It is, thus, not surprising that transregional co-operation met with hesitant regional administration and project planning was delayed. Structural funds for transregional projects were limited. The financing came mainly from the CI Interreg which supported co-operation of administrations and other associations, but was reserved with infrastructure investment, which the regional authorities would have preferred. Outside the structural funds transregional co-operation was very limited. Existing agreements were used as an instrument for the promotion of exportation, such as an office of the IFA in Tokyo or representations in South America. Despite restricted resources, administrators did not think that the lack of funds constrained co-operation.

In the first CSF, transregional co-operation was not taking place since regional authorities were too absorbed in planning and implementing other structural interventions. What had occurred were impromptu visits to external regions in conjunction with the holding of international conferences and work contacts between regional planners on the basis of personal professional relations. The second CSF saw a rise of activities, especially towards the end of the planning period. The most prominent programmes were established with Portugal and Morocco. Since both countries do not have regional institutions, but rather national institutions at the regional level, true transregional co-operation was hard to find. Contacts were usually state-initiated and fields of co-operation were negotiated according to national priorities. However, regional administrations were responsible for the planning and implementation of those priorities. Generally, contacts between administrations were good regarding the technical aspects of management. In political terms, the co-operation was reported to be somewhat difficult since central ministries, closely following what was going on at the regional level, were intervening when they thought the competence of foreign policy was touched. The co-operation with Morocco, an important trade partner of Andalusia, was complicated since the European regulations did not foresee structural fund investments outside of its territory. The number of private visitors from abroad, usually entrepreneurs, had substantially increased.

## 8.5    Synopsis

Andalusia is one of the most backward regions in the European Union. The main obstacle to economic development has been the shortage of qualified labour which hampered an increase in productivity and competitivity. Further deficits were insufficient basic infrastructure, an underdeveloped industrial sector and the lack of a diversified economy. These deficits resulted in a low GDP income and very high unemployment rates, especially among the young population. On the downside, Andalusia displays a largely intact environment with rich natural resources, a young workforce and a rich cultural heritage. The aim of substantial European structural transfers has been to strengthen the potential and to overcome the drawbacks for development. The analysis of structural interventions revealed that regional actors focused mainly on infrastructure investments and neglected the development of intangible assets. The main actor in regional development policy was the JdA, though its realm was restricted strongly to the regionalised part of European funds whereas the bigger pluri-regional part was under the competence of national authorities which has been a constant source of conflict between the Andalusian and central governments. For the preparation of regional CSFs, there existed close collaboration among the regional, national and European levels. The most important role was played by the JdA as a translator of CSFs into OPs, a process which has improved considerably during the observed period of time (1989-2000). The obligation to monitor and evaluate structural interventions met with strong resistance from the regional authorities in the first years after the European regional policy reform. However, the Commission's insistence on evaluating all programmes co-financed by European funds led to a spread of an evaluation culture in the entire JdA, including *ex ante*, ongoing and *ex post* assessments for most public policies. In terms of the facilitator role many private actors have been involved in European regional policy. Most of them took part only in the implementation phase where they were benefiters of structural payments. The involvement of private sector agents in other phases of the regional policy process was small, which had to do with the long-standing tradition of the public sector's dominance in Andalusia. An overwhelming majority of participants regarded the planning approach of CSFs and OPs as extremely valuable. Technical shortcomings in the first CSF were overcome during the second planning period. The attitude of the JdA towards innovative development actions was characterised by caution and risk aversion. Policy planners and implementers universally agreed that they preferred investments in infrastructure than soft projects. An improvement in this field could be observed in recent years. Interregional co-operation occurred mainly informally between those responsible for structural policy. On the contrary, transregional co-operation has become common over time, especially with Portuguese and Moroccan border areas.

# 9 ALGARVE: THE RISE OF A WEAK REGIONAL BASE

The second case study is on Algarve in Portugal. The first section of the chapter presents the region's geographical characteristics, population, economy and administrative system. The second section is about European structural interventions in the Algarve. The institutions that are involved in regional development are discussed in the third section. Finally, institutional performance is analysed.

## 9.1 Portrait of the Region

### 9.1.1 Physical Environment

The region of Algarve is situated at the western end of the Iberian Peninsula, in the south of Portugal. The mildness of the region's climate and its natural heritage have proved to be the greatest natural assets attracting people to produce and settle there. With a surface of 4'989 square kilometres, which is divided into sixteen municipalities, Algarve covers about six per cent of the total area of the country. It is separated from the north by the Alentejo, from Spain by the River Guadiana to the east and it is bathed by the Atlantic Ocean in the south and west.

**Figure 9-1: The Region of Algarve**

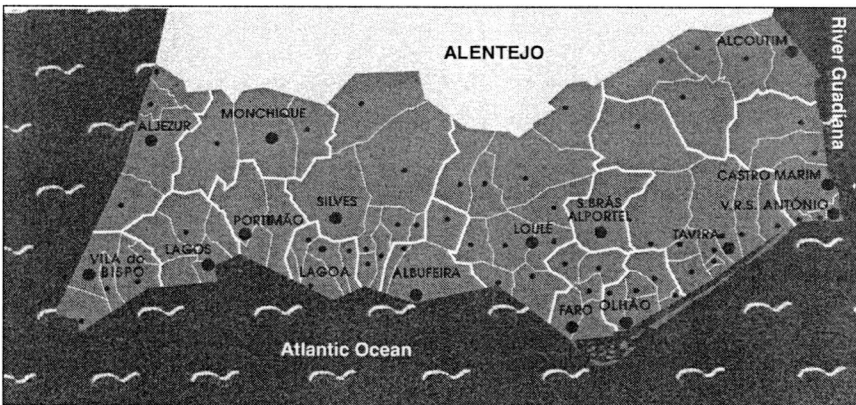

*Source: CCR 1997b: 19.*

The Algarve is composed of three distinct physical units that all more or less run parallel to the south coast (AMAL 1999b: 25f; CCR Algarve 1997b: 15, 17; Gaspar 1993: 175-177). A mountainous area lies in the north which is sparsely populated and where even agriculture is limited because the terrain is made up chiefly of forest and heathland. The capital of Faro and all the bigger cities are situated in the flat coastal strip (except Loulé) and is therefore the most densely populated part of the Algarve with the most diversified economy. The coast is dominated by sun and sea tourism (and related services), with some agriculture that is found mainly in the eastern part. Fishing, the extraction of sea salt and aquaculture offer other possibilities of economic activity. Between the coastal area and the northern mountains lies the intermediate zone with a band of gentle slopes and many rocky outcrops. This part of the Algarve has been the reserve of food and human resources throughout the centuries. This role still exists today but it is not limited to the supply of foodstuffs anymore; it also provides logistic support and labour for the main coastal activities (tourism and construction). In recent years, the area has become famous for its crafts, which are sold in tourist resorts along the coastline.

### 9.1.2    Demographic Characteristics

In 1997 Algarve had a resident population of about 350'000, only 3.5 per cent of the total population of Portugal (see Figure 9-2). However, the region's population varies strongly between seasons. Tourism brings in more than three million visitors each year (most of them in summer), which means that the population triples at certain times of the year. The population is unevenly distributed in the region. Despite the fact that the hilly areas represent sixty per cent of the surface, they account for little over 10 per cent of the population. This imbalance in human settlement is reflected in the population density of the parishes which ranges from eight to several hundred inhabitants per square kilometre. This situation is unlikely to change, as the densely populated areas on the coast are the ones where immigrants find work.

The population of Algarve has been the fastest growing, over 30 per cent in the last 25 years. Up until the start of the 1970s, the emigration of the population to other regions of Portugal where employment was available in industry, or to countries of northern Europe, led to a rapid decrease in the resident population which reached its lowest level in 1970. The strong economic growth of the 1980s changed the migration pattern and made the region more attractive for immigrants, resulting in a positive population growth rate. The proportion of young people (under 25) lies today around 32 per cent and is close to the national average. In the last twenty years (1980-1998) this category of age declined in the Algarve, as throughout Portugal, although the drop is the smallest of all the Portuguese regions. The overall positive population balance is due to a strong positive migration balance (AMAL 1999b: 26-28; Briesemeister 1997: 100-102; Eurostat and European Commission 1998: 92f).

**Figure 9-2: Demographic Data of Algarve**

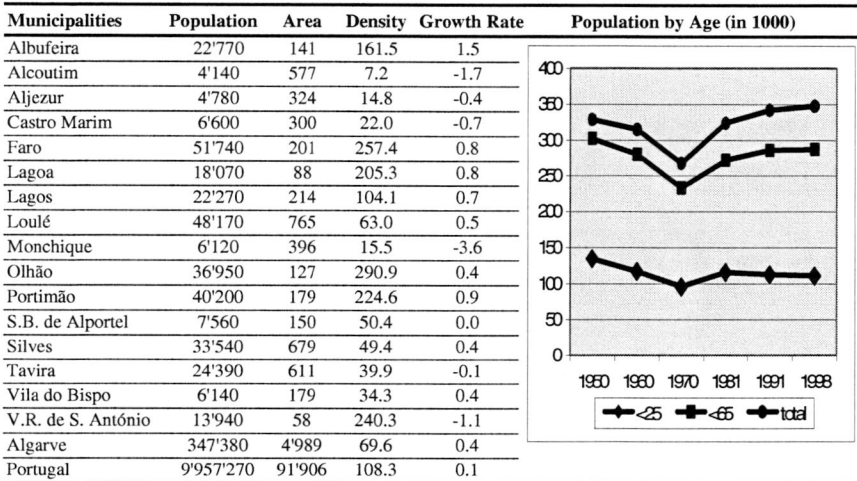

| Municipalities | Population | Area | Density | Growth Rate | Population by Age (in 1000) |
|---|---|---|---|---|---|
| Albufeira | 22'770 | 141 | 161.5 | 1.5 | |
| Alcoutim | 4'140 | 577 | 7.2 | -1.7 | |
| Aljezur | 4'780 | 324 | 14.8 | -0.4 | |
| Castro Marim | 6'600 | 300 | 22.0 | -0.7 | |
| Faro | 51'740 | 201 | 257.4 | 0.8 | |
| Lagoa | 18'070 | 88 | 205.3 | 0.8 | |
| Lagos | 22'270 | 214 | 104.1 | 0.7 | |
| Loulé | 48'170 | 765 | 63.0 | 0.5 | |
| Monchique | 6'120 | 396 | 15.5 | -3.6 | |
| Olhão | 36'950 | 127 | 290.9 | 0.4 | |
| Portimão | 40'200 | 179 | 224.6 | 0.9 | |
| S.B. de Alportel | 7'560 | 150 | 50.4 | 0.0 | |
| Silves | 33'540 | 679 | 49.4 | 0.4 | |
| Tavira | 24'390 | 611 | 39.9 | -0.1 | |
| Vila do Bispo | 6'140 | 179 | 34.3 | 0.4 | |
| V.R. de S. António | 13'940 | 58 | 240.3 | -1.1 | |
| Algarve | 347'380 | 4'989 | 69.6 | 0.4 | |
| Portugal | 9'957'270 | 91'906 | 108.3 | 0.1 | |

*Note: All figures are for 1997. Population figures are based on resident population; density figures are persons per square kilometre; growth rates are annual average rates in per cent (1981-1997); area in square kilometres.*

*Source: CCR Algarve 1990a: 18-21; 1990b: 19; Eurostat; INE 1998a: 15-17.*

### 9.1.3   Evolution and Characteristics of the Economy (1980s and 1990s)

The Algarve economy generates some four per cent of Portugal's GDP. Despite its small size, compared to the rest of Portugal, Algarve makes an important contribution to the national economy since revenue from tourist spending helps to reduce the balance of payments deficit. Algarve is also the most important foreign currency earner and is a major employer in the summer season (Corkill 1993: 81). In the beginning of the 1980s, the Algarve economy was faced with three problems which stemmed from the national and international environments (Bornhorst 1997: 24-26; Economist Intelligence Unit 1999b: 5). Firstly, the oil crisis at the end of the 1970s hit the economy particularly hard, as Portugal was highly dependent on oil importation. Secondly, the revolution (1974-1976) did not bring a stable government but political uncertainty, with low domestic and foreign investment activities for several years. Moreover, the revolution led to the loss of traditional markets in the colonies and to a diminished human capital due to the anti-fascist movement. State interventionism (e.g., nationalisation of enterprises, or fixed prices in agriculture, etc.), finally, not only prevented Portugal from modernisation, but led also to an over-sized public sector and heavy debts. In terms of output, the Algarve economy was based (and still is) on only three fields which exploit its natural resources: agriculture, fishing and tourism (Eurostat and European Commission 1998: 95). Agriculture and fishing in the early

1980s were still traditional and domestically oriented but they delivered inputs for the small industrial base in Algarve, namely the canning, food processing and ship building industries. Moreover, the wood and cork industries were of some importance. The service sector was dominated by tourism, which grew rapidly but could not exploit its full potential due to limited accommodation and basic infrastructure capacities. As a result of the negative national and international environments, economic growth was slow. Unemployment stayed at a low level due to state interventions (see Figure 9-3).

**Figure 9-3: Unemployment and Growth Rate of Regional GDP in Algarve (1983-1998; in per cent)**

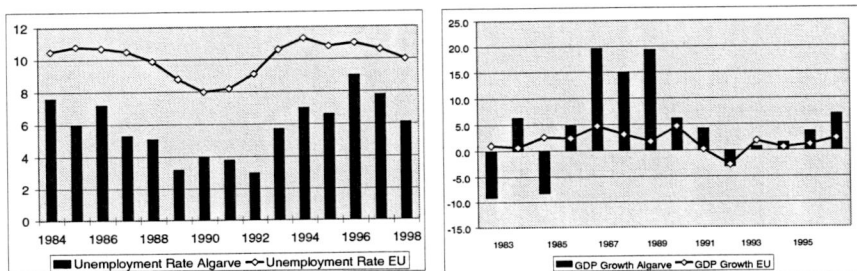

*Note: GDP growth rates are based on PPS figures, inflation adjusted (at 1986 prices).*

*Source: Data from European Commission 1999k; Eurostat.*

The second intervention of the IMF (1983) and the prospects of entering the European Community brought the turn around of the Portuguese economy by the mid-1980s (Bornhorst 1997: 27f). The Social Democratic Party (PSD; *Partido Social Democrático*) replaced the frequently changing and unstable minority coalitions with a solid majority, which resulted in a consequent transition of a heavily regulated Portugal into a modern market economy. The boom in the Algarve led to annual GDP growth rates of above fifteen per cent between 19871989 (Economist Intelligence Unit 1999b: 5f). The base of the economic development lay in tourism, with overnight hotel stays at record levels through the second half of the 1980s. Tourism also brought projects for the fast growing construction industry. However, the boom in tourism depended heavily on the English (40 per cent) and German (29 per cent) market. Another negative effect was a speculation bubble in real estate, which led to rising living costs for the population (Gaspar 1993: 180). Agriculture experienced specialisation and modernisation. The combination of using intensive systems of production, combined with the region's climate, made the agricultural sector strongly competitive since it allowed products to be exported at the start of the season and, hence, to benefit from added value resulting from early sales. The industrial sector continued to be small. Furthermore, the traditional wood and cork processing industries came under pressure due to rising labour costs.

The growth of the Algarve economy rapidly ended in the beginning of the 1990s. The unfavourable environment with the rest of Europe in recession led to slower growth and higher unemployment. The small industrial sector lost further ground with only the food processing industry being able to stand the international pressure on prices. Agriculture was less vulnerable due to its modern and specialised production system. Despite the recession, aquaculture was developing and, in addition to the traditional production of molluscs and fish farming, replaced some of the lost employment in industry (Eurostat and European Commission 1998: 95). Tourism was growing but at lower rates, which meant also slower development of the entire service sector. It was in this period that Algarve experienced the negative sides of the excessive dependence on the "sun-and-beach" tourists from England, who used to be low spenders and used to switch to alternative cheap destinations (Corkill 1993: 82). Moreover, unplanned construction activities, the promotion of real estate and the destruction of a considerable part of natural and cultural values threatened to destroy the image of the region (Gaspar 1993: 180).

The recovery of the Algarve economy took place in 1995. It is not surprising that tourism acted as the main driver of the recovery. The sector profited, on the one hand, from the fact that the entire European economy was recovering. On the other hand, the combined efforts of the central and local administration with the support of European financial transfers helped to overcome some negative effects of tourism. The fact that large areas of the Algarve reached their saturation point could be mitigated by an increasing demand for inland tourism, which was less seasonal (INE 1998a; Corkill 1993: 83). The rise in unemployment through the decline of certain sectors of the manufacturing industry during the recession of the 1990s has been partially reduced. Despite this positive picture, the structure of the labour market in Algarve has featured some specialities that make it vulnerable against external shocks (Eurostat and European Commission 1998: 93; Delegão Regional do Algarve do IEFP 1998a: 5, 10). Firstly, the high percentage of activities related to tourism such as the buying and selling of property, the construction of hotel complexes, transport, recreation, leisure and provision of personal services make employment in the region increasingly dependent on tourism. Secondly, employment in tourism strongly varied according to the sector's seasons. The labour market absorbs a large number of workers in the summer months whereas employment is 20 per cent lower during the winter season. Thirdly, women are the group most affected by seasonal fluctuations. Finally, there has been a large number of young people under 25 without work.

The level of education of those in employment is below the national average (AMAL 1999b: 57f; Eurostat and European Commission 1998: 92). According to the 1991 census, 20 per cent of the work force had educational qualifications beyond the statutory minimum period of schooling (INE: www.ine.pt). The situation has been greatly improved by the existence of a range of vocational and professional schools, which, in association with the tourism industry, have assisted the training and placement of professionals in the sector (see Figure 9-4). Major efforts in vocational training have also been undertaken in agriculture in recent years. At the tertiary level, the University of Algarve, which was set up in 1983 in Faro, has developed fields of study of regional interest, such as marine biology, agriculture and fruit-growing, tourism and ecology. The university has also been highly instrumental in meeting the demand for managerial staff (CCR Algarve 1997b: 29).

**Figure 9-4: Educational Level of the Working Population in Algarve**

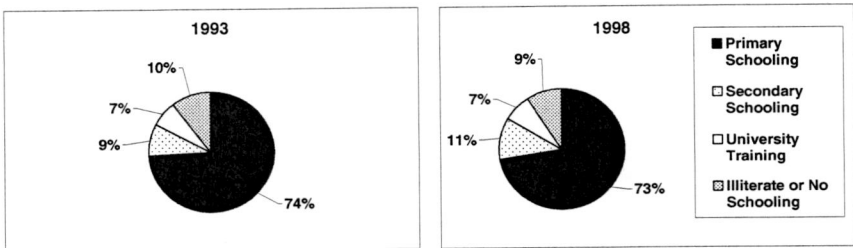

Source: Data from INE; Eurostat and European Commission 1998: 92.

The regional economic structure has followed the European trend and has been transformed from an agricultural to a service dominated economy in the last 30 years (Delegão Regional do Algarve do IEFP 1998a: 1; INE 1998a; 1998b). In 1960, agricultural workers accounted for 59 per cent of employment whereas the figure in 1998 was just under 11 per cent. The sector has gone through a decline of traditional production in the mountainous region (figs, almonds and carob beans) to intensive farming concentrated in the coastal areas. The fishing sector is still of importance, though to a smaller degree than in former times. The secondary sector accounts only for 17 per cent of total employment (including the construction business). It lacks a solid base, with the exception of the canning and cork industries. In recent years, as a result of speculation in real estate and the seasonal nature of the labour supply, the situation in industry has become worse and the industrial sector has found itself in a major crisis. The service sector, which employed 18 per cent of workers in 1960, now accounts for almost 72 per cent of employment in the region. The main branch in services is tourism, which has also been responsible for the development of other activities in the tertiary sector, such as the construction industry or transport services (Eurostat and European Commission 1998: 96).

## Figure 9-5: Welfare Indicators for Algarve

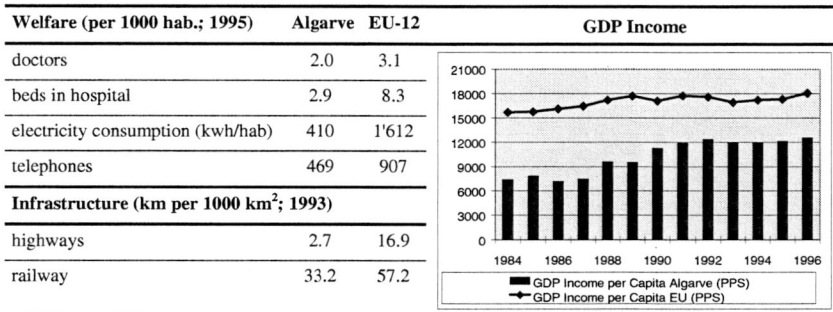

| Welfare (per 1000 hab.; 1995) | Algarve | EU-12 | GDP Income |
| --- | --- | --- | --- |
| doctors | 2.0 | 3.1 | |
| beds in hospital | 2.9 | 8.3 | |
| electricity consumption (kwh/hab) | 410 | 1'612 | |
| telephones | 469 | 907 | |
| Infrastructure (km per 1000 km²; 1993) | | | |
| highways | 2.7 | 16.9 | |
| railway | 33.2 | 57.2 | |

GDP Income per Capita Algarve (PPS)
GDP Income per Capita EU (PPS)

*Source: CEPI 1996: 14, 19; Eurostat; IEA 1998d.*

Tourism has brought a considerable improvement of the socio-economic situation (see Figure 9-5). The region's GDP *per capita* (in PPS) was 70 per cent of the European average in 1996. In 1986 regional GDP *per capita* was only 45 per cent of the European average. The strength of the Algarve economy is also mirrored in the fact that the region is a net contributor to the national transfer system (INE 1998). On the other hand, tourism is responsible for aggravating intra-regional imbalances both of the income situation as well as of the distribution of facilities, with the main facilities (health care, education, social security, culture and sport) being concentrated along the coast. The region, furthermore, still suffers from a lack of basic infrastructure such as a train connection to Spain or access to the European gas and fibre optic network.

Striking the balance in potentials and drawbacks the Algarve has significant potential for further development. The main assets of the region are the Mediterranean climate with a mild winter attracting visitors from the north, and competitive advantages of the agricultural sector. There are, however, negative aspects most of which derive from unbalanced development. The main problems of Algarve have been an unequal development, favouring the coastal strip at the expense of the interior, uncoordinated urban development as a result of the tourism boom, the abandonment of large tracts of land in the interior, formerly used for farming and livestock rearing as a result of the emigration of manpower, and the lack of a solid industrial basis which sustained local and regional suppliers.

### 9.1.4    Regional Government and Administration

In strict institutional terms, the authorities of the region of Algarve in Faro are an extension of the central government. In practice, however, they are rooted in the regional and local environment. The system of only loose co-operation of representatives of the various national ministries in Algarve dates back to the waning years of the *Estado Novo* [86] during the dictatorship, when technicians recognised the need to regionalise the planning process (Corkill 1993: 21f). A new Constitution was promulgated after the revolution in 1976 in order to democratise and decentralise the state apparatus built up over the nearly half century of dictatorship (Sänger 1993b: 294-297). Institutional decentralisation, however, has not been achieved to date, which is the reason why contemporary regional authorities of Algarve are still heavily controlled by the central government.

The Constitution enshrines three types of regions: autonomous, administrative and planning (Opello 1993: 164-167). The status of an autonomous region with special measures of independence has been granted only to Azores and Madeira, because of their separation from the mainland and unique economic and political conditions. The administrative regions, which have not yet been created, would replace the district level of government. The Constitution requires all administrative regions to be created simultaneously but only after a favourable vote of a majority of the counties that would be contained in the proposed area. When introduced, the main bodies of the regional tier of government will be the regional assembly (*Assembleia Regional*) and the regional board (*Junta Regional*). The regional assembly will be composed of members directly elected by citizens enrolled in the electoral register for the regional area. The regional board will be the corporate executive organ for the region, elected by the members of the regional assembly from among their number. As regards the sphere of competence (Pereira 1995: 276), the regional government would be empowered to direct the region's public services and co-ordinate the activities of their municipal executives. Each region would be expected to prepare its own regional development plan and participate in the national planning process. Although a number of regionalisation proposals have been under intense discussion and despite the almost universal agreement among Portugal's political class that administrative regions are absolutely necessary, their creation has been delayed to date (Opello 1993:173f). The reason for this is, on the one hand, an intense disagreement about what criteria ought to be used to delineate regional boundaries. On the other hand, there is a lack of political will, of the prevailing party in power in Lisbon, which showed its reluctance to hand over power to the regional level once they were not in opposition any more (Pereira 1993: 273-275). This is true for the centre-right Social Democratic Party (PSD; *Partido Socialistico Democratico*) between 1985 and 1995, as well as for the centre-left Socialist Party (PS; *Partido Socialistico*) which has stayed in power since 1995. Even the PS, which promised in the electoral campaign to establish a regional

---

[86]   The Estado Novo was a corporate state under Antonio de Oliveira Salazar based on vague but generally rightist ideals. Politically, Salazar wanted to preserve Portugal as a rural and religious society where industrialisation, democracy and other modernising influences would be excluded (Economist Intelligence Unit 1999b: 4).

political system, did not fiercely defend its own referendum on regionalisation, which was rejected by the electorate in November 1998 (Gallagher 1998: 7; *Neue Zürcher Zeitung*, 103/1996: 5; *Neue Zürcher Zeitung*, 259/1998: 5).

The failure to create an administrative region means that Algarve, divided into 16 municipalities, is still a non-democratic and centralist planning region. The regional territory is administered by government organisations represented through extensions of the national ministries. In the field of regional policies, the central government keeps its influence through the Commission of Regional Co-ordination (CCR; *Comissão de Cordenação Regional*), an entity which is recognised by the EU.[87] Despite the fact that the CCR is the extended arm of the central government, the regional and local tier of government have some weight in the formulation of regional development policies because the CCR is composed of representatives from the municipal councils,[88] the directors of the region's Units of Technical Assistance (GAT; Gabinete de Apoio Técnico), and of regional representatives from national ministries. Created in the late 1960s and early 1970s, the CCR was organised as a study commission to feed into the national development plan. It acquired greater technical capacity and significant political weight during the 1980s. The CCR of today is concerned with planning of projects, support of municipalities and dialogue with the university and business associations. It has specific executive functions in urban and countryside planning, co-ordinates closely with local municipalities in the selection of projects to be financed by European and national funds, and manages those funds (CCR Algarve w.y.). In the absence of self-governing regions, the CCR has also played the part of a regional forum in debating national or Community policies which could affect regional interest (Opello 1993: 168; Pereira 1993: 277f). In spite of these competencies the authorities of the regional level considered their competencies in regional development as inappropriate. They would have liked an increase in power in many policy fields, especially in territorial planning, environment and transport.

## 9.2    European Regional Policy Interventions

According to the size of the Algarve population, the region received a relatively small part of the European structural transfers designated to Portugal, although the part has been growing (see Table 9-1). Public spending in Algarve reached Euro 342 million in the first CSF. Thirty per cent of these funds were managed by (but not entirely under the competence of) the CCR Algarve, including the regionalised part of the Portuguese CSF and some sectoral investments which were under the competence of national

---

[87]    Further details on the structure of the administrative body are in Chapter 9.3, where I focus on the actors involved in regional development.

[88]    The municipalities and parishes are the main territorial and administrative units at the local level. Although both of them have representative bodies directly elected by the population, decision-making power is concentrated in the municipal councils (Magone 1997: 62f).

ministries. The rest of the (sectoral) investments were under the competence of various national ministries, e.g. the Ministry of Environment or the Ministry of Transport (CEPI 1996: 46-49; 52f).[89] In the CSF 1994-1999, public spending amounted to Euro 1'002 million. The percentage of resources managed by the CCR Algarve was significantly reduced (to about 7.5 per cent) as all sectoral interventions were administered by national ministries (European Commission 1995e: 87). The financial planning for the CSF 2000-2006 estimates public investments in Algarve at Euro 1'748 million. The current planning period returns to the first system of fund administration, so that the region of Algarve is responsible for a part of the sectoral investments. The part of funds under regional authorities will, therefore, increase to about 44 per cent, which is even above the levels of the first CSF (AMAL 1999c). This development should not only be seen as the result of a learning effect of the negative experience with the system in the second CSF, but also as an effect of the regionalisation referendum in 1998. The national government tries to decentralise decision-making by increasing the financial competencies of the regional level, since the referendum failed.

**Table 9-1: Interventions of Structural Funds in Algarve (1989-2006)**

|           | CSF 1989-1993 | | CSF 1994-1999 | | CSF 2000-2006 | |
|-----------|-----------|-------------|-----------|-------------|-----------|-------------|
|           | Mio Euro  | % of Port.  | Mio Euro  | % of Port.  | Mio Euro  | % of Port.  |
| Andalusia | 221       | 3.0         | 657       | 4.7         | 1'009     | 5.8         |
| Portugal  | 7'368     | 100.0       | 13'980    | 100.0       | 19'800    | 100.0       |

*Source: AMAL 1999c; CEPI 1996: 46-49, 52f; European Commission 1995e: 86f; MEPAT, SEDR 1989: 48f, 55f.*

Figure 9-6 shows how European structural interventions were organised. The first CSF was characterised by a variety of axes of intervention in the field of infrastructure and enterprise support. These axes were brought together in the second CSF. The relative amount of funds for these investments, however, was more or less the same for both periods. A major change between the first and the second CSFs was the diminution of the first axe (development of human resources). This trend was against the intentions of the Commission, but the Portuguese government succeeded in pushing through its position, which favoured investments in "hard" infrastructure, instead of "soft" intangibles. The rationale behind the Portuguese position was that the country had shown an insufficient absorption capacity for these funds in the first CSF and could, thus, not profit from all the available funds. The remaining funds were allocated in a newly created axis instead (improving the quality of life and social cohesion). The CF,

---

[89]   Structural interventions, co-financed by the European Union, can be separated into sectoral and regionalised interventions. Sectoral investments were under the competence of various national ministries. Regionalised funds aimed at the strengthening of the regional economic base and were administered by the CCR. The final decision on regionalised investments, however, also lay at the national level (MEPAT).

which has financed in the Algarve only environmental projects, increased the tendency to invest in infrastructure (DGDR 1998b). According to the Portuguese RDP, the relative weight of the axes of intervention in the 2000-2006 period is about the same as in the case of the second CSF period.

The structure of interventions was similar in all three CSFs, including one regional OP for Algarve (two in the 1989-1993 CSF), global grants and CIs (see Table 9-2). The number of (national) sectoral OPs (such as the OP transport or the OP health) was considerably reduced in the second CSF (European Commission 1995e: 36). The major difference between the two CSFs was that the regional and local level could not apply any more to the national authorities for project financing in the second CSF. The CSF 2000-2006 is going to see a simplified structure of CIs (European Commission 1999h: 2).

**Table 9-2: Structure of Structural Interventions in Algarve (1989-2006)**

| CSF 1989-1993 | |
| --- | --- |
| 2 regional OPs Algarve | |
| projects out of various sectoral OPs | |
| global grants | |
| CIs: | • Prisma (services to businesses in connection with SEM) |
| • Interreg (transregional co-operation) | |
| • Leader (stimulation of rural development) | • Retex (diversification and modernisation of the textile sector) |
| • Envireg (protection of environment) | • Stride (development of R&D capacity) |
| **CSF 1994-1999** | |
| 1 regional OP Algarve | |
| projects of various sectoral OPs | |
| global grants | |
| CIs: | • Retex (diversification and modernisation of the textile sector) |
| • Interreg II | |
| • Leader II | |
| • SME (strengthening of competitivity) | • Urban (regeneration of crisis-struck areas in medium-sized and large towns) |
| • Pescas | |
| **CSF 2000-2006** | |
| 1 regional OP Algarve | |
| projects of various sectoral OPs | |
| global grants | |
| CIs: | • Equal (former Employment and Adapt) |
| • Interreg III | |
| • Leader III | |

*Source: CEPI 1996: 49; www.inforegio.org.*

## Figure 9-6: Axes of Structural Interventions in Algarve (1989-2006)

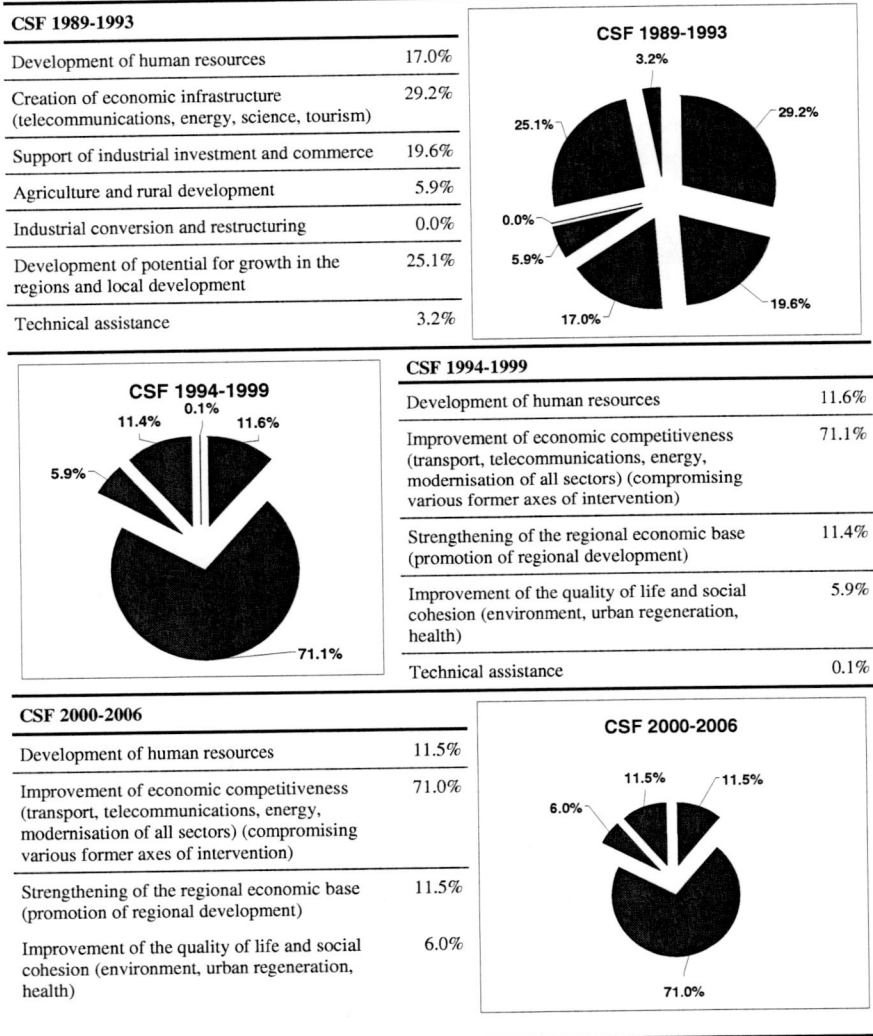

**CSF 1989-1993**

| | |
|---|---|
| Development of human resources | 17.0% |
| Creation of economic infrastructure (telecommunications, energy, science, tourism) | 29.2% |
| Support of industrial investment and commerce | 19.6% |
| Agriculture and rural development | 5.9% |
| Industrial conversion and restructuring | 0.0% |
| Development of potential for growth in the regions and local development | 25.1% |
| Technical assistance | 3.2% |

**CSF 1989-1993**

3.2%
29.2%
25.1%
0.0%
5.9%
19.6%
17.0%

**CSF 1994-1999**

0.1%
11.4%
11.6%
5.9%
71.1%

**CSF 1994-1999**

| | |
|---|---|
| Development of human resources | 11.6% |
| Improvement of economic competitiveness (transport, telecommunications, energy, modernisation of all sectors) (compromising various former axes of intervention) | 71.1% |
| Strengthening of the regional economic base (promotion of regional development) | 11.4% |
| Improvement of the quality of life and social cohesion (environment, urban regeneration, health) | 5.9% |
| Technical assistance | 0.1% |

**CSF 2000-2006**

| | |
|---|---|
| Development of human resources | 11.5% |
| Improvement of economic competitiveness (transport, telecommunications, energy, modernisation of all sectors) (compromising various former axes of intervention) | 71.0% |
| Strengthening of the regional economic base (promotion of regional development) | 11.5% |
| Improvement of the quality of life and social cohesion (environment, urban regeneration, health) | 6.0% |

**CSF 2000-2006**

11.5%
11.5%
6.0%
71.0%

*Note: The calculations are based on regional and sectoral interventions, of which the latter are managed by national ministries.*

*Source: CEPI 1996: 41, 52; European Commission 1995e: 86f; MEPAT, SEDR 1999d: VI-3ff.*

## 9.3    Institutions Concerned with Regional Development

The actors involved in Algarve structural policy are best analysed by following the process of European regional policy. Algarve institutions were not involved in the first two phases of the policy process because national authorities excluded regional actors from the negotiations on the budget and institutional design. The CCR at the regional level was interested in information on those issues. However, it has never developed any political activity in order to have a stronger role in those two phases. Information on structural funds was delivered through the Ministry of Regional Equipment, Development and Administration of Territory (MEPAT: *Ministério do Equipamento, do Planeamento e da Administração do Território*) which had as one of its functions the distribution of information on the European Union across regional districts.

**Figure 9-7: Actors of European Regional Policy in Algarve**

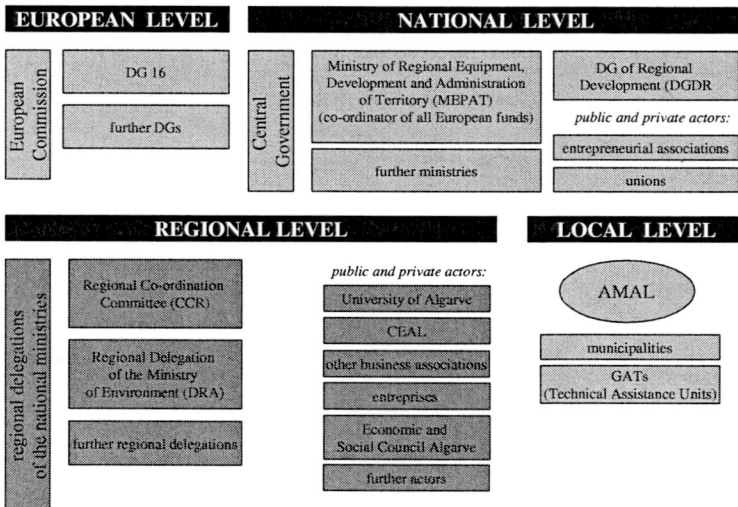

| EUROPEAN LEVEL | | NATIONAL LEVEL | |
|---|---|---|---|
| European Commission | DG 16 | Central Government | Ministry of Regional Equipment, Development and Administration of Territory (MEPAT) (co-ordinator of all European funds) |
| | further DGs | | DG of Regional Development (DGDR *public and private actors:* |
| | | | entrepreneurial associations |
| | | further ministries | unions |

| REGIONAL LEVEL | | | LOCAL LEVEL |
|---|---|---|---|
| regional delegations of the national ministries | Regional Co-ordination Committee (CCR) | *public and private actors:* University of Algarve | AMAL |
| | Regional Delegation of the Ministry of Environment (DRA) | CEAL other business associations entreprises | municipalities GATs (Technical Assistance Units) |
| | further regional delegations | Economic and Social Council Algarve further actors | |

*Source: own figure.*

National authorities also played a key role in policy-making, but the involvement of regional actors was more active in the four sub-phases of policy-making (see Figure 9-7). Despite a bottom-up process with the CCR Algarve presenting a RDP to Lisbon (DGDR 1998a), the preparation of CSFs was dominated by the Directorate General for Regional Development (DGDR; *Direcção-Geral do Desenvolvimento Regional*) in the MEPAT. The DGDR used the Algarve RDP as input for the Portuguese development plan but it was not bound to follow the investment propositions of the CCR, neither for sectoral nor for regionalised parts of the CSF. There was no involvement of other private and local actors (both private and public). In the process of negotiating the Portuguese development plan the CCR did not participate. The main actors in this phase were the DGDR and the DG-16 of the European Commission.

The formulation and implementation of the regional OPs (third and fourth phases), consisting of specific projects and investments, saw more involvement of regional actors. The CCR Algarve was responsible both for the preparation and management of OPs aiming at strengthening the regional economic base. The CCR relied mainly on inputs from the Algarve municipalities, and to a smaller degree on other regional delegations of national ministries, such as the delegation of the Ministry of Environment (DRA; *Delegação Região do Ambiento*), the delegation of the Ministry of Education, or the delegation of the Ministry of Social Affairs. In terms of sectoral interventions, which were under the competence of national ministries, the CCR was responsible for the management (but not planning) of projects, as well as directing information from the local and regional base to Lisbon. Units of Technical Assistance (GAT; Gabinete de Apoio Técnica) assisted local actors in the elaboration of project proposals for financial assistance within sectoral and regional OPs. The Algarve municipalities organised themselves in 1994 within the Association of Algarve municipalities (AMAL; *Associação de Municípios do Algarve*) in order to have a common, stronger voice in their claim for structural funds. Other private actors could also propose and realise development actions. The most prominent private actors were the University of Algarve and the Entrepreneurial Association of Algarve (CEAL; *Confederação dos Empresarios do Algarve*). The CEAL, which was created in 1990, represented most of the companies of Algarve as well as other entrepreneurial associations.

## *9.4    Analysis of Institutional Performance*

### 9.4.1    Contributor

In all three planning periods, the involvement of regional institutions in the elaboration of CSFs was restricted to the preparation phase since the regional level was excluded from the negotiations with the European Commission. But even in the preparation phase the competencies of the Algarve institutions were restrained, since the national authorities used RDPs as an indication only and felt free to change investment priorities listed by the regional level. This was entirely the case for sectoral axes of interventions, but held also for the regionalised part of funds which were aiming at the strengthening of the regional base.

In the first CSF period (1989-1993), the CCR Algarve delivered a rudimentary RDP to the DGDR, which was a part of the MEPAT (CCR Algarve 1989). The document only partially identified regional development problems both in terms of a sectoral and territorial approach. It neither offered a coherent strategy for endogenous development, nor strongly reflected the (infrastructure) needs of international real estate business. Furthermore, the plan suffered from poor co-ordination between the CCR and other regional extensions of the central government, such as the DRA or the Regional Delegation of Education. The low quality of the first Algarve RDP was, on the one hand, due to the novelty and complexity of the requirements of European regional policy. The poor result reflected, on the other hand, the lack of an active political and administrative force at the regional level. The involvement of the local level in the preparation of the CSF was low since municipalities were excluded from the debate on investment priorities and regional development strategies. The CCR viewed the municipalities mainly as executors of planned investments. Overall, there existed only a small influence of the CCR both on the formulation of sectoral and regionalised parts of the CSF, since the DGDR in Lisbon rejected the idea that partnership should be regionally based.

In the second CSF period (1994-1999), the technical quality of the RDP delivered by the CCR to the MEPAT had improved strongly (which was mainly due to the help of external consultants; CCR Algarve 1993), but the plan still lacked an endogenous development strategy. Furthermore, the influence of the CCR in the formulation of the regionalised part of European structural interventions decreased because all the sectoral interventions in the axis of "strengthening the regional economic base", formerly administered by the CCR, came under the management of national ministries (see Chapter 9.2; DGDR w.y.a; w.y.b; MEPAT, SEDR 1993a; 1993b; 1993c; 1994). The co-ordination between the regional branches of the national government was not improved, rather the situation worsened, since the second CSF period did not allow any longer financing of the same project (although in different phases) from different structural funds. This meant that the national ministries in charge of a specific structural fund (e.g. the MEPAT for the ERDF or the Ministry of Labour and Social Affairs for the ESF), and of course their regional extensions, too, exchanged less information between each other. Contrary to the first period, the municipalities were more active in trying to influence the investment priorities of the CCR. However, the newly created AMAL (1994) was still too preoccupied with setting up its own organisation in order to give the sixteen municipalities one strong voice.

The formulation of the third CSF (2000-2006) worked according to the same logic as the two previous CSFs with the almost nonexistent involvement of the CCR in the sectoral parts of the Portuguese CSFs (CCR Algarve 1999b; 1999c). The co-ordination between regional branches of the national ministries should be improved by allowing multi-fund financing again. In reality, however, the heavily centralised and hierarchical structure of the Portuguese administration prevented intensive horizontal co-ordination (MEPAT, SEDR 1999a; 1999b). The wish of municipalities to participate more in regional development planning was not granted by the CCR, which caused the AMAL to launch its own regional development plan (AMAL 1999b; 1999c). The document, which was established with professional assistance, reflected the common view of all the Algarve municipalities. It aimed, on the one hand, at raising the negotiation power of the AMAL against the CCR. On the other hand, the development plan of the AMAL needed to prove that the local level was indeed capable of taking over more responsibility in regional development planning. Finally, the AMAL document provided the European Commission with information from the local base. The impact of the document was marginal, though, and led to frustration of the AMAL since the Algarve municipalities perceived their weak position in structural policy.

In all the three periods, the influence of the regional level on the planning of regionalised and sectoral investments was severely limited. The same has been true for all CF interventions which were under the co-ordination of the DGDR (DGDR 1998b). The situation is partially explained by the relatively small weight of Algarve in terms of population and economic output. The main reason for the low activity of the regional level, however, was the lack of a democratically elected regional government, which had a true interest (and responsibility) in the development of the Algarve. The CCR has been active in budget maximising, though, but its interest has not been the development of the Algarve from a regional point of view. In fact, the CCR and the national authorities consolidated together the view that only a national perspective was able to guarantee the best payback of structural investments. The result of the national perspective was that the region of Algarve has not yet been regarded as a territorial identity, worthy of developing the potential for endogenous growth, but as a part of a sectoral approach, which focused mainly on the development of tourism. The possibilities of the European Commission to strengthen the involvement of the regional and local level in the preparation of CSFs has been limited because it had to respect the national territorial system which did not foresee much involvement of these actors in the preparation of CSFs.

### 9.4.2 Translator

The CCR was more involved in the process of translating Portuguese CSFs into OPs, especially in terms of regionalised interventions (the DGDR was still an important player). Concerning the regionalised part of investments, regional authorities were responsible for both the planning and implementation of structural measures. In the planning and implementation of sectoral OPs, the CCR was mostly excluded.

In the first period, the CCR was responsible for the planning of two regional OPs: OP Algarve Sotavento and OP Algarve Barlavento (CCR Algarve 1990a; 1990b). Members of the CCR felt overwhelmed by the requirements of the Commission in the beginning, but adapted towards the end of the first framework. The main tasks of the CCR were the preparation of the regional OPs, the co-ordination of regional actors and the assistance of the local level in their requests for structural funds. Both regional OPs of the first period had no sub-programmes, but they contained (sectoral) investments of national ministries. This was, on the one hand, welcomed by the CCR since it gave regional authorities the opportunity to voice their concerns in national development actions. The CCR complained, on the other hand, that large sectoral projects of the national government heavily delayed the completion of Algarve OPs, which retarded also the implementation of their (already prepared) smaller regional and local projects. Infrastructure made the biggest share of development interventions co-financed by European structural funds. The Algarve regional authorities would have liked at their disposal more funds in the field of economic dynamisation. The experiences with the ESF were positive (CCFSE 1998). Not all ESF funds were absorbed, though. Some problems occurred with investments in human resources in the private sector where cases of embezzlement were reported. The extent of corruption, however, should not be exaggerated. The most common forms of corruption were client and nepotist relationships (Della Porta and Mény 1997: 81-83).

The involvement of municipalities in planning regional investments was ambiguous, since the CCR depended much on inputs from the local base for the presentation of projects to Lisbon and Brussels, but the CCR did not want to give away its discretionary power in decisions on regionalised investments. For the preparation of the OPs, each municipality was asked to present ten important projects, which the CCR took as the basis of the document. The implementation itself was facilitated by the GATs (Units of Technical Assistance) which provided municipalities with basic infrastructure and help in filling application forms. The requests were then negotiated with the CCR and finally approved by the respective ministries in Lisbon (this was the case for both actions financed by regional and sectoral OPs). The relations between the CCR and the Algarve municipalities in terms of implication were reported to be intense but not distressed. The CCR kept the role of managing and controlling the funds both of regionalised and (Algarve) sectoral investments (but not of the CF which was administered by the MEPAT). The municipalities were responsible for the final execution of specific measures. An exception to this was the Community Initiative Leader, which promoted decentralised management by local action groups. In terms of sectoral OPs, the CCR delivered information to Lisbon, which was in need of regional input for the planning of structural interventions. The national authorities, though, were not obliged to follow regional propositions. Overall, participation of the regional level in terms of sectoral OPs was therefore restricted.

In the 1994-1999 period, there was only one regionalised OP, containing three sub-programmes (CCR Algarve 1994; 1995a; 1996a; 1997a; 1998a). The first sub-programme (39 per cent) was meant for municipal investments only. The financial management of the entire sub-programme was given to the AMAL in 1996. The second sub-programme (49 per cent) aimed at sectoral measures.[90] The third sub-programme, finally, was spent on economic dynamisation. Both of them stood under the management of the CCR, but municipalities and other regional (private) actors could apply to them, which led to competition among regional actors. The strict separation of national and regional interventions – which meant that regional and local actors did not participate in the planning of sectoral investments – caused problems in the second period. Firstly, they caused severe information asymmetries, since the national authorities lacked the knowledge from the base in the planning phase. There was, secondly, an obvious lack of co-ordination between various national ministries which planned their own interventions, but were not forced to co-ordinate them at the regional level. The separation did not allow local actors to present projects co-financed by the structural funds to the authorities in Lisbon. This was only possible for projects co-financed by the Cohesion Fund. The part of funds reserved for the qualification of human resources was smaller, since not all of the available funds had been absorbed in the first period. The fight against unemployment, however, was successful. The regional delegation of the Institute for Employment and Professional Training (IEFP; Instituto do Emprego e Formação Profissional) showed innovative measures, such as special training of the large tourism workforce during the winter season (Delegão Regional do Algarve do IEFP 1998b; 1999; Ministério Para a Qualificação e o Emprego, IEFP 1999). The involvement of local actors was the same as in the first period. The main change concerned the co-ordination between municipalities and the CCR which was done via the AMAL, the association of all Algarve municipalities. This simplified, on the one hand, the co-ordination since the CCR had to deal with only one actor (instead of sixteen). On the other hand, it gave rise to tension in the beginning of the second period, especially with the national level, because Lisbon was not interested in a strong local level taking over the tasks of their regional branches. The main argument against a stronger role of the local level in structural policy built on the argument that local actors were incapable of producing a development strategy. This argument, however, was disproved by the positive results of local actors.

In the third planning period there is one OP for Algarve, containing three sub-programmes including sectoral (national) and regional measures (similar to the first framework). The first sub-programme, which is managed by municipalities, is planned for local investments. The second sub-programme contains measures of territorial integration and is managed by the CCR. The third sub-programme unites the sectoral measures of various ministries. Many details were still unclear at the time of editing this study.[91] The most important issues were, firstly, how much sectoral interventions

---

[90]   These sectoral measures had nothing to do with the national (sectoral) programmes which were, contrary to the 1989-1993 period, not included in the Algarve OP any more.

[91]   The completion of the Portuguese OP was delayed.

each ministry would give away to the local level. It was, secondly, not clear who would co-ordinate the three sub-programmes. The latest available information thought about strengthening the role of the CCR, that is to link it directly to the prime minister, so that it would have the power to co-ordinate the regional extensions of other national ministries. The role of local actors was also thought to be strengthened, according to the promise of the socialist government. Details on the role of municipalities were not available.

A major problem in all three periods was the co-ordination between the regional and national levels. This was not so much the case between the CCR Algarve and the DGDR in Lisbon, which worked together closely in many aspects since they belonged both to the same ministry. The real problem lay in the combination of the strictly vertical organisation of the Portuguese administration and the fact that the DGDR, responsible for the co-ordination of all Portuguese structural interventions co-financed by European funds, did not have competencies in other ministries (e.g., the Ministry of Transport, or the Ministry of Environment). The consequence of this structure was that most ministries had their own regional representation in the Algarve which was directly responsible to Lisbon. Therefore, a real vacuum of co-ordination among regional delegations existed. The following example shows the problem. When the CCR Algarve had to co-ordinate a development project in the field of environment, the DRA did not have the competencies to decide on its own. The CCR could neither contact the Ministry of Environment since it did not belong to the same ministry. The CCR was thought to direct the request via the DGDR in the MEPAT, which would then contact the Ministry of Environment. The Ministry of Environment itself would, finally, co-ordinate with the DRA Algarve. The situation was worsened by uncooperative competition between national ministries and the structure of the second CSF period with no more (national) sectoral actions at the regional level under CCR management.

In general, Lisbon did not reject contacts between the CCR Algarve and Brussels, since the CCR was strongly linked to the national level. The relations between the CCR and the European Commission in the first CSF, however, were reported by interviewees at all levels as difficult, even in terms of technical questions. The reason for this was the pressure of the European Commission to strengthen some axes of interventions, which Lisbon interpreted as an interference in internal affairs.[92] The communication improved strongly and became regular during the second CSF period. The management of the Algarve OP reported that good relationships with the

---

[92]   The European Commission wanted to increase the funds of the ESF at the expense of the ERDF since the fiercest development problem of Portugal has not been a deficit in infrastructure but a deficit of qualified human resources.

Commission even helped to influence two reprogrammings in favour of the regional level. It will be interesting to await the reaction of the national authorities on the further activities of the AMAL. The European Commission welcomed the additional source of information at the base. Both national authorities and the DG-16 neglected, however, an influence of the AMAL development plan on the Portuguese 2000-2006 CSF.

### 9.4.3 Monitor

The Algarve authorities (that is the chairman of the CCR) were included in the Monitoring Committee of national CSFs, which was chaired by the MEPAT in Lisbon. The regional authorities, together with representatives of the DG-16, DGDR, AMAL and CEAL were also present in the Monitoring Committee of regional OPs (and sub-programmes). The committees were responsible for the co-ordination of structural interventions, proposing the allocation of the resources annually generated by deflator application and the monitoring/evaluation of OPs on the basis of financial, physical and impact indicators. The CCR could influence outcomes in both types of committees (sectoral and regional), especially when it came to specific issues of implementation.

Another important task of regional actors in monitoring was the performance of *ex ante*, *ex post* and ongoing evaluations of the Algarve OPs.[93] The performance of regional evaluations in the first CSF period was poor in all aspects. *Ex ante* assessments were delayed for almost three years because the development of OPs had taken more resources than expected. The CCR also lacked qualified personnel and a solid data base at the regional level for *ex ante* evaluations. Ongoing evaluations were not done as mentioned above. In the field of *ex post* assessment, there existed only evaluations on (national) sectoral OPs (CEDRU 1994; MEPAT, SEDR 1996) but not on Algarve OPs. Overall, the first experiences with evaluations could be fruitful, but the assessments were not taken seriously,  and the Commission did not have the resources to reinforce European regulations. Therefore, the learning effects in the first CSF period were not optimal.

Monitoring was reinforced by the European Commission in the second CSF period which lead to a substantial improvement of evaluations. The Portuguese authorities established an *ex ante* monitoring system at the national level, including a range of quantitative indicators which were measured at the regional level (CEPI 1996). The system helped to standardise evaluation studies in the country. The main deficiency of the system, however, lay in its application, because regional and national authorities were reluctant in defining the quantitative effects of structural measures. The database

---

[93]    Ongoing evaluations were introduced in the second CSF period. The impact evaluation of projects co-financed by the Cohesion Fund was under the responsibility of the national ministries and the European Commission.

was improved partially. Regional and national authorities reported positive experiences with ongoing evaluations (CEDRU 1997; CIDEC 1999). They gave policy planners at the regional, national and European level an opportunity to rethink their actions and were viewed as a real contribution to partnership. *Ex post* evaluations were still underway at the time of editing. The lack of concise objectives in the *ex ante* evaluations, however, will limit the scope of these assessments. Evaluations for the third period foresee a stronger focus on regional aspects, especially in terms of socio-economic and environmental effects and the equality of women and men.

Regional authorities reported widespread dissatisfaction with the emphasis on quantitative indicators required by the European Commission. They thought that the definition of quantified goals restricted them too much in their actions. Training in evaluations during the second CSF period, financed within the axis of technical assistance, helped to overcome technical problems and the resistance of managers in charge of OPs. Overall, the need of evaluating structural interventions has become accepted. It is restricted to actions co-financed by the European funds, though, and the Portuguese authorities do not apply evaluations for structural policy programmes solely financed by national funds. The interest in insights from evaluations was generally high, although many interviewees doubted that evaluation changed the way that structural polices were designed and implemented. A newly created national supervisor of evaluations (1998) aimed to ensure the long-term effects of evaluations. The CCR, for instance, will have to report what measures will be taken to implement the recommendations of the evaluations. The results of this policy have to be awaited.

### 9.4.4 Facilitator

Overall, the involvement of Algarve private actors in European regional policy has been small. If there was any participation, it has been in the implementation phase when private companies profited from structural measures. However, the interest of private actors in influencing structural policy has grown in the last three years. The main reasons for the under-representation of the private sector were on the one hand, the traditional dominance of the public sector in the Algarve. On the other, there was the sheer scarcity of (active) private associations and confederations. Unions were not organised at the regional level so that the social accords took place at the national level. The majority of business associations, such as for tourism, restaurants, the promotion of the airport or real estate business, have been literally inactive. In fact, there was just one single strong regional entrepreneurial association in the form of the CEAL. The CEAL has been representing almost all the Algarve enterprises and other business associations.

The preparation phases of the first and second CSFs/OPs were characterised by a total absence of private sector activity. The European Commission tried to initialise private actions through the provision of information of structural funds. The Eurocabinet, which supported enterprises to find the best practices, or the Business Innovation Centre (BIC) played a prominent but not very successful role. An attempt for stronger involvement of the private sector was made with the creation of various national sectoral associations, such as the Confederation of Industry Portugal (CIP; *Confederação do Industria Portugal*), the Confederation of Agriculture Portugal (CAP; *Confederação do Agricultura Portugal*) or the Confederation of Tourism Portugal (CTP; *Confederação do Turismo Portugal*). The attempt, however, showed little success since there are no partners in Algarve that could have copied the idea of an economic and social council at the regional level.

It was only in the preparation of the third period that a significant change occurred when the CEAL contacted the CCR in order to participate in the planning of the Algarve RDP. As a preparation for the desired co-operation, the CEAL elaborated a (professional) development plan with its own priorities and recommendations for each economic sector (CEAL 1995). The proposition of the CEAL was different from the CCR plan, insofar as it proposed to look at Algarve development from a regional (territorial) point of view and less from the common national (sectoral) perspective, which had aimed mainly at developing the tourism industry. The partnership between the CCR and the CEAL was described as difficult from the CCR's side, whereas the CEAL was totally disappointed by the co-operation. The CEAL criticised the "simulation of participation" since it was listened to but its ideas had no impact at all on the RDP. The CEAL was also an opponent of the current form (not of the idea in general) of the Economic and Social Council Algarve, which was created in summer 1999. It was criticised that the council had too weak a position with more than thirty permanent members. It was not clear what role the council should take in the partnership with the CCR.

The CEAL intensified its lobbying activity in an attempt to give its regionalist point of view more weight. It presented its ideas to the head of the MEPAT, the prime minister and the DG-16 in Brussels. Furthermore, the CEAL tried to profit from the general elections in 1999, when it negotiated pacts on economic policy with each political party for the next government period. Overall, the political activities strongly strengthened the role of the CEAL. It has to be seen, though, whether private actors will have a stronger role in the preparation of CSFs/OPs in the future.

Private actors were mainly benefiters of the implementation phase. Interventions with private actors in general did not work as well as with their counterparts of the public sector. Evaluations even revealed causes of fraud, especially in the first period when private actors had wider competencies and profited from a high degree of confidence of public authorities (CEDRU 1994). In spite of its opposing role, the CEAL became an important partner during the second planning period. Due to its close relation to the entrepreneurial base, it was successfully engaged in professional training, the dissemination of quality management techniques in industry, the promotion of Algarve products and assistance for the introduction of the Euro.

### 9.4.5 Stimulator

Regional planning had already been known in the Estado Novo. It revived when Portugal entered the European Community in the mid-1980s. The first development plan was characterised by a short-term, project-based approach and suffered from an insufficient co-ordination of development goals (CCR Algarve 1985). Participants and managers of CSFs/OPs universally welcomed long-term, integrated programmes introduced by the European regional policy reform. Some complaints were voiced in the beginning of the first CSF period, because the regional actors were not well instructed in what was demanded by the European Commission. Technical deficiencies became rare after the support delivered by the axis of technical assistance in the second CSF. Those responsible did not expect any surprises in the planning for the third period.

### 9.4.6 Experimenter

Interviewees at the regional and national levels universally agreed that they preferred investments in infrastructure. The reason for this lay in the higher predictability of success of hard projects, compared to more innovative measures, which were time and resource consuming. The analysis of the allocation of structural funds revealed that the tendency to invest in infrastructure was indeed strong. Those responsible, however, showed interest in experimental projects and would have liked more funds for the axis of economic dynamisation. The absorption of available funds was above the European average in the first two CSF periods, though not all funds were absorbed. Experimental projects usually needed more time to take off since they involved more actors and demanded deeper analysis (due to higher risks). Innovative projects were usually done with partners from the public sector. They included projects such as the strengthening of inland and winter season tourism, or the promotion of Algarve handcrafts in holiday resorts.

### 9.4.7 Co-ordinator

The CCR was not able to play a co-ordinating role vis-à-vis other Portuguese regions since multi-regional projects financed by European structural funds were strictly under the control of the national ministries. The MEPAT had as one of its functions the distribution of information across regional districts. In an informal manner, however, exchanges among regional districts were commonplace, constrained only by budgetary realities when travel was involved. If the CCR needed to exchange information, usually with the neighbouring region Alentejo in the north of Algarve, this was done directly between the respective managers of the regional OPs. No regional co-operation outside the European structural funds was established by the CCR. Overall, there was little interest in increased interregional co-operation.

### 9.4.8    Initiator

Examples of true transregional co-operation were hard to find since Algarve lacked a veritable regional administration. The CCR Algarve, however, was interested in transregional co-operation. Interviewees reported that transregional co-operation had an explicit experimental character since this kind of co-operation was not known before. Some regional authorities, however, were not convinced that projects in this field helped to promote economic development. Transregional co-operation was solely financed by funds available through the CI Interreg, which supported either transregional infrastructure investments or co-operation projects of administration and other regional actors.

In the first CSF, regional authorities were interested mainly in projects to improve the infrastructure between the two regions, since the Spanish neighbouring region is an important exterior market for Algarve. These projects, however, were never executed due to a variety of reasons. First of all, the CCR lacked the resources for their co-financing part. More important, the authorities in Lisbon were not much interested in infrastructure projects in Andalusia. The Portuguese authorities preferred to improve transport facilities between Lisbon and Madrid. This example shows that transregional co-operation was not only hampered by technical and administrative problems at the regional level, but that the success of a project depended heavily on the national authorities, which followed closely what the regional level was doing in terms of transregional co-operation.

In the second CSF, fewer funds were available for infrastructure so that only minor improvement of road connections between Algarve and Andalusia could be carried out. Co-operation between governmental and private actors became more popular and included conferences or studies on specific development topics. It existed with Andalusia and Morocco, with the latter one only since 1999 (Universidad de Sevilla 1999: 186f). The CCR, furthermore, participated in the Commission of European Regions and the Commission of Peripheral Maritime Regions. Towards the end of the second CSF, regional authorities reported contacts with CEECs, which were interested in the possibilities of structural funds. Transregional co-operation between enterprises was rare. This seems to be surprising in the case of co-operation with Andalusia. It can be explained, however, by the small complementarity between the two neighbouring regions (rather there is competition, such as in tourism or agro-food products).

## 9.5    Synopsis

Algarve belongs to the poorest regions of the European Union. The region's most valuable asset has been its mild climate, which provided competitive advantages in tourism and agricultural production. The main problem has been an unbalanced development with the coastal strip being favoured at the expense of interior areas. The region has also suffered from uncoordinated urban development due to intensive tourism. Finally, the lack of a solid industrial base and the specialisation in tourism and related activities resulted in a highly vulnerable economy. European structural transfers aimed to overcome these drawbacks for development. The analysis of structural interventions revealed that regional actors preferred infrastructure investments instead of investments in intangible assets. There were two main actors in structural policy: the DGDR and the CCR. The DGDR belonged to the national level, which had the final word in regional planning both for the sectoral and regionalised part of European structural funds. The CCR at the regional level participated very little in the preparation and negotiation of CSFs. The exclusion of the CCR from this phase did not lead to any political activity by the regional authorities. However, municipalities organised themselves within the AMAL in order to give their claim for structural funds more weight. The translation of CSFs into OPs reflected the need of national authorities for information from the regional and local base. The CCR played an important role in the planning of OPs for regionalised investments. In terms of sectoral investments, regional authorities were only implementing national plans. The translation phase suffered from heavy co-ordination problems among actors both at the regional and local level, which demonstrated the limits of the vertical and hierarchical administrative system in Portugal. The obligation to monitor and evaluate structural interventions met with the strong resistance of regional authorities. The Commission's insistence on monitoring improved evaluations. It did not lead to a spread of an evaluation culture, but all programmes co-financed by European funds have been evaluated to European regulations. The involvement of the private sector in European structural policy was small. It happened mainly when private actors benefited from structural funds. The reason for this lay in the inactivity of private actors, with the exception of the CEAL, which became more and more politically active. Participants highly welcomed the European planning approach. Technical shortcomings in the first CSF were overcome during the second planning period. Regional authorities were interested in innovative structural projects. Overall, little had been undertaken by the CCR in this field because experimental development actions were resource consuming and involved higher risk than conventional projects. Interregional co-operation under the Algarve authorities was not observed because sectoral programmes were under the control of national ministries. On the contrary, transregional co-operation has become common over time, especially with the Andalusia and Morocco border areas.

# 10 COMPARING THE CASES OF ANDALUSIA AND ALGARVE

This chapter analyses the relation between the partnership principle of the 1988 European regional policy reform and institutional performance in the observed period of time. The variation of variables is observed over time and between the cases. The analysis detects on the one hand, in which roles the partnership principle supported the development of institutional performance. On the other hand, the chapter discusses additional variables that promoted or hampered the rise of institutional performance.

## 10.1 Similarities and Differences in Institutional Performance

### 10.1.1 Contributor: The Territorial System Defines the Degree of Partnership

The degree of partnership in terms of CSFs can be broken down in the phases of preparing and negotiating support frameworks. Both Andalusia and Algarve were entirely excluded from the negotiations of CSFs, and it is thus not surprising that the two regions did not develop any kind of institutional performance in this field. In the case of Andalusia, there existed close collaboration between the regional, national and European level for the preparation of regional CSFs, as a result of which the JdA was able to advance from the poor RDP of the first planning period to an endogenous regional development strategy for the third planning period. Pluri-regional CSFs did not inhibit elements of co-operation between Madrid and Seville despite strong (but unsuccessful) political lobbying of the JdA in Brussels. The national level viewed partnership in pluri-regional interventions mainly as financial and the Andalusian government was incapable of influencing the decision of the national ministries.

In the case of Algarve, the concept of partnership was endorsed by national authorities since the MEPAT asked regional authorities to deliver RDPs. The idea, however, that partnership should be truly region-based was rejected. National authorities saw the formulation of RDPs more as an exercise in bureaucratic and technocratic rationality, and less as a participatory process of regional planning. The role of the CCR was, therefore, of a rather symbolic, formalistic nature, not a substantive one since the MEPAT held the sole authority to decide on the content of both sectoral and regional programmes. Regional authorities had in general a bit more planning competencies in the latter. Despite the limited competencies, the Algarve authorities did not develop political activities to strengthen their position. The institutional capacity of the CCR in regional planning was low throughout the entire period of observation, with RDPs lacking a coherent approach to regional development. The result of the piecemeal drawing up of RDPs was that instead of being integrated strategic plans for endogenous development, they were essentially lists of proposed actions on the basis of demands of regional and local agencies.

The comparison of the cases of Andalusia and Algarve suggests that institutional capacity was higher where regional authorities had the competence to participate as full partners and where the role of the regions in economic development was recognised. Partnership and, consequently, institutional capacity depended therefore strongly on the structure of the territorial system.[94] Andalusia is an autonomous region with a democratically elected government that lobbied for pluri-regional funds and defended their competencies in the planning of regional funds. Conversely, the CCR has had no autonomous power-base since Portugal's territorial structure exhibited only planning regions. The regional authorities were political appointees, who had ultimately to bow to the central authorities. The fact that the regional level did not develop any kind of serious pressure for more competencies in regional planning points to the democratic deficits of the current status of Portuguese planning regions.

The impact of the partnership principle on the structure of the territorial system itself has been marginal. The institutional balance of power between the centre and the region has not been altered, either in Andalusia or Algarve. And if the regionalisation referendum in Portugal had been successful, the creation of administrative Portuguese regions would have been mainly the result of domestic political ideological commitments, not that of European regional policy. Despite the fact that there has been no direct impact of the partnership principle on the balance between the centre and the periphery at the institutional level, the involvement of the regional level in European regional policy constituted an external shock for the territorial system. This resulted in some pressure for more involvement of sub-national authorities, especially in the case of the Algarve municipalities. The AMAL refuted the prevailing attitude of the central administration, which was one of contempt towards the abilities of local and regional actors to develop economically meaningful proposals. Conversely, the Andalusian municipalities were confronted with a tendency to centralise structural policy at the regional level. Overall, I repeat, national authorities in Spain and Portugal have succeeded in resisting the pressure from the European Commission for the extended involvement of sub-national actors. Regional participation in the process of European regional policy still aims more at a semblance of democratic planning, a legitimisation of the whole exercise, rather than at a genuine "synergy" between central, local and regional actors.

---

[94]   The structure of the territorial system prescribes how different levels of government rely on each other and how they co-operate. The territorial system defines therefore the degree of autonomy and power relations among levels of government.

## 10.1.2   Translator: Partnership Raises the Responsibility for the Impact of Own Structural Interventions

In the case of Andalusia, the degree of both partnership and institutional performance was low for the planning of pluri-regional OPs. The implementation phase, on the contrary, reflected the need of the central Spanish authorities for information from the base. The involvement of the regional level was therefore somewhat higher. There was, however, no difference between the quality of interventions implemented by national and regional actors. In the case of regional OPs, there was a positive relationship between the degree of partnership and institutional performance, especially in the planning phase of OPs. The second OP of the planning period 1994-1999 (because of the reprogramming of interventions) started an important learning process of the Andalusian authorities which accepted, on the one hand, that structural funds not only obliged a transparent financial management, but that European funds also meant an increased responsibility for the impact of structural interventions. Regional policy, on the other hand, became more strategically oriented since regional authorities allocated financial resources according to medium- and long-term development priorities and less to short-term political needs. Policy planners and makers also broadened their scope in analysing structural impacts of other public policies. A further feature of the second period was the establishment of the DG of European Funds which was a step in synchronising the institutional organisation with the national and European structure.

The planning of Portuguese sectoral OPs was characterised by a low level of partnership between national and regional authorities. This led to structural interventions on Algarve territory which were characterised by a strong national and sectoral perspective. The implementation of sectoral OPs was partially done by regional representatives which helped national programmes to overcome the formidable information deficits of the highly centralist administrative system. Partnership in the planning of regionalised OPs was a hybrid form of co-operation because the CCR could set up their own plans, but national authorities were responsible for final decisions on regionalised OPs. As a result of this process, regionalised OPs were also driven by a sectoral perspective. The implementation of regionalised OPs, which was characterised by a high degree of partnership, worked well and led to an increased responsibility for the impact of interventions. Despite the positive experience with regionalised OPs, interviewees reported that the implementation phase could have been better if the co-ordination among regional delegations of national ministries had been better.

The comparison between Andalusia and Algarve unveils that institutional performance in the role of translating CSFs into OPs follows a similar pattern as in the case of the contributor role, with the structure of the territorial system being an additional variable for institutional performance at the regional level. In general, the partnership principle induced in both regions higher responsibility for the impact of their own structural interventions. This effect was weaker in Algarve where the centralist administrative system blurred responsibilities between the actors to some degree. Partnership with regional actors helped furthermore to absorb European funds quickly. This result was contrary to the expectations of national authorities, especially in the case of Portugal, who believed that it would be easier to spend funds on large-scale projects. The impact of the partnership principle on the structure of the territorial system (in terms of institutional change) was small in both regions. The partnership principle of 1988, however, created a bottom-up demand for more involvement, since the European funds constituted additional resources that gave hitherto marginal actors an opportunity to gain financial support for projects of particular interest to them, and to increase their presence in the regional policy process in general.

### 10.1.3   Monitor: Between a Necessary Evil and a System to Design and Manage Structural Interventions

The involvement of the Andalusian authorities in terms of monitoring pluri-regional CSFs and OPs – both Monitoring Committees and evaluations – was formalistic, and the influence, and respectively institutional performance, was small. Conversely, the JdA was an equal partner in monitoring functions for regional CSFs and OPs. It could, thus, influence outcomes according to the demands of public and private actors. The JdA has also developed a substantial level in assessing structural programmes. Evaluations were not only seen as an answer to regulatory obligations by the European Commission, but they had become a system to aid the design and management of interventions by the end of the second planning period. There remained a range of deficits, though, mainly in the field of quantified indicators of *ex ante* evaluations. The positive aspects of increased performance in monitoring were a stricter discipline concerning available budgets and the establishment of development priorities.

In the case of Algarve, the CCR was not an equal but an important partner in the Monitoring Committees of both sectoral and regionalised CSFs/OPs. The influence of the regional authorities in these committees could be significant, especially when it came to specific problems of the implementation phase. The CCR was also mainly responsible for evaluations of the Algarve OPs, a task which regional authorities viewed primarily as a constraint and an additional workload weighing on managers and less as a system to reflect and design structural policies. Impact assessments still displayed a range of technical deficits at the beginning of the third planning period.

Comparing the two cases reveals that Andalusia displayed a higher degree of institutional performance in terms of evaluating structural interventions. This had consequences for performance in the translator role, since evaluations constituted the start of institutional learning processes which were less marked in the case of Algarve.

The reason for this situation is not straightforward, but it can be argued that the democratically elected officials in Andalusia welcomed evaluations as a tool to control and ensure the desired policy results of their own administration, whereas the regional delegates of the national ministries had less incentives to use evaluations in this sense. The democratic use of evaluations, however, has not yet been established either in Andalusia or in Algarve. The discussion of evaluation results has not become a political act, in which policy makers inform the public on the efficiency and effectiveness of structural policy. Regarding the variables in terms of involvement of regional actors in Monitoring Committees, Algarve displays a higher value both for partnership and institutional performance, because the national authorities decided to rely on inputs from their regional delegations. This suggests that the territorial system acted as a weaker variable as it was the case in the contributor and translator role. It should be mentioned, though, that the development of the institutional capacity in monitoring was not only due to the partnership principle, but owes a lot to the pressure of the European Commission in the beginning of the second planning period to fulfil European regulations.

### 10.1.4  Facilitator: The Rise and Strengthening of the Private Sector

The Andalusian private actors' involvement was concentrated on regional CSFs and OPs. The partnership principle was strengthened in the preparation of the second planning with the establishment of the social accord between entrepreneurial associations, trade unions and the JdA. The accord allowed the private sector to put forward its demands in structural policy, as a result of which the co-operation between the partners significantly improved, both in the planning and implementation phases. The involvement of the private sector in terms of pluri-regional CSFs/OPs was restricted to benefiting from European funds.

In the Algarve region, partnership between the public and private sector was not marked, mainly because the latter was not organised at the regional level, as a result of which the demands of regional private actors were hardly taken into consideration by public authorities. The rise of the CEAL in the last few years was a reaction to this deplorable state of affairs. The realm of the CEAL, however, was limited to the regionalised part of structural funds, and even there the CCR was not always interested in co-operation with the entrepreneurial association.

Comparing the two cases is difficult since the two regions started from a very different level of the private sector's activity in regional policy. The partnership approach was successful in both regions since the private sector became more lively and interested in defending its interests in terms of European regional policy. Monitoring Committees especially proved to be successful in raising the performance in the facilitator role since they allowed solutions to be found for concrete issues between a variety of actors concerned. The higher degree of performance of the JdA in facilitating was due to two factors. Firstly, there was the historically stronger private base in Andalusia. Secondly, the Spanish authorities accepted that facilitating takes place at the regional level. Conversely, the initiative of the central Portuguese authorities to create national sectoral associations was not successful – and not even necessary as the Algarve case demonstrates. The private sector organised itself and exerted pressure in order to be listened to by structural policy planners. European funds played an important role in the process of strengthening associations of the private sector, since they enabled associations to modernise their organisational structures, to acquire modern equipment and to set up highly specialised "EU agencies". Another important factor for more involvement of the private sector was the decision of the European Commission to promote assistance for the strengthening of the regional economic base, instead of supporting big infrastructure projects. This led to pressure for national ministries to collaborate with regional and local private actors since planning and implementation decisions in building an economic network were more appropriate when they were taken together with regional actors.

### 10.1.5 Stimulator: Rise in Institutional Performance, But Not Because of the Partnership Principle

The stimulator role concerned solely technical aspects of planning structural policy. Both regions developed a high level of institutional performance in this role, though it was restricted to regional CSFs/OPs since regional actors did not have planning competencies in pluri-regional and sectoral affairs. The main variable for explaining the rise of capacity in this role is less the partnership principle than specific planning techniques introduced by the European Commission, with features such as multi-annual planning or matching development priorities with available resources. The partnership principle only became important when plans entered the public debate about investment priorities. It could, then, guarantee that different levels of the territorial system as well as private actors could put forward their demands for European structural policy (see the roles of contributor, translator and facilitator).

### 10.1.6 Experimenter: The Partnership Principle Does Not Explain the Low Level of Institutional Performance

The capacity (and interest) to perform innovative projects has risen a little bit within the last ten years in both regions. The overall capacity, however, at the beginning of the third planning period was still small. The degree of partnership did not prove to be the main variable in determining the level of institutional capacity. The low level of the dependent variable was mainly due to the risk aversion of public actors since experimental projects were time and resource consuming with the uncertain success of projects.

### 10.1.7 Co-ordinator: Little Interest of Regional Actors in Inter-Regional Co-operation

The partnership principle found no application in the field of inter-regional co-operation. Neither the Andalusian nor the Algarve authorities have developed a strong role in co-ordinating structural polices with other regions in their own country. The CCR did not have the competency to take over a co-ordinating role, since this policy arena stood entirely under the control of national ministries. In the case of the JdA, regional authorities were not interested in co-ordinating inter-regional structural programmes because they were time and resource consuming. Another reason for the absence of institutional performance in the co-ordinator role was that the European Union did not provide the financial means for this kind of projects, which might have led to more co-ordinating activities of regional actors in order to absorb such funds.

### 10.1.8 Initiator: Better Result When Partnership Principle Was Applied

Institutional performance in the initiator role has developed significantly in both regions during the observed period of time, although regional authorities had many problems with transregional co-operation in the first planning period. Transregional co-operation has been strongly focused on co-operation with neighbouring regions, namely Andalusia, Algarve and Morocco. Applying the partnership principle in transregional projects, that is to include regional actors and national representatives of both countries in the planning and implementation phases, led to better results and took public and private actors' needs more into consideration than projects where regional actors were excluded from decision-making.

A comparison of the two cases also reveals that the structure of the territorial system has been an important factor in explaining the variation of performance in the initiator role. The Algarve authorities heavily depended on the approval of transregional projects by the national level, whereas in the case of Andalusia, the JdA had the competency to establish relations with regional representatives from abroad. Further explanatory variables of the degree of institutional capacity in the initiator role were the amount of available funds and time, the latter showed to be a handicap in the first planning period when regional authorities were absorbed by the novelty of European regional policy procedures.

## 10.2  Synopsis

This chapter examined the relation between the partnership principle of the 1988 European regional policy reform and institutional performance. On the one hand, I analysed the evolution of institutional performance over time in each of the eight roles proposed by the analytical framework. On the other hand, the variables were compared between the two cases of Andalusia and Algarve. Figure 10-1 summarises the results of the analysis.

In general, the degree of partnership in pluri-regional and sectoral CSFs and OPs was small (with minor exceptions) and, thus, was institutional performance in any role. In terms of interventions within regional CSFs, there was a positive relation between partnership and institutional performance in the contributor role. The degree of applying the partnership principle itself was strongly defined by the structure of the territorial system. The partnership approach, however, constituted an external shock to the territorial system, which put pressure on national authorities to rethink their strategy of centralist planning. In the translator role, partnership was responsible for a higher absorption rate of funds, more responsibility of regional actors for the impact of their own structural interventions, and institutional convergence in the case of Andalusia (through the creation of the DG of European Funds). The structure of the territorial system again proved to be an additional variable determining the effects of the partnership principle. The quality of evaluations improved in both cases, with Andalusia having quite an established evaluation culture today. In terms of the facilitator role, the partnership principle strengthened institutional performance in both regions. The effects were different, though, since the two regions started from a very different level. Monitoring Committees, where partnership was particularly high, proved to be highly suitable for raising the capability to respond to the demands of private actors. In the case of Algarve, where a network of private actors was almost nonexistent at the beginning of the first planning period, European funds enabled sectoral associations to modernise their organisational structures. This led, eventually, to a bottom-up demand for more involvement in regional policy.

In the stimulator, experimenter and co-ordinator roles, no relation between the partnership principle and institutional performance was found. In the case of the stimulator role, institutional performance rose mainly through planning techniques imposed by the European Commission. In the experimenter role, risk aversion of public actors was responsible for low performance concerning innovative projects. Institutional performance in the co-ordinator role was hampered by the territorial structure and the fact that the European Union did not foresee financial transfers for such projects. Institutional performance in the initiator role, finally, showed that it was fostered by the partnership principle.

**Figure 10-1: Empirical Results of the Relation Between Partnership and Institutional Performance**

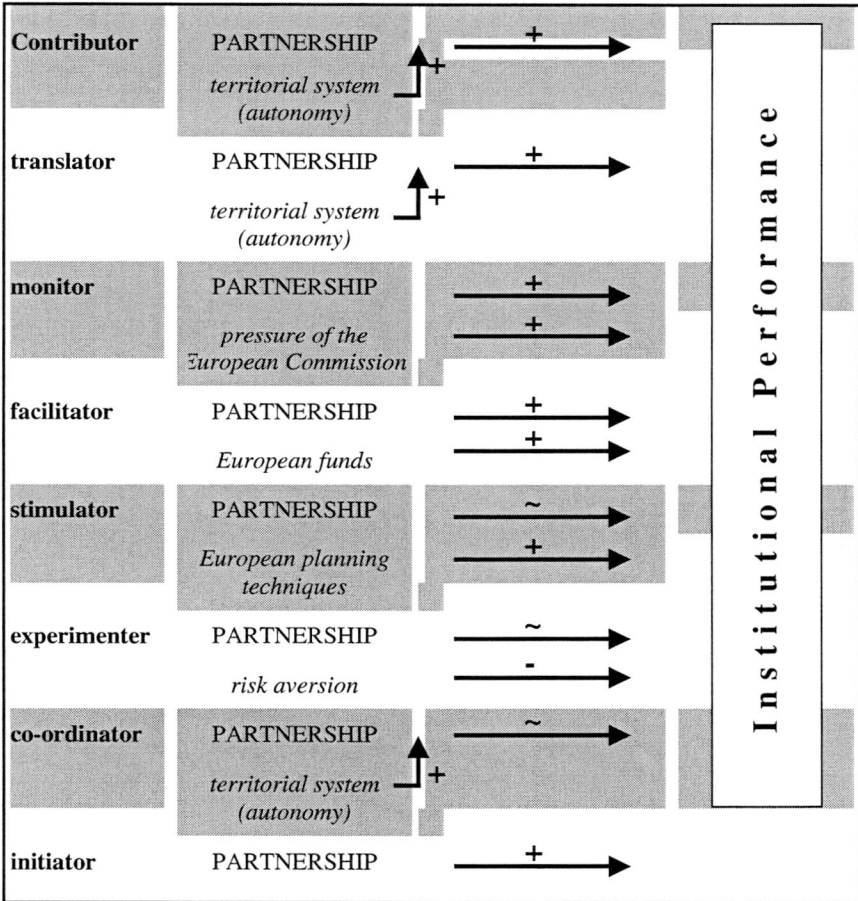

Note: +/- means that there is a positive/negative relation between the independent and dependent variable. ~ indicates there is no relation between variables.

Source: own figure.

# 11 CONCLUSIONS AND OUTLOOK

The principal aim of this work has been to analyse the impact of the two main features of the 1988 European regional policy reform: the increased European structural transfers and the partnership principle. For the former, I was specifically interested in determining the impact of structural funds on the convergence process of GDP *per capita* growth and unemployment rates. For the latter, I analysed the partnership principle, which involves close collaboration between the Commission and all the relevant authorities at national, regional or local levels in regional policy. With respect to the partnership principle, I questioned how the partnership principle enhanced institutional performance. The concept of institutional performance was defined as the capacity to respond to the demands of the public and private environments. I answered the research questions using quantitative and qualitative methods. Firstly, I used a macro-quantitative approach, applying a multiple regression technique on data of forty southern European regions, including seven Greek, seven Portuguese, eighteen Spanish and eight Italian regions. Secondly, two case studies on the Spanish region of Andalusia and the Algarve in Portugal helped to understand how the European regional policy reform induced institutional performance.

What can be said with respect to the impact of European structural transfers? Firstly, my results showed that agglomeration effects were an important (divergence) factor in explaining the cohesion of southern European regions. Secondly, I found evidence for the "natural" convergence process since the initial regional income lag reacted according to the prediction of the neo-classical convergence theory. The results on urbanisation effects and natural neo-classical convergence effects confirm previous empirical research on regional economic development. Thirdly, we can conclude that European financial transfers resulted in having a positive effect on cohesion. Multiple regression of European transfers on GDP growth and unemployment rates revealed significant positive parameters. This finding closes a gap in the research on the impact of European regional transfers. Before I go on to discuss these results, I would like to voice a word of caution. Some regression analyses display rather low values of the coefficient of determination ($R^2$). But the above-mentioned variables are significant. There are two explanations for the low coefficient of determination. On the one hand, the scarcity of data - both for various macro-economic indicators and over a long period of time - represents a serious handicap for explaining regional economic processes. There exist, on the other hand, additional variables for the explanation of regional economic processes, especially the national economic "climate", which has been found to influence regional development (Easterly *et al.* 1993; Levine and Renelt 1992).

What does the insight into the impact of structural transfers mean for the future of European funds? Opponents of public intervention in economic development usually criticise the fact that structural transfers have often been overestimated as a means of resolving regional problems and that European transfers constitute solely a side-payment to the less developed regions within the EU for not blocking deeper economic integration. My results allow us to reject this hypothesis. Critics have to acknowledge the fact that structural transfers indeed have a positive cohesion effect (which does not rule out the fact that they have been used as an instrument of convincing the less competitive member states of deeper European integration). Thus, the claim of abolishing European regional policy does not seem to be justified. From a point of view of fairness, it is likewise obsolete to think about halting structural transfers since they constitute an important element of European solidarity. On the contrary, the advocates of European regional policy, who take the moderate pace of the "natural" (neo-classical) convergence process as an argument for the increase in structural transfers, should be aware that the financial constraints of the European Union prevent an infinite extension of European regional policy. They should, furthermore, try to distinguish between the effects of European regional policy, for example, the consumption effects and investments supporting the development of endogenous growth potential. This kind of analysis is not yet possible with the data currently available. It will be possible, however, with the improvement of the regional statistical database.

For neither the extension, nor the abolishment of European regional policy, are potential options from a pragmatic and scientific point of view, the EU should focus on improving the disbursement of European funds. Opponents of structural transfers usually point to the lack of efficiency and efficacy of European regional transfers - two issues, which lead us to analyse the role of the institutions involved in economic development and structural policies. For institutions form rules and standard operating procedures that leave their imprint on political outcome, for example economic development, by structuring political behaviour. With respect to the question of the impact of the partnership principle on institutional performance, the empirical findings confirm the theoretical predictions of *new institutionalism*. We found a positive relationship between the degree of partnership and institutional performance for the majority of the eight roles that regional institutions have to carry out in economic development.[95] This statement is true, without reservation, for the roles of monitor, initiator and facilitator. Evaluations of public policies and transregional co-operation have become common in both regions. The function of involving the private sector in European regional policy exemplifies the advantages of the partnership principle over

---

[95]    In terms of the roles of stimulator, experimenter and co-ordinator the study refutes the hypothesis that there is a positive or any relation between the partnership principle and institutional performance.

a unilateral approach. Regional government and institutions have played a significant role in the formation of networks and in achieving a closer interaction between public and private actors. Where there was a lack of active regional private actors (as in the case of Algarve), the initial development strategy of Portuguese authorities was based on the involvement of private actors at the national level only. This approach, irrespective of its efficacy and efficiency, was not successful and inhibited rather than facilitated the bottom-up learning and adaptation process.

The analysis of the contributor and translator roles also revealed a positive relationship between the partnership principle and institutional performance. The degree of partnership, however, depended on the structure of the territorial system. This was exemplified by the case of the autonomous region of Andalusia. The partnership principle was applied to policy fields where the region had competencies. Institutional performance was, consequently, higher than in the case of structural policies under national competency. The region of Algarve - operating in a centralist territorial structure and having an administrative status - was largely excluded from the European regional policy process. It is true that national politicians were obliged to open the door for regional demands in Portugal. For the partnership principle forced Lisbon to share responsibility in the policy formulation with subnational actors. Partnership led, thus, to a widening of the number of regional actors involved in the policy formulation process. But whatever the participation of regional actors in the policy process, the power of the regional level to influence policy outcomes was strongly limited because there exists no true autonomy in Algarve. The application of the partnership principle appeared more as a semblance of democratic planning - a legitimisation of the whole exercise - rather than a genuine "synergy" among central, regional and European actors. The fact that regional authorities have found a partner in the European Commission in their attempt at securing a place in policy-making bodies and processes of European regional policy did not guarantee a strengthening of regional actors. These results fit the findings of research on multi-level governance that European regional policy is a system of continuous negotiation among governments at several territorial tiers. My work, however, questions the optimistic point of view of the multi-level governance school that the process of institutional creation and decisional reallocation among different levels of government in the EU inevitably leads to the strengthening of subnational actors (Marks: 1996a; 1996b).

Does the finding that the territorial system strongly defines regional institutional power generally question the usefulness of the partnership principle as a means of enhancing institutional performance? The answer to this question must be a "no" because the territorial system, firstly, does not affect all regional development roles identified by the analytical framework. It is, secondly, from a methodological point of view not possible to generalise the findings to other regions in the European Union. Only a broader research programme including a number of various case studies would allow a valid generalisation of my findings. Such research should ask for factors allowing regional actors to give more weight to the regional point of view, and what strategies they use in preventing and counterbalancing the centralisation of regional competencies. Despite this comment, one should bear in mind the strength of the qualitative method applied in this work, which helped to better understand both the impact of the partnership principle and the role that regions play in regional economic development.

Combining the findings of this study on structural transfers and institutions, we can draw the following conclusions on European regional policy. Structural funds support the European Union's effort to lower the welfare differences between the poor and rich regions. They should therefore be continued. An increase in transfers is not likely both in view of the budget constraints and the Eastern enlargement of the European Union. Thus, the convergence process among European regions should be promoted by improving the current system. The present multi-stage, multi-fund, multi-level procedures provide potential for a more efficient European regional policy. The cumbersome, transparency-lacking and bureaucratic processes should be streamlined, and European regional policy should be better co-ordinated with other European policies, namely the Common Agricultural Policy and state aids subsidies.

Concentration of regional assistance is another issue. In the planning period 2000-2006 nearly fifty per cent of the EU population lives in eligible areas despite the initial yardstick of 35 per cent listed in the *Agenda 2000*. Nevertheless, while regional support should be more concentrated on the poorest European regions, it should also be kept in mind that an overemphasis on "balanced" spatial development within these areas is likely to reduce efficiency. In economic terms, it can be more meaningful to allocate European regional support to the most productive regions of member states. This policy option could both maximise national growth and the income surplus available for national redistribution mechanisms to less developed regions - which is good for national *and* European cohesion. To go further in this analysis, and to have a solid basis for a choice between these two strategies, it would be necessary to build a dynamic model explaining what the best strategy is, and in which countries should funds be redistributed between regions (according to inter-regional differences in marginal productivity and the marginal propensity of the budget). A first step towards such an analysis has recently been undertaken by the European Commission (1998a).

My work reveals that regional institutions concerned with structural policies offer another possibility of making European regional policy more successful, because SMEs and micro-enterprises depend on well functioning institutions at the regional level. The partnership principle proved to be an efficient way of enhancing institutional performance, leading to coherent strategies for endogenous regional development and accurate implementation of structural interventions. This is especially the case when regional government and institutions do have autonomous power in structural policy. The European Commission should, thus, improve the co-operation between national and regional authorities whenever European funds co-finance structural investments through the reinforcement of the partnership principle. It is further recommended to increase the resources available for regional CSFs/OPs (at the expense of the pluri-regional/sectoral CSFs/OPs). Surprisingly and contradicting to the 1988 reform, the *Agenda 2000* and the regulations for the Community Support Framework 2000-2006 work contrary to these recommendations. They foresee the strengthening of the national level in European regional policy, which *de facto* amounts to a renationalisation of the governance of structural funds. The reason for this development is that the European Commission's own bureaucracy is not prepared for the involvement of regions in the policy-making. In short, the transaction costs to the Commission involved in participating in increasingly pluralist partnerships are simply too high. As the number of actors in the cohesion policy field proliferates, it is increasingly difficult for the Commission to identify the key partners which it can trust. The implications of this step are not yet clear but it is suggested that the increased application of the partnership principle becomes less likely.

# 12 REFERENCES

## 12.1 Andalusia Documents

Arenal Grupo Consultor (1998), Informe de Evaluación Intermedia: Subvención Global de Andalucía, 1994-1999. Sevilla: JdA. (Evaluation Study (ongoing) of the Global Interventions 1994-1999).

CEA (Confederación de Empresarios de Andalucía) (w.y.a), CEA, un Compromiso con Andalucía. Sevilla: CEA. (Information Brochure about the Andalusian Confederation of Entreprises).

CEA (Confederación de Empresarios de Andalucía) (w.y.b), CEA: Departamento de Relaciones Internacionales. Sevilla: CEA. (Information Brochure about the International Department of the Andalusian Confederation of Entreprises).

Comisión Europea (1990), España: Marco Comunitario de Apoyo 1989-1993. Luxemburgo: Oficina de Publicaciones Oficiales de las Comunidades Europeas. (Community Support Framework 1989-1993).

Comisión Europea (1996), España: Marco Comunitario de Apoyo 1994-1999. Luxemburgo: Oficina de Publicaciones Oficiales de las Comunidades Europeas. (Community Support Framework 1994-1999).

ESECA (Sociedad de Estudios Económicos de Andalucía) (1990a-1998a), Informe Económico Financiero de Andalucía 1990 (-1998). Málaga: Eseca-Unicaja. (Financial Information about Andalusia 1990 (-1998).

ESECA (Sociedad de Estudios Económicos de Andalucía) (1992b), Atlas Económico de Andalucía 1992. Málaga: Eseca-Unicaja. (Economic Atlas of Andalusia).

Fundación BBV (1998), Renta Nacional de España y su Distribución Provincial. Serie Homogénea Años 1955 a 1993 y Avances 1994-1998, Tomo 1. Bilbao: Fundación BBV. (National Income and Provincial Distribution).

Idom (1998), Informe de la Primero Fase de Evaluación Intermededia del Programa Operative (FSE) 1994-99 de Andalucía. Sevilla: JdA, CTI. (First Evaluation Study (ongoing) of the ESF Activities 1994-1999).

Idom (1999), Informe de la Segunda Fase de Evaluación Intermededia del Programa Operative (FSE) 1994-99 de Andalucía. Sevilla: JdA, CTI. (Second Evaluation Study (ongoing) of the ESF Activities 1994-1999).

IDR (Instituto de Desarrollo Regional) (1996), Informe Preparación del Programa Operativo Andalucía 1994-1999: Avance del Análisis de Evaluabilidad. Sevilla: IDR. (Study on the Evaluability of the OP Andalusia 1994-1999).

IDR (Instituto de Desarrollo Regional) (1997a), Evaluación Intermedia: Programa Operativo Doñana, 2da Fase, 1994-1999. Sevilla: IDR. (Evaluation Study (ongoing) of the Operational Programme for Doñana (an environmentally protected area in Andalusia), 2nd phase, 1994-1999).

IDR (Instituto de Desarrollo Regional) (1997b), Capacidad de Gestión de la Administración en Relación al Seguimiento y la Evaluación de las Acciones de los P.O.s: Andaluciía y Doñana II Fase. Sevilla: IDR. (Meta-Evaluation Study on the Evaluations in the JdA).

IDR (Instituto de Desarrollo Regional) (1998), Evaluación Intermedia: Programa Operativo de Andalucía, 1994-1999. Sevilla: IDR. (Evaluation Study (ongoing) of the Operational Programme 1994-1999).

IEA (Instituto de Estadística de Andalucía) (1988b-1998b), Anuario Estadístico de Andalucía 1988 (-1998). Sevilla: IEA. (Statistical Yearbook of Andalusia 1988 (-1998)).

IEA (Instituto de Estadística de Andalucía) (1990a-1998a), Indicadores Economicos de Andalucía 1990 (-1998). Sevilla: IEA. (Economic Indicators of Andalusia 1990 (-1998)).

IEA (Instituto de Estadística de Andalucía) (1994c), Contabilidad Regional y Tablas Input - Output de Andalucía 1990: Análisis de Resultados. Vol. 1 & 2. Sevilla: IEA. (Regional Accounting and Input-Output Tables 1990: Analysis of Results).

IEA (Instituto de Estadística de Andalucía) (1995c-1999c), Andalusia: Basic Data 1995 (-1999). Sevilla: IEA.

IEA (Instituto de Estadística de Andalucía) (1995d), Contabilidad Regional y Tablas Input - Output de Andalucía 1990: Presentación de Resultados. Sevilla: IEA. (Regional Accounting and Input-Output Tables 1990: Presentation of Results).

IFA (Instituto de Fomento de Andalucía) (1998a), Selección de algunos proyectos de interés de la subvencion global de Andalucía. Sevilla: IFA. (Selection of Interesting Projects Financed by the Global Grant).

IFA (Instituto de Fomento de Andalucía) (1998b), Manual de Calidad del IFA. Sevilla: IFA. (Manual of the Quality Management of IFA (Institute for Promotion).

IFA (Instituto de Fomento de Andalucía) (1998c), Memoria 1997. Sevilla: IFA. (Annual Report 1997).

IFA (Instituto de Fomento de Andalucía) (1999), 99Andalucí@ 10.000 Empresas: Directorio e Informe Económico Financiero. Sevilla: IFA. (Yellow Pages of Andalusian Enterprises including Financial Information).

IFA (Instituto de Fomento de Andalucía) (w.y.), Programas Comunitarias en los que participa el IFA. Sevilla: IFA. (List of EU Programmes in which IFA (Institute for Promotion) participates).

JdA (1990-1999), Boletín Oficial de la Junta de Andalucía. Andalucía: Junta. Sevilla: JdA. (Official Bulletin of the JdA).

JdA (1999b), Organigramma de la Junta de Andalucía. Available at (10.9.1999) http://www.junta-andalucia.es/guiafys/org_pres.htm. (Organisational Structure of the Junta of Andalusia).

JdA, CEH (1984), Plan Económico para Andalucía 1984-1986. Sevilla: JdA. (Economic Plan for Andalusia 1984-1986).

JdA, CEH (1987), Programa Andaluz de Desarollo Económico 1987-1990. Sevilla: JdA. (Economic Programme for the Economic Development of Andalusia 1987-1990).

JdA, CEH (1989a), Plan Andaluz de Desarrollo Económico 1989-1994. Sevilla: JdA. (Regional Development Plan 1989-1993).

JdA, CEH (1989b), Programa Nacional de Interés Comunitario del Almería-Levante 1989-1992. Sevilla: JdA. (Operational Programme of Sub-CSF for Almería-Levante1989-1992).

JdA, CEH (1990a-1996a), Memoria de Actividades 1989 (-1995). Sevilla: JdA. (Annual Report of the Consejeria de Economía y Hacienda, 1989 (-1995)).

JdA, CEH (1991b), Programa Andaluz de Desarollo Económico 1991-1994. Sevilla: JdA. (Programme for the Economic Development of Andalusia 1991-1994).

JdA, CEH (1992b-1998b), Informe Económico de Andalucía 1992 (-1998). Sevilla: JdA. (Information on the Economic Situation in Andalusia 1992 (-1998)).

JdA, CEH (1992c), Programa Operativo de la Comarca del Sur y Este de Jaen y Norte de Granada, 1991-1993. Sevilla: JdA. (Operational Programme of Sub-CSF for Sur y Este de Jaen y Norte de Granada, 1991-1993).

JdA, CEH (1992d), Programa Operativo de Malaga, 1990-1993. Sevilla: JdA. (Operational Programme of Sub-CSF for Malaga, 1990-1993).

JdA, CEH (1993c), Programa Operativo de la Comarca del Bajo Guadalquivir, 1991-1993. Sevilla: JdA. (Operational Programme of Sub-CSF for Bajo Guadalquivir, 1991-1993).

JdA, CEH (1993d), Programa Operativo de la Comarca del Norte de Huelva, 1989-1993. Sevilla: JdA. (Operational Programme of Sub-CSF for Norte de Huelva, 1989-1993).

JdA, CEH (1994c), Plan Andaluz de Desarrollo Económico 1994-1999. Sevilla: JdA. (Regional Development Plan 1994-1999).

JdA, CEH (1994d), Andalucía: Programa Operativo (1° Fase), (Objetivo no. 1) 1994-1999. Sevilla: JdA. (Operational Programme for Andalusia, 1st phase, 1994-1999).

JdA, CEH (1994e), Andalucía: Marco Comunitario de Apoyo, 1989-1993. Sevilla: JdA. (Community Support Framework in Andalusia, 1989-1993).

JdA, CEH (1996c), Andalucía: Programa Operativo, 2da Fase (Objetivo no. 1) 1994-1999. Sevilla: JdA. Sevilla: JdA. (Operational Programme for Doñana (an environmentally protected area in Andalusia), 2nd phase, 1994-1999).

JdA, CEH (1996d), Andalucía: Programa Operativo de Doñana, 2da Fase (Objetivo no. 1) 1994-1999. Sevilla: JdA. Sevilla: JdA. (Operational Programme for Doñana (an environmentally protected area in Andalusia), 2nd phase, 1994-1999).

JdA, CEH (1996e), Andalucía: Subvención Global (Objetivo no. 1) 1994-1999. Sevilla: JdA. (Operational Programme for Global Interventions in Andalusia, 1994-1999 (managed by the IFA - Instituto de Fomenta de Andalucía)).

JdA, CEH (1997a), Economic Report on Andalusia 1996. Sevilla: JdA.

JdA, CEH (1999a), Plan de Desarrollo Económico de Andalucía, 2000-2006. Sevilla: JdA. (Regional Development Plan 2000-2006).

JdA, CEH (1999b), Plan Económico Andalucía Horizonte 2000. Sevilla: JdA. (Economic Plan for Andalusia: Horizon 2000).

JdA, CP (1999), Pactos por el Empleo: El Modelo Andaluz. Sevilla: JdA. (Employment Pact: The Andalusian Model).

JdA, CTAS (1991a), Andalucía: Programa Operativo de Valorizacion de los Recursos Humanos (FSE), 1989-1993. Sevilla: JdA. (Operational Programme for Human Resources Investments (FSE), 1989-1993).

JdA, CTAS (1991b), Andalucía: Programa Operativo de Fomento de Empleo (FSE), 1989-1993. Sevilla: JdA. (Operational Programme for Employment (FSE), 1989-1993).

JdA, CTAS (1994a), Evaluación Final del Programa Operative (FSE) 1989-93 de Andalucía. Sevilla: JdA. (Evaluation Study (ex post) of the Operational Programme (ESF), 1989-1994).

JdA, CTAS (1994b), Andalucía: Programa Operativo de Valorizacion de los Recursos Humanos (FSE), 1994-1999. Sevilla: JdA. (Operational Programme for Human Resources Investments (FSE), 1994-1999).

JdA, CTI (1994), Programa Industrial para Andalucía 1994-1997. Sevilla: JdA. (Programme for Industrial Planning 1994-1997).

JdA, CTI (1999), Programa Industrial para Andalucía 1998-2001. Sevilla: JdA. (Programme for Industrial Planning 1998-2001).

MEH, DGAPP, Secretaría de Estado de Presupuestos y Gastos (1993-1998), La Planification Regional y sus Instrumentos, Informe Anual. Madrid: MEH. (Annual Regional Plannification Documentation).

Ministerio de la Presidencia, Secretaría de Estado de la Comunicación (1999). Agenda de la Comunicación 1999. Madrid: Ministerio de la Presidencia. (Agenda and Guidebook of Spain).

Sevilla Siglo XXI (Diputacion de Sevilla) (w.y), Plan Director para el Fomento de la Cultura Emprendedora. Sevilla: Sevilla Siglo XXI. (Director Plan for the Promotion of the Enterprising Culture).

Universidad de Sevilla (1999), Las Regiones Españolas en Europa. Libro de Resumen de la XXV Reunión de Estudios Regionales. Sevilla: Asociación Española de Ciencia Regional y Asociación Andaluza de Ciencia Regional.

## 12.2   Algarve Documents

AMAL (Associação de Municípios do Algarve) (1999a), Análise ao Programa Operacional do Algarve (PROA) 1994-1999. Faro: Associação de Municípios do Algarve. (Analysis of the OP Algarve 1994-1999).

AMAL (Associação de Municípios do Algarve) (1999b), PEDRA: Plano Estratégico de Desenvolvimento da Região do Algarve. Faro: Associação de Municípios do Algarve. (Strategic Plan of the Regional Development Algarve).

AMAL (Associação de Municípios do Algarve) (1999c), Análise ao Quadro Global da Programação Financeira do PDR 2000-2006. Working Document. (Financial Analysis of the Provisional CSF 2000-2006).

Banco de Fomento e Exterior (1995), Sistema de Incentivos Regionais (SIR). Lisbon: Banco de Fomento e Exterior. (System of Regional Incentivos).

CCFSE (1998), The European Social Fund in Portugal. Lisbon: CCFSE.

CCR Algarve (1985), Programa de Desenvolvimento Regional Algarve 1986-1990. Faro: CCR Algarve. (Regional Development Plan 1986-1990).

CCR Algarve (1989), Contributo para o Plano Nacional de Desenvolvimento Económico e Social 1989-1993. Faro: CCR Algarve. (Regional Development Plan Algarve 1989-1993).

CCR Algarve (1990a), Programa Operacional Plurifundos do Sotavento Algarvio 1989-1993. Faro: CCR Algarve. (Operational Programme Algarve (Sotavento) 1989-1993).

CCR Algarve (1990b), Programa Operacional Plurifundos do Barlavento Algarvio 1989-1993. Faro: CCR Algarve. (Operational Programme Algarve (Barlavento) 1989-1993).

CCR Algarve (1993), Enquadramento Estratégico para a Região do Algarve 1994-1999. Faro: CCR Algarve. (Regional Development Plan Algarve 1994-1999).

CCR Algarve (1994), Programa Operacional do Algarve 1994-1999. Faro: CCR Algarve. (Operational Programme Algarve 1994-1999).

CCR Algarve (1995a-1999a), Programa Operacional do Algarve: Relatório de Execução 1994 (-1998). Faro: CCR Algarve. (Annual Report of OP Algarve Activities 1994 (-1998)).

CCR Algarve (1997b), Algarve: Challenge for the Future. Faro: CCR Algarve.

CCR Algarve (1999b), Diagnóstico da Região do Algarve: Contributo para o Plano Nacional de Desenvolvimento Económico e Social. Faro: CCR Algarve. (Regional Development Plan 2000-2006: Analysis of the Region of Algarve).

CCR Algarve (1999c), Período de Programação 2000-2006: Intervenção Operacional do Algarve. Faro: CCR Algarve. (Regional Development Plan 2000-2006).

CCR Algarve (w.y.), Information Leaflet. Faro: CCR Algarve.

CEAL (1995), Plano de Desenvolvimento Económico Algarve. Faro: CEAL.

CEDRU (Centro de Estudos e Desenvolvimento Regional e Urbano) (1994). Estudo de Avaliação Ex-Post do QCA I: Área do Desenvolvimento Regional. Lisbon: CEDRU (Evaluation Study (ex-post) of the CSF 1989-1993).

CEDRU (Centro de Estudos e Desenvolvimento Regional e Urbano) (1997). Estudo de Avaliação Intercalar do Programa Operacional do Algarve. Lisbon: CEDRU (Evaluation Study (ongoing) of the Operational Programme Algarve 1994-1999).

CEPI (Centro de Estudos de Problemas de Informação) (1996), The Contribution of the Community Structural Policies to the Economic and Social Cohesion of the European

Union: The Case of Portugal. Lisbon: CEPI (Evaluation Study of the Structural Policies in Portugal [1989-1993 (ex post); 1994-1999 (ex ante)]).

CIDEC (Centro Interdisciplinar de Estudos Económicos) (1999), Estudo Relativo às Sínteses das Avaliações Intercalares Efectuadas aos Programas e Intervenções Operacionalis que Intergram o QCM 1994-1999. Lisbon: CIDEC (Meta Evaluation Study of all OPs in Portugal 1994-1999).

Delegão Regional do Algarve do IEFP (1998a), Brève Charactérisation de la Région Algarve. Faro: IEFP. (Short Portrait of the Region of Algarve).

Delegão Regional do Algarve do IEFP (1998b), Relatório de Actividades 1998. Faro: IEFP. (Annual Report of the Institute of Employment and Vocational Training 1998).

Delegão Regional do Algarve do IEFP (1999), Plano de Actividades e Orçamento para 1999. Faro: IEFP. (Action Plan of the Institute of Employment and Vocational Training 1999).

DGDR (1994), Plano de Desenvolvimento Regional 1994-1999: Avaliaçao do Impacte Esperado das Intervenções Operacionais. Lisbon: DGDR. (Portuguese Regional Development Plan 1994-1999).

DGDR (1998a), Information Leaflet. Lisbon: DGDR.

DGDR (1998b), The Cohesion Fund in Portugal. Lisbon: DGDR.

DGDR (w.y.a), Community Support Framework 1994-99. Lisbon: DGDR. (Internal Working Paper).

DGDR (w.y.b), Information on the Portuguese Community Support Framework. Lisbon: DGDR. (Internal Working Paper).

INE (Instituto Nacional de Estatística) (1993a-1999a), Anuário Estatístico: Região Algarve 1992 - (1998). Faro: INE. (Statistical Yearbook of Algarve 1992 - (1998)).

INE (Instituto Nacional de Estatística) (1993b-1999b), Anuário Estatístico de Portugal 1992 - (1998). Lisboa: INE. (Statistical Yearbook of Portugal 1992 - (1998)).

INE (Instituto Nacional de Estatística) (1998c), Os Municípios do Algarve. Faro: INE. (The Municipalities of Algarve: A Statistical Portrait).

INE (Instituto Nacional de Estatística) (1998d), Números do Algarve 1997. (Statistical Data about Algarve).

MEPAT, SEDR (1989), Quadro Comunitário de Apoio do PDR 1989-1993. Lisbon: MEPAT. (Portuguese CSF 1989-1993).

MEPAT, SEDR (1993a), Preparar Portugal Para o Séc. XXI: Plano de Desenvolvimento Regional. Lisbon: MEPAT. (Portuguese Regional Development Plan 1994-1999).

MEPAT, SEDR (1993b), Preparar Portugal Para o Séc. XXI: Opções Estratégicas. Lisbon: MEPAT. (Portuguese Regional Development Plan 1994-1999: Strategic Options).

MEPAT, SEDR (1993c), Análise Económica e Social. Lisbon: MEPAT. (Portuguese Regional Development Plan 1994-1999: Socio-Economic Analysis).

MEPAT, SEDR (1994), Quadro Comunitário de Apoio do PDR 1994-1999. Lisbon: MEPAT. (Portuguese CSF 1994-1999).

MEPAT, SEDR (1995), Fundos Estruturais em Portugal: 10 Anos. Lisbon: MEPAT. (10 Years of Structural Funds in Portugal).

MEPAT, SEDR (1996), Avaliação Ex-Post do Quadro Comunitário de Apoio 1989-1993: Relatório de Síntese. Lisbon: MEPAT. (Evaluation (ex post) of CSF 1989-1993).

MEPAT, SEDR (1999a), Portugal Plano Nacional de Desenvolvimento Económico e Social: Diagnóstico e Prostpectivo. Lisbon: MEPAT. (Portuguese Regional Develoment Plan: Analysis and Perspectives).

MEPAT, SEDR (1999b), Portugal Plano Nacional de Desenvolvimento Económico e Social: Uma Visão Estratégica para Vencer o Séc XXI. Lisbon: MEPAT. (Portuguese National Plan for Economic and Social Development: Vision for the 21st Century).

MEPAT, SEDR (1999c), Quadro Comunitário de Apoio, 1994-1999: Balanço Final. Draft Version. Lisbon: MEPAT. (Evaluation Study (ex post) for the CSF 1994-1999).

MEPAT, SEDR (1999d), Portugal Plano de Desenvolvimento Regional. Lisbon: MEPAT. (Portuguese Regional Development Plan).

Ministério Para a Qualificação e o Emprego, IEFP (1999), Relatório Final do Estudo de Avaliação dos Programas Ocupacionais: Síntese. Faro: IEFP. (Evaluation (ex post) of Occupational Programmes of the Institute of Employment and Vocational Training).

MQE, IEFP (1996), La Formation Professionnelle au Portugal. Lisbon: Ministério Para a Qualififcação e o Emprego.

Secretariado para a Modernização Administrativa (1999), Roteiro da Administracção Pública 1999. Lisbon: Secretariado para a Modernização Administrativa. (Guidebook of the Public Administration).

## 12.3 Literature

Alshuth, Stefan (1993), Die internationale Wettbewerbsfähigkeit Spaniens: Die spanische Volkswirtschaft vor der Europäischen Wirtschafts- und Währungsunion. Diss. Frankurt: Peter Lang.

Amtsblatt der Europäischen Gemeinschaften (1987), Einheitliche Europäische Akte. L 169.

Amtsblatt der Europäischen Gemeinschaften (1992), Vertrag über die Europäische Union. C 191.

Armstrong, Harvey (1995a), Convergence Among Regions of the European Union. In: Papers in Regional Science 74/2, 143-152.

Armstrong, Harvey (1995b), An Appraisal of the Evidence from Cross-Sectional Analysis of the Regional Growth Process Within the European Union 1950-1990. In: Armstrong, Harvey and Vickermann, Roger (Eds.), Convergence and Divergence Among European Regions. London: Pion, 40-65.

Armstrong, Harvey and Kervenoael, Ronan (1997), Regional Economic Change in the European Union. In: Bachtler, John and Turok, Ivan (Eds.), The Coherence of EU Regional Policy: Contrasting Perspectives on the Structural Funds. Regional Policy and Development Series 17. London: Jessica Kingsley, 29-47.

Artobolevsky, Sergey (1997), Regional Policy in Europe. Regional Policy and Development Series 11. London: Jessica Kingsley.

Aschinger, Gerhard (1996), Ist die Europäische Währungsunion realisierbar? In: Zohlnhöfer, Werner (Ed.), Europa auf dem Wege zur Politischen Union? Berlin: Dunker & Humblot, 49-74.

Aume and Niesr (1992), Maastricht und was dann? Perspektiven der Europäischen Wirtschafts- und Währungunion. Übersetzung aus dem Englischen. Landsberg/Lech: Moderne Industrie.

Bachtler, John and Turok, Ivan (1997), Conclusions. In: Bachtler, John and Turok, Ivan (Eds.), The Coherence of EU Regional Policy: Contrasting Perspectives on the Structural Funds. Regional Policy and Development Series 17. London: Jessica Kingsley, 346-372.

Baltensperger, Ernst and Jordan, Erich (1996), Fiskalpolitische Konsequenzen einer Währungsunion. In: NZZ 22, 89.

Barro, Robert and Sala-i-Martin, Xavier (1991), Convergence Across States and Regions. In: Brookings Paper on Economic Activity 1, 107-182.

Barro, Robert and Sala-i-Martin, Xavier (1992), Convergence. In: Journal of Political Economy 100, 223-251.

Barro, Robert and Sala-i-Martin, Xavier (1995), Economic Growth. New York/London/ Tokyo: McGraw-Hill.

Becattini, G. (1994), The Development of Light Industry in Tuscany. In: Leonardi, Robert and Nanetti, Raffaella (Eds.), Regional Development in a Modern European Economy: The Case of Tuscany. London: Pinter, 238-255.

Beck, Nathaniel and Katz, Jonathan (1995), What to Do (and Not to Do) with Time-Series Cross-Section Data. In: American Political Science Review 89/3, 634-647.

Becker, Wolf-Dieter (1995), Eine Währungsunion ist mehr als ein System fixer Wechselkurse. In: NZZ 121, 89.

Begg, Iain and Mayes, David (1993), Cohesion, Convergence and Economic and Monetary Union in Europe. In: Regional Studies 27/2, 149-157.

Bellers, Jürgen and Häckel, Erwin (1990), Theorien internationaler Integration und internationaler Organisationen. In: Politische Vierteljahresschrift, Sonderheft 21/1990, 286-303.

Bellini, Nolli (1990), The Management of the Economy in Emilia-Romagna: The PCI and the Regional Experience. In: Leonardi, Robert and Nanetti, Raffaela (Eds.), The Regions and European Integration: The Case of Emilia-Romagna. London/New York: Pinter, 109-124.

Berry, William and Feldman, Stanley (1985), Multiple Regression in Practice. Quantitative Applications in the Social Sciences 50. London: Sage Publications.

Bianchi, Guliano (1993), The IMPs: A Missed Opportunity? In: Leonardi, Robert (Ed.), The Regions and the European Community. London: Frank Cass, 47-70.

Bieber, Roland (Ed.; 1997), Europarecht: Textausgabe. Baden-Baden: Nomos.

Blomström, Magnus und Kokko, Ari (1997), Regional Integration and Foreign Direct Investment. Working Paper 6019, National Bureau of Economic Research, 1-36.

Böckenförde, Wolfgang (1997), Wenn der europäische Stier vom goldenen Kalb überholt wird. In: Frankfurter Allgemeine 169.

Bohley, Peter (1992), Statistik: Einführendes Lehrbuch für Wirtschafts- und Sozialwissenschaftler. München/Wien: Oldenburg.

Booz, Allen and Hamilton (1989), Effects of the Internal Market on Greece, Ireland, Portugal and Spain. Study for the EC Commission. Luxembourg: Office of Official Publications of the European Communities.

Bornhorst, Fabian (1997), Die Wirtschaft Portugals im Überblick: Grundlagen, Daten, Zusammenhänge, Perspektiven. In: Briesemeister, Dietrich and Schönberger, Axel (Eds.), Portugal heute: Politik, Wirtschaft, Kultur. Frankfurt: Vervuert, 15-93.

Börzel, Tanja (1999), Towards Convergence in Europe? Institutional Adaptation to Europeanization in Germany and Spain. In: Journal of Common Market Studies 37/4, 573-596.

Bretschger, Lucas (1996), Wachstumstheorie. München/Wien: Oldenbourg.

Bretschger, Lucas (1997a), Eine makroökonomische Synthese zur Dynamik der realwirtschaftlichen Integration. Forschungsberichte der Universität des Saarlandes 9706.

Bretschger, Lucas (1997b), Integration und langfristige Wirtschaftsentwicklung. München: Oldenburg.

Briesemeister, Dietrich (1997), Die Bevölkerungsentwicklung in Portugal. In: Briesemeister, Dietrich and Schönberger, Axel (Eds.), Portugal heute: Politik, Wirtschaft, Kultur. Frankfurt: Vervuert, 95-116.

Bröcker, Johannes (1997), Economic Integration and the Space Economy: Lessons from New Theory. In: Peschel, Karin (Ed.), Regional Growth and Regional Policy Within the Framework of European Integration. Heidelberg: Physika, 20-35.

Bullmann, Udo (1994), Die Politik der dritten Ebene: Regionen im Europa der Union. Baden-Baden: Nomos.

Buschmann, Peter (1991), Realökonomische Integration im Lichte der Neuen Politischen Ökonomie. Diss. St. Gallen: Studentendruckerei.

Button, Kenneth and Pentecost, Eric (1995), Testing for Convergence of the EU Regional Economies. In: Economic Inquiry 33/4, 664-671.

Caesar, Rolf (1987), Finanzpolitische Konvergenz in der EG. In: Scharrer, Hans-Eckart (Ed.), Stabilität durch EWS? Koordination und Konvergenz im europäischen Währungssystem. Bonn: Europa Union Verlag, 255-302.

Cheshire, Paul and Carbonaro, Gianni (1997), Testing Models, Describing Reality or Neither? Convergence and Divergence of Regional Growth Rates in Europe During the 1980s. In: Peschel, Karin (Ed.), Regional Growth and Regional Policy Within the Framework of European Integration. Heidelberg: Physika, 36-65.

Commission Européenne (1997), Rapport annuel du fonds de cohésion. Louxembourg: Bureau de Publications Officielles de la Communitée Européenne.

Conzelmann, Thomas (1998), "Europeanisation" of Regional Development Policies Linking the Multi-Level Governance Approach with Theories of Policy Learning and Policy Change. In: European Integration Online Paper 2/4. Available at http://eiop.or.at/eiop/texte/1998-004a.htm.

Corkill, David (1993), The Portuguese Economy since 1974. Edinburgh: University Press.

Cutanda, Antonio and Paricio, Joaquina (1994), Infrastructure and Regional Economic Growth: The Spanish Case. In: Regional Studies 28/1, 69-77.

Dammeyer, Manfred (1997), Das Europa der Regionen. In: Europa Archiv (Internationale Politik) 52/11, 57-60.

Dasgupta, Partha (1997), Economic Development and the Idea of Social Capital. Working Paper of the Beijer International Institute of Ecological Economics, Stockholm. March 1997.

De Grauwe, Paul (1996), Monetary Union and Convergence Economic. In: European Economic Review 40, 1091-1101.

De la Fuente, Angel and Vives, Xavier (1995), Infrastructure and Education as Instruments of Regional Policy: Evidence from Spain. In: Economic Policy 20, 13-51.

Della, Porta and Mény, Yves (1997), Democracy and Corruption in Europe. London/Washington: Pinter.

Dessler, David (1991), Beyond Correlation: Toward a Causal Theory of War. In: International Studies Quarterly 35/3, 337-355.

Dieckheuer, Gustav (1995), Internationale Wirtschaftsbeziehungen. München/Wien: Oldenburg.

Dinan, Desmond (1998), Encyclopedia of the European Union: Cohesion Policy. London: Macmillan, 47-51.

Dollar, David and Pritchett, Lant (1998), Assessing Aid: What Works, What Doesn't and Why. Washington: World Bank.

Dunford, Mick (1993), Regional Disparities in the European Community: Evidence from the REGIO Databank. In: Regional Studies 27/8, 727-743.

Dyson, Kenneth (1994), Elusive Union: The Process of Economic and Monetary Union in Europe. London/New York: Longman.

Easterly, William et al. (1993), Good Policy or Good Luck? Country Growth Performance and Temporary Shocks. In: Journal of Monetary Economics 32, 459-483.

Economist Intelligence Unit (1999a), Country Profile: Greece 1999-2000. London: Economist.

Economist Intelligence Unit (1999b), Country Profile: Portugal 1999-2000. London: Economist.

Economist Intelligence Unit (1999c), Country Profile: Spain 1999-2000. London: Economist.

Eichengreen, Barry et al. (1995), The Political Economy of European Integration. Heidelberg: Springer.

Eissel, Dieter (1994), Disparität oder Konvergenz im "Europa der Regionen". In: Bullmann, Udo (Ed.), Die Politik der dritten Ebene: Regionen im Europa der Union. Baden-Baden: Nomos, 45-60.

Europäische Kommission (1989), Leifaden zur Reform der Strukturfonds der Gemeinschaft. Luxemburg: Amt für amtliche Veröffentlichungen der Europäischen Gemeinschaften.

Europäische Kommission (1991), Zweiter Jahresbericht über die Durchführung der Strukturfonds 1990. Luxemburg: Amt für amtliche Veröffentlichungen der Europäischen Gemeinschaften.

Europäische Kommission (1992a), Der ERFE im Jahr 1990. Luxemburg: Amt für amtliche Veröffentlichungen der Europäischen Gemeinschaften.

Europäische Kommission (1992b), Dritter Jahresbericht über die Durchführung der Strukturfonds 1991. Luxemburg: Amt für amtliche Veröffentlichungen der Europäischen Gemeinschaften.

Europäische Kommission (1992c), Von der Einheitlichen Akte zu der Zeit nach Maastricht: Ausreichende Mittel für unsere ehrgeizigen Ziele. Mitteilung der Kommission (KOM (92) 2000). In: Bulletin der EG, Beilage 1.

Europäische Kommission (1994a), Wachstum, Wettbewerb, Beschäftigung: Herausforderungen der Gegenwart und Wege ins 21. Jahrhundert (Weissbuch). Luxemburg: Amt für amtliche Veröffentlichungen der Europäischen Gemeinschaften.

Europäische Kommission (1994b), Wettbewerbsfähigkeit und Kohäsion: Tendenzen in den Regionen. Luxemburg: Amt für amtliche Veröffentlichungen der Europäischen Gemeinschaften.

Europäische Kommission (1995a), Die Durchführung der Strukturfondsreform 1993. Luxemburg: Amt für amtliche Veröffentlichungen der Europäischen Gemeinschaften.

Europäische Kommission (1995b), Wettbewerbsfähigkeit und Kohäsion: Tendenzen in den Regionen. Luxemburg: Amt für amtliche Veröffentlichungen der Europäischen Gemeinschaften.

Europäische Kommission (1996a), Die Strukturfonds in 1994: Sechster Jahresbericht. Luxemburg: Amt für amtliche Veröffentlichungen der Europäischen Gemeinschaften.

Europäische Kommission (1996b), Die Strukurfonds in 1995: Siebter Jahresbericht. Luxemburg: Amt für amtliche Veröffentlichungen der Europäischen Gemeinschaften.

Europäische Kommission (1996c), Strukturfonds und Kohäsionsfond 1994-99: Verordnungen und Erläuterungen. Luxemburg: Amt für amtliche Veröffentlichungen der Europäischen Gemeinschaften.

Europäische Kommission (1997a), Agenda 2000: Eine stärkere und erweiterte Union. Luxemburg: Amt für amtliche Veröffentlichungen der Europäischen Gemeinschaften.

Europäische Kommission (1997b), Europäisches Kohäsionsforum: Reden und Zusammenfassungen (28.-30. April). Luxemburg: Amt für amtliche Veröffentlichungen der Europäischen Gemeinschaften.

Europäisches Parlament (1991), Die regionalen Auswirkungen der Gemeinschaftspolitiken. Reihe Regionalpolitik und Verkehr 17. Luxemburg: Europäisches Parlament.

Europäisches Parlament (1993), Effizienz der Regionalpolitik in der Europäischen Union: Bewertung der direkten und indirekten Auswirkungen der Strukturfonds. Reihe Regionalpolitik W-4/10. Luxemburg: Europäisches Parlament.

European Commission (1976-1989), European Regional Development Fund: Annual Reports. Luxembourg: Office for Official Publications of the European Communities.

European Commission (1989a), Spain: Community Support Framework, 1989-1993. Luxembourg: Office for Official Publications of the European Communities.

European Commission (1989b), Portugal: Community Support Framework, 1989-1993. Luxembourg: Office for Official Publications of the European Communities.

European Commission (1990a), Annual Report on the Implementation of the Reform of the Structural Funds 1989. Luxembourg: Office for Official Publications of the European Communities.

European Commission (1990b), An Empirical Assessment of Factors Shaping Competitiveness in Problem Regions. Luxembourg: Office for Official Publications of the European Communities.

European Commission (1990c), Community Support Framework 1989-93 (Portugal). Luxembourg: Office for Official Publications of the European Communities.

European Commission (1991), The Regions in the 1990s: Fourth Periodic Report on the Social and Economic Situation of the Regions of the Community. Luxembourg: Office for Official Publications of the European Communities.

European Commission (1992), Second Annual Report on the Implementation of the Reform of the Structural Funds 1990. Luxembourg: Office for Official Publications of the European Communities.

European Commission (1993a), Community Structural Funds 1994-1999. Luxembourg: Office for Official Publications of the European Communities.

European Commission (1993b), Annual Report on the Implementation of the Reform of the Structural Funds 1991. Luxembourg: Office for Official Publications of the European Communities.

European Commission (1994a), Guide to the Community Initiatives 1994-1999. Luxembourg: Office for Official Publications of the European Communities.

European Commission (1994b), The Implementation of the Reform of the Structural Funds 1992: Fourth Annual Report. Luxembourg: Office for Official Publications of the European Communities.

European Commission (1994c), Employment in Europe 1994. Luxembourg: Office for Official Publications of the European Communities.

European Commission (1994d), Spain: Community Support Framework 1994-1999. Luxembourg: Office for Official Publications of the European Communities.

European Commission (1995a), Cohesion Financial Instrument: Cohesion Fund. Luxembourg: Office for Official Publications of the European Communities.

European Commission (1995b), The Implementation of the Reform of the Structural Funds 1993: Fifth Annual Report. Luxembourg: Office for Official Publications of the European Communities.

European Commission (1995c), Development Prospect of the Central Mediterranean Regions (Mezzogiorno-Greece). Luxembourg: Office for Official Publications of the European Communities.

European Commission (1995d), Greece: Community Support Framework 1994-99. Luxembourg: Office for Official Publications of the European Communities.

European Commission (1995e), Portugal: Community Support Framework 1994-1999. Luxembourg: Office for Official Publications of the European Communities.

European Commission (1995f), Regional Development Programmes 1994. Luxembourg: Office for Official Publications of the European Communities.

European Commission (1996b), First Report on Economic and Social Cohesion 1996. Luxembourg: Office for Official Publications of the European Communities.

European Commission (1997a), The Structural Funds in 1996: Eighth Annual Report. Luxembourg: Office for Official Publications of the European Communities.

European Commission (1997b), The Impact of Structural Policies On Economic and Social Cohesion in the Union 1989-1999. Luxembourg: Office for Official Publications of the European Communities.

European Commission (1998a), Economic and Social Cohesion in the European Union: The Impact of Member States' Own Policies. Luxembourg: Office for Official Publications of the European Communities.

European Commission (1998b), The Structural Funds in 1997: Ninth Annual Report. Luxembourg: Office for Official Publications of the European Communities.

European Commission (1999a), Presidency Conclusions of Berlin European Council 1999. Luxembourg: Office for Official Publications of the European Communities. (currently available at http://inforegio.cec.eu.int/document/doc/news/berlin_en.doc).

European Commission (1999b), Reform of the Structural Funds 2000-2006: Comparative Analysis. Luxembourg: Office for Official Publications of the European Communities.

European Commission (1999c), The Structural Funds and Their Co-ordination with the Cohesion Fund. Draft Guidance for Programmes in the Period 2000-2006. Working Paper of the Commission.

European Commission (1999d), The Socio-Economic Impact of Projects Financed by the Cohesion Fund: A Modelling Approach (Vol. 1-3). Luxembourg: Office for Official Publications of the European Communities.

European Commission (1999e), The Socio-Economic Impact of Projects Financed by the Cohesion Fund in Spain and Portugal: Simulation Report. Working Paper of DG 16.

European Commission (1999f), Better Management Through Evaluation. Luxembourg: Office for Official Publications of the European Communities.

European Commission (1999g), Evaluating Socio-Economic Programmes. Vol. 1-6. Luxembourg: Office for Official Publications of the European Communities.

European Commission (1999h), The Community Initiatives 2000-2006. Commission Working Document 97/020.

European Commission (1999i), The Structural Funds and Their Co-ordination with the Cohesion Fund. Working Paper of the Commission.

European Commission (1999j), Structural Funds: Presentation Kit (CD-ROM). Luxembourg: DG 16.

European Commission (1999k), Employment in Europe 1999. Luxembourg: Office for Official Publications of the European Communities.

European Parliament (1991), Regional Impact of EC Policies. Regional Policy Series No.17 (September). Luxembourg: European Parliament.

European Parliament (1993), Alternative Indicators of Regional Development and Hidden Economy and the Regions of the European Union. Regional Policy Series 11 (November). Luxembourg: European Parliament.

Eurostat (1996a), Eurostat Jahrbuch 1996: Europa im Blick der Statistik 1985-1995. Luxemburg: Amt für amtliche Veröffentlichungen der Europäischen Gemeinschaften.

Eurostat (1996b), Regionen: Statistisches Jahrbuch. Luxemburg: Amt für amtliche Veröffentlichungen der Europäischen Gemeinschaften.

Eurostat and European Commission (1993), Portrait of the Regions: Portugal, Spain, Italy and Greece. Vol. 3. Brussels/Luxembourg: Office for Official Publications of the European Communities.

Eurostat and European Commission (1998), Portrait of the Regions: Portugal. Brussels/Luxembourg: Office for Official Publications of the European Communities.

Fagerberg, Jan and Verspagen, Bart (1996), Heading for Divergence? Regional Growth in Europe Reconsidered. In: Journal of Common Market Studies 34/3, 432-448.

Featherstone, Kevin and Yannopoulos, George (1995), The European Community and Greece: Integration and the Challenge to Centralism. In: Barry, Jones and Keating, Michael (Eds.), Regions in the European Community. Oxford: Clarendon, 232-248.

Feld, Lars and Savioz, Marcel (1996), Direct Democracy Matters for Economic Performance: An Empirical Investigation. Discussion Paper of the SIASR, University of St.Gallen.

Fischer, Tobias (1996), Aufteilung Portugals in administrative Regionen: Bindeglied zwischen Lissabon und den Gemeinden. In: NZZ 103, 5.

Fischer, Tobias (1997), Feinschliffe an der portugiesischen Verfassung: die vierte Revision vom Parlament gebilligt. In: NZZ, 205, 5.

Fischer, Tobias (1998), Demagogie gegen die Gebietsreform in Portugal: Die Opposition erwartet einen Sieg beim Referendum. In: NZZ 259, 5.

Frankfurter Allgemeine Zeitung (1995), In Spanien und Portugal greift der Subventionsbetrug um sich. 12. Dezember, 16.

Franz, Wolfgang (1997), "Schattenseiten" des Euro: Erhebliche Flexibilitätsanforderungen an die Lohnpolitik. In: NZZ 266, 23.

Frei, Daniel (1983), Integrationsprozesse: Theoretische Erkenntnisse und praktische Folgen. In: Weidenfeld, Werner (Ed.), Die Identität Europas: Positionen und Perspektiven. Bonn: Hanser, 113-131.

Frenkel, Michael (1989), Integrationsprobleme und ökonomische Wirkungen der europäischen Binnenmarktliberalisierung. In: Europa Archiv (Internationale Politik) 44/8, 241-250.

Frey, Bruno (1997), Ein neuer Föderalismus für Europa: Die Idee der FOCJ. Tübingen: Mohr.

Frey, Bruno and Kirchgässner, Gebhard (1994), Demokratische Wirtschaftspolitik. München: Franz Vahlen.

Fuster, Thomas (1997), Die "Good Governance" Diskussion der Jahre 1989 bis 1994: Ein Beitrag zur jüngeren Geschichte der Entwicklungspolitik unter spezieller Berücksichtigung der Welbank und des DAC. Diss. Bern/Wien: Haupt.

Gallagher, Tom (1998), Portugal Reject Regional Devolution as Threat to Nation. In: The Scotsman, November 9th, 7.

Garofoli, Giuseppe (1992), Endogenous Development in Southern Europe. Aldershot: Gower.

Gaspar, Jorge (1993), The Regions of Portugal. Lisbon: DGDR.

Gillis, Malcolm et al. (1992), Economics of Development: Growth and Structural Change. London/New York: Norton, 36-69.

Glen, Carol (1995), Growing Together or Coming Apart? The Causes and Consequences of National and Regional Disparities in the European Union. Diss. Florida: Uuniversity Press.

Grossmann, G. and Helpman, E. (1994), Endogenous Innovation in the Theory of Growth. In: Journal of Economic Perspectives 8/1, 23-44.

Grote, Jürgen (1996), Regionalpolitik. In: Nohlen, Dieter (Ed.), Lexikon der Politik. Vol. 5 (Die Europäische Union). München: Beck, 232-237.

Grote, Jürgen (1998), Regionale Vernetzung: Interorganisatorische Strukturdifferenzen regionaler Politikgestaltung. In: Kohler-Koch, Beate (Ed.), Interaktive Politik in Europa: Regionen im Netzwerk der Integration. Opladen: Leske + Budrich, 62-96.

Guerrero, Daniel (1997), La politica regional de la Union Europea: Una evaluacion del fondo Europeo de desarrollo regional en Andalucia. Cadiz: Servicio de publicaciones univerdidad.

Guerrero, Daniel Coronado and Seró, Manuel Acosta (1996), Spatial Distribution of Patents in Spain: Determing Factors and Consequences on Regional Development. In: Regional Studies 31/4, 381-390.

Hall, Robert and Jones, Charles (1998), Why Do Some Countries Produce So Much More Output Per Worker Than Others? In: NBER Working Paper Series 6564.

Harbrecht, Wolgang and Schmid, Jürgen (1987), Die monetären Konvergenzwirkungen des EWS. In: Scharrer, Hans-Eckart (Ed.), Stabilität durch EWS? Koordination und Konvergenz im europäischen Währungssystem. Bonn: Europa Union Verlag, 213-254.

Harrop, Jeffrey (1992), The Political Economy of Integration in the European Community. London: Edward Elgar.

Harrop, Jeffrey (1996), Structural Funding and Employment in the European Union: Financing the Path to Integration. Brookfield: Edward Elgar.

Held, Gerhard (1994), Konstitutiver Regionalismus – Ein spanisches Modell für das mediterrane Europa? In: Bullmann, Udo (Ed.), Die Politik der dritten Ebene: Regionen im Europa der Union. Baden-Baden: Nomos, 197-213.

Hellmann, Rainer (1987), Folgen von EG-Erweiterung für die Konvergenz. In: Scharrer, Hans-Eckart (Ed.), Stabilität durch EWS? Koordination und Konvergenz im europäischen Währungssystem. Bonn: Europa Union Verlag, 389-426.

Heywood, Paul (1995), The Government and Politics of Spain. New York: St. Martin's Press.

Heywood, Paul (1997), From Dictatorship to Democracy: Changing Forms of Corruption in Spain. In: Della, Porta and Mény, Yves (Eds.), Democracy and Corruption in Europe. London/Washington: Pinter, 65-84.

Hildenbrand, Andreas (1998), Regionalismus und Auntonomiestaat (1977-1997). In: Bernecker, Walther and Dirscherl, Klaus (Eds.), Spanien heute: Politik, Wirtschaft, Kultur. Frankfurt: Vervuert, 101-139.

Hooghe, Liesbet (1996), Building a Europe with the Regions: The Changing Role of the European Commission. In: Hooghe, Liesbet (Ed.), Cohesion Policy and European Integration: Building Multi-Level Governance. Oxford: University Press, 89-126.

Hrbek, Rudolf (1996), Regionen in Europa und die regionale Ebene in der EU: Zur Einführung. In: Fäber, Gisela and Forsyth, Murry (Eds.), The Regions - Factors of Integration or Disintegration in Europe? Baden-Baden: Nomos, 13-22.

Inforegio Newsletter (1998, 1999). Newsletter.en@lists.inforegio.org

Ioakimidis, C. (1996), EU Cohesion Policy in Greece: The Tension Between Bureaucratic Centralism and Regionalism. In: Hooghe, Liesbet (Ed.), Cohesion Policy and European Integration: Building Multi-Level Governance. Oxford: University Press, 342-362.

Jones, Charles (1998), Introduction to Economic Growth. New York/London: Norton.

Jouve, Bernard and Négrier, Emmanuel (1998), Das Europa der Regionen auf dem Prüfstand: Konvergenzen und Gegensätze. In: Kohler-Koch, Beate (Ed.), Interaktive Politik in Europa: Regionen im Netzwerk der Integration. Opladen: Leske + Budrich, 32-61.

Kearny, Conor (1997), Development Programming, Negotiation and Evaluation: Lessons for the Future. In: Bachtler, John and Turok, Ivan (Eds.), The Coherence of EU Regional Policy: Contrasting Perspectives on the Structural Funds. Regional Policy and Development Series 17. London: Jessica Kingsley, 305-321.

Keating, Michael (1995), Europeanism and Regionalism. In: Jones, Barry and Keating, Michael (Eds.), Regions in the European Community. Oxford: Clarendon, 1-22.

Knodt, Michèle (1998a), Die Prägekraft regionaler Politikstile. In: Kohler-Koch, Beate (Ed.), Interaktive Politik in Europa: Regionen im Netzwerk der Integration. Opladen: Leske + Budrich, 97-124.

Knodt, Michèle (1998b), Tiefenwirkung europäischer Politik: Eigensinn oder Anpassung regionalen Regierens? Baden-Baden: Nomos.

Kohler-Koch, Beate (1998), Europäisierung der Regionen: Institutioneller Wandel als sozialer Prozess. In: Kohler-Koch, Beate (Ed.), Interaktive Politik in Europa: Regionen im Netzwerk der Integration. Opladen: Leske + Budrich, 13-31.

Kohler-Koch, Beate and Jachtenfuchs, Markus (1996), Regieren in der Europäischen Union – Fragestellung für eine interdisziplinäre Europaforschung. In: Politische Vierteljahresschrift 37/3, 537-556.

Kohler-Koch, Beate and Schmidberger, Martin (1996), Integrationstheorien. In: Kohler-Koch, Beate and Woyke, Wichard (Eds.), Lexikon der Politik. Band 5. München: Beck, 152-161.

Kotler, Philip et al. (1994), Standort-Marketing: Wie Städte, Regionen und Länder gezielt Investitionen, Industrien und Tourismus anziehen. Düsseldorf: Econ.

Kreyenbühl, Thomas (1999), Wie können sie wieder aus dem Schatten treten? Italienische Erfahrungen im Umgang mit der Schwarzarbeit. In: NZZ 69, 83.

Krugman Paul (1991b), Increasing Returns and Economic Geography. In: Journal of Political Economy 99/3, 483-499.

Krugman, Paul (1991a), Geography and Trade. Cambridge/London: MIT Press.

Krugman, Paul (1993a), First Nature, Second Nature, and Metropolitan Location. In: Journal of Regional Science 33/2, 129-144.

Krugman, Paul (1993b), Economic Geography: On the Number and Locations of Cities. In: European Economic Review 37, 293-298.

Krugman, Paul (1995), Development, Geography and Economic Theory. Cambridge: MIT Press.

Lawlor, Teresa and Rigby, Mike (1998), Contemporary Spain: Essays and Texts on Politics, Economics, Education, Employment, and Society. London/New York: Longman.

Leonard, Dick (1998), Guide to the European Union. London: The Economist, 152-159.

Leonardi, Robert (1993), The Regions and the European Community: The Regional Response to the Single Market in the Underdeveloped Areas. Portland: Frank Cass.

Leonardi, Robert (1995), Convergence, Cohesion and Integration in the Euopean Union. New York: St. Martin's Press.

Leonardi, Robert and Nanetti, Raffaella (1990), The Regions and European Integration: The Case of Emilia-Romagna. London/New York: Pinter.

Levine, Ross and Renelt, David (1992), A Sensitivity Analysis of Cross-Country Growth Regressions. In: The American Economic Review 82/4, 942-963.

Liebermann, Sima (1995), Growth and Crisis in the Spanish Economy: 1940-1993. London/New York: Routledge.

Lijphart, Arend (1971), Comaparative Politics and the Comparative Method. In: American Political Science Review 65/3, 682-693.

Magone, José (1997), European Portugal: The Difficult Road to Sustainable Democracy. London: Macmillan.

Mancha Navarro, Thomás and Cuadrado Roura, Juan (1996), La convergencia de las regiones españolas: una difícil tarea. In: Cuadrado Roura, Juan and Mancha Navarro, Thomás (Eds.), España frente a la Union Economica y Monetaria, 329-372.

Mankiw, Gregory, Romer, David and Weil, David (1992), A Contribution to the Empirics of Economic Growth. In: Quarterly Journal of Economics 107, 407-437.

Maresso, Anna (1996), Chronology of important political events in Italy - 1994. In: Leonardi, Robert and Nanetti, Raffaella (Eds.), Italy: Politics and Policy. Aldershot: Dartmouth, 1-31.

Marks, Gary (1996a), Exploring and Explaining Variation in EU Cohesion Policy. In: Hooghe, Liesbet (Ed.), Cohesion Policy and European Integration: Building Multi-Level Governance. Oxford: University Press, 388-420.

Marks, Gary (1996b), Politikmuster und Einflusslogik in der Strukturpolitik. In: Kohler-Koch, Beate and Jachtenfuchs, Markus (Eds.), Europäische Integration. Opladen: Leske & Buldrich, 313-343.

Markus, Gregory (1979), Analyzing Panel Data. Quantitative Applications in the Social Sciences 18. London: Sage.

Martín, Manuel and Lizarraga, Mollinedo (1994), Evolución de las Disparidades Económicas Comarcales en Andalucía, 1970-1991: Principales Tendencias Evolutivas. In: Revista de Estudios Regionales 38, 197-224.

Martin, Reiner (1998), Regional Policy in the EU: Economic Foundations and Reality. Brussels: Centre for European Policy Studies.

Martin, Ron (1999), The New "Geographical Turn" in Economics: Some Critical Reflections. In: Cambridge Journal of Economics 23, 65-91.

Martínez-Pujalte López, Vicente *et al.* (1998), El papel de las regiones en la Unión Europea. Valencia: Fundació Bancaixa.

Mas, Matilde *et al.* (1996), Infrastructures and Productivity in the Spanish Regions. In: Regional Studies 30/7, 641-650.

Mauro, Paolo (1995), Corruption and Growth. In: Quarterly Journal of Economics 110, 681-712.

McDonald, Frank and Dearden, Stephen (1992), European Economic Integration. London/New York: Longman.

Meister, Ulrich (1999), Spanien hängt am Kohäsionsfonds: Auslegungskampf um eine Sonderhilfe durch die EU. In: NZZ 62, 23.

Michie, Rona and Fitzgerald, Rona (1997), The Evolution of the Structural Funds. In: Bachtler, John and Turok, Ivan (Eds.), The Coherence of EU Regional Policy: Contrasting Perspectives on the Structural Funds. Regional Policy and Development Series 17. London: Jessica Kingsley, 14-28.

Miles, Matthew and Huberman, Michael (1994), Qualitative Data Analysis. London/New Delhi: Sage.

Miller, Jody and Glassner, Barry (1997), The "Inside" and the "Outside": Finding Realities in Interviews. In: Silverman, David (Ed.), Qualitative Research: Theory, Method and Practice. London/New Delhi: Sage, 99-112.

Mitchell, Ronald and Bernauer, Thomas (1997), Empirical Research on International Environment Policy: Designing Qualitative Case Studies. Studien zur Politikwissenschaft 301. Zürich.

Mittendorfer, Roland (1994), Wirtschafts- und Währungsunion und Föderalismus: Ein interdisziplinärer Beitrag zur "Optimum Currency Area Theory", zum Europarecht und zur Föderalismustheorie. Wien/New York: Springer.

Molle, Willem (1988), Regional Impact of Community Policies in Europe. Hong Kong/Sydney: Dartmouth.

Molle, Willem (1990a), The Economics of European Integration: Theory, Practice, Policy. Hong Kong/Sydney: Dartmouth.

Molle, Willem (1990b), Will the Completion of the Internal Market Lead to Regional Divergence? In: Siebert, Horst (Ed.), The Completion of the Internal Market. Tübingen: Mohr, 174-196.

Molle, Willem *et al.* (1980), Regional Disparity and Economic Development in the European Community. Westmead: Saxon House.

Morata, Francesc (1993), Regions and the European Community: A Comparative Analysis of Four Spanish Regions. In: Leonardi, Robert (Ed.), The Regions and the European Community: The Regional Response to the Single Market in the Underdeveloped Areas. Portland: Frank Cass, 187-216.

Morata, Francesc (1995), Spanish Regions in the European Community. In: Barry, Jones and Keating, Michael (Eds.), Regions in the European Community. Oxford: Clarendon, 115-134.

Morata, Francesc and Munoz, Xavier (1996), Vying for European Funds: Territorial Restructuring in Spain. In: Hooghe, Liesbeth (Ed.), Cohesion Policy and European Integration: Building Multi-Level Governance. Oxford: University Press, 195-218.

Müller-Graff, Peter Christian (1997), Die europäischen Regionen in der Verfassung der EU. In: integration 3, 145-159.

Mundell, Robert (1961), A Theory of Optimum Currency Area. In: American Economic Review 51, 657-664.

Myrdal, Gunnar (1957), Economic Theory and the Underdeveloped Regions. London: Duckworth.

Nanetti, Raffaella (1987), The Strategy of Region-Specific Development in Italy. In: Geoforum 18: 81-88.

Nanetti, Raffaella (1996), EU Cohesion and Territorial Restructuring in the Member States. In: Hooghe, Liesbet (Ed.), Cohesion Policy and European Integration: Building Multi-Level Governance. Oxford: University Press, 59-88.

Neven, Danien and Gouyette, Claudine (1994), Regional Convergence in the European Community. In: CEPR Discussion Paper 914.

Newton, Michael (1997), Institutions of Modern Spain: A Political and Economic Guide. Cambridge: University Press.

Nijkamp, Peter and Blaas, Eddy (1995), Comparative Regional Policy Impact Analysis: Ex Post Evaluation of the Performance of the European Regional Development Fund. In: Journal of Regional Science 35/4, 579-597.

Nohlen, Dieter and Hildenbrand, Andreas (1992), Spanien: Wirtschaft, Gesellschaft, Politik. Opladen: Leske + Budrich.

North, Douglas (1990), Institutions, Institutional Change, and Economic Performance. Cambridge: Cambridge University Press.

North, Douglas (1992), Institutions, Ideology and Economic Performance. In: Cato Journal 11, 477-488.

North, Douglass (1994), Economic Performance Through Time. In: American Economic Review 84, 359-368.

Obinger, Herbert (1999), Politische und institutionelle Determinanten des Wirtschaftswachstums 1960-1992. In: Zes-Arbeitspapier (Zentrum für Sozialpolitik, Universität Bremen), 1-43.

Opello, Walter (1993), Portuguese Regionalism in the Transition from the Estado Novo to the Single Market. In: Leonardi, Robert (Ed.), The Regions and the European Community: The Regional Response to the Single Market in the Underdeveloped Areas. Portland: Frank Cass, 162-186.

Ostrom, Elinor (1990), Governing the Commons: The Evolution of Institutions for Collective Action. New York: Cambridge University Press.

Pajuelo, Alfonso (1994), El Submarco Regional y las Iniciativas Comunitarias en Andalucía: 1994-1999. In: Europa-Junta 29/Julio, 13-23. (Sub-CSF and Community Initiatives in Andalusia 1994-1999).

Paraskevopoulos, Christos (1998), Social Capital, Institutional Learning and Europen Regional Policy: Evidence from Greece. In: Regional & Federal Studies 8/3, 31-64.

Pereira, Armando (1995), Regionalism in Portugal. In: Barry, Jones and Keating, Michael (Eds.), Regions in the European Community. Oxford: Clarendon, 269-280.

Pérez-Alcalá (1998), Die spanische Wirtschaft auf dem Weg nach Maastricht. In: Bernecker, Walther and Dirscherl, Klaus (Eds.), Spanien heute: Politik. Wirtschaft, Kultur. Frankurt a.M: Vervuert, 225-265.

Pfeil, Susanne (1993), Die Konvergenz der wirtschaftlichen Entwicklung in den Staaten der Europäischen Gemeinschaft. Diss. Düsseldorf: Studentendruckerei.

Pintarits, Sylvia (1996), Die regionale Dimension der politischen und wirtschaftlichen Integration und Desintegration EU-Europas. Diss. Wien: Studentendruckerei.

Putnam, Robert (1993), Making Democracy Work: Civic Traditions in Modern Italy. Princeton: Princeton University Press.

Pyndick, Robert and Rubinfeld, Daniel (1997), Econometric Models & Economic Forecasts. New York: McGraw-Hill.

Quah, Danny (1993), Empirical Cross-Section Dynamics in Economic Growth. In: European Economic Review 37, 426-434.

Ragin, Charles (1987), The Comparative Method: Moving Beyond Qualitative and Quantitative Strategies. Berkley/London: University of California Press.

Rodríguez-Pose, Andrés (1998), The Dynamics of Regional Growth in Europe: Social and Political Factors. Oxford: Clarendon.

Rossi, Angelo (1992), Der wirtschaftliche Strukturwandel und die Regionen: Am Beispiel der Schweiz und der angrenzenden Länder. Institut für Orts-, Regional- und Landes-planung 93. Zürich: Hochschulverlag der ETH Zürich.

Sala-i-Martin, Xavier (1990), On Growth and States. Diss. Cambridge: Cambridge University Press.

Sala-i-Martin, Xavier (1994), Cross-Sectional Regressions and the Empirics of Economic Growth. In: European Economic Review 38, 739-747.

Sala-i-Martin, Xavier (1996a), The Classical Approach to Convergence Analysis. In: The Economic Journal 106, 1019-1036.

Sala-i-Martin, Xavier (1996b), Regional Cohesion: Evidence and Theories of Regional Growth and Convergence. In: European Economic Review 40, 1325-1352.

Salmon, Keith (1991), The Modern Spanish Economy: Transformation and Integration Into Europe. London/New York: Pinter Publishers.

Salmon, Keith (1992), Andalucia: An Emerging Regional Economy in Europe. Sevilla: JdA.

Samland, Detlev (1997), Wenn jeder zweite EU-Bürger in einem "Fördergebiet" lebt. In: Frankfurter Rundschau 160.

Sänger, Ralf (1993a), Die Auswirkungen der Europäischen Strukurfonds auf die regionale Entwicklung in Portugal. In: Aus Politik und Zeitgeschichte, Beilage zur Wochenzeitung "Das Parlament", B 20-21, 14. Mai, 30-36.

Sänger, Ralf (1993b), Portugals langer Weg nach "Europa". Diss. Giessen: Studentendruckerei.

Sarris, Alexander (1992), Inflexibility and Adjustment of the Greek Economy under Liberalisation. In: Skouras, Thanos (Ed.), The Greek Economy: Economic Policy for the 1990s. Issues in Contemporary Economics. Vol. 5. , 161-169. Hong Kong: Macmillan, 161-169.

Sayrs, Lois (1989), Pooled Times Series Analysis. Quantitative Applications in the Social Sciences 70. London: Sage.

Scharpf, Fritz (1996), Politische Optionen im vollendeten Binnenmarkt. In: Kohler-Koch, Beate and Jachtenfuchs, Markus (Eds.), Europäische Integration. Opladen: Leske & Buldrich, 109-140.

Schmid, Erich (1998), Europas Integration – eine reale Herausforderung. In: NZZ 18, 8.

Schmidt, Hansjörg (1997), Konvergenz wachsender Volkswirtschaften. Diss. Zürich: Studentendruckerei.

Schneider, Hans-Peter (1996), The Regions in Europe - From a Constitutional Perspective. In: Fäber, Gisela and Forsyth, Murry (Eds.), The Regions - Factors of Integration or Disintegration in Europe? Baden-Baden: Nomos, 45-56.

Scobie, H.M. (1998), The Spanish Economy in the 1990s. London/New York: Routledge.

Serna, Angel (1996), Eine dezentrale Steuerordnung für Spanien: Hoffen auf positive Wachstumseffekte. In: NZZ 101, 25.

Silverman, David (1997), Introducing Qualitative Research. In: Silverman, David (Ed.), Qualitative Research: Theory, Method and Practice. London/New Delhi: Sage, 1-7.

Sodupe, Kepa (1999), The European Union and Inter-regional Co-operation. In: Regional and Federal Studies 9/1, 58-81.

Stadlmann, Heinz (1986), Die Süderweiterung der Europäischen Gemeinschaft. In: Europa Archiv (Internationale Politik) 41/5, 129-137.

Stieger, Cyrill (1997), Griechenlands mühsame Modernisierung: Beschwerlicher Weg in die europäische Währungsunion. In: NZZ 286, 9.

Stimson, James (1985), Regression in Space and Time: A Statistical Essay. In: American Political Science Review 29/4, 914-947.

Teutemann, Manfred (1993), Interpersonal vs. Interregional Redistribution at the European Level - As Seen from the Perspective of Fiscal Federalism and Public Choice Theory. In: Commission of the European Communities (Ed.), European Economy 5, 395-411.

The Economist, various issues.

Thibaut, Bernhard (1996), Europäische Investitionsbank - EIB. In: Nohlen, Dieter (Ed.), Lexikon der Politik. Vol. 5 (Die Europäische Union). München: Beck, 79-81.

Tridimas, George (1996), Greek Fiscal Policy and the European Union. In: Featherstone, Kevin and Ifantis, Kostas (Eds.), Greece in a Changing Europe: Between European Integration and Balkan Disintegration. Manchester/New York: Manchester University Press, 53-71.

Trigilia, C. (1989), Small-Firm Development and Political Subculture in Italy. In: Goodman, E. et al. (Eds.), Small Firms and Industrial Districts in Italy. London/New York: Routledge, 174-197.

Tsoukalis, L. (1993), The New European Economy: The Politics and Economics of Integration. Oxford: Oxford University Press.

Unger, Brigitte (1995), Europa zwischen Integration und Desintegration: Zum Spannungsfeld zwischen ökonomischer und politischer Integration. In: Althaler, Karl. (Ed.), Sozioökonomische Forschungsansätze: Historische Genese, Methoden, Anwendungsgebiete. Marburg: Metropolis, 243-264.

Van Evera, Stephan (1997), Guide to Methods for Students of Political Science. Ithaca/London: Cornell.

Verspagen, Bart (1994), Technology and Growth: the Complex Dynamics of Convergence and Divergence. In: Silverberg, Gerald and Soete, Luc (Eds.), Economics of Growth and Technical Change: Technologies, Nations, Agents. Cornwall: Edward Elger, 154-184.

Walz, Uwe (1996), Long-Run Effects of Regional Policy in an Economic Union. In: Annals of Regional Science 30, 165-183.

Weidenfeld, Werner and Wessels, Wolfgang (1994b), Europa von A-Z: Taschenbuch der europäischen Integration. Bonn: Europa Union Verlag.

Wishlade, Fiona (1996), EU Cohesion Policy: Facts, Figures, and Issues. In: Hooghe, Liesbet (Ed.), Cohesion Policy and European Integration: Building Multi-Level Governance. Oxford: University Press, 27-58.

www.europe.eu.int (European Union)

www.iea.junta-andalucia.es (Regional Statistical Institute of Andalusia)

www.ine.es (National Statistical Institute of Spain)

www.inforegio.org (European Regional Policy)

www.junta-andalucia-es (Government and Administration of Andalusia)

www.mzes.uni-mannheim.de/arb3/dfg.html (Deutsches Forschungsschwerpunkt Programm)

www.odci.gov/cia (CIA World Facts Book)

www.oecd.org (OECD)
www.unibas.ch/euro/ (Europa-Institut Universität Basel)
www.worldbank.org (World Bank)
Yin, Robert (1994), Case Study Research: Design and Methods. London: Sage.

# 13 APPENDIX

## A.1 List of Southern European Regions

| European Union | |
|---|---|
| EU | Average of EU (12) |

| Greece | |
|---|---|
| GR1 | Western Macedonia (& Islands), Attica<br>(Ditiki Macedonia, Attiki) |
| GR2 | Middle and Eastern Macedonia, Thrace<br>(Kentriki Macedonia, Anatoliki Macedonia, Thraki) |
| GR3 | Peloponnese, Western Greece, Continental Greece<br>(Peloponnisos, Ditiki Ellada, Sterea Ellada) |
| GR4 | Thessaly<br>(Thessalia) |
| GR5 | Crete<br>(Kritis) |
| GR6 | Epirus, Ionian Islands<br>(Ipeiros, Ionia Nisia) |
| GR7 | Islands of the Eastern, Northern and Southern Aegean<br>(Voreio Aigaio, Notio Aigaio) |

| Portugal | |
|---|---|
| PT1 | Norte |
| PT2 | Centro |
| PT3 | Lisboa e Vale do Tejo |
| PT4 | Alentejo |
| PT5 | Algarve |
| PT6 | Acores |
| PT7 | Madeira |

## Spain

| ES1 | Galicia |
|-----|---------|
| ES2 | Asturias |
| ES3 | Cantabria |
| ES4 | Pais Vasco |
| ES5 | Navarro |
| ES6 | La Rioja |
| ES7 | Aragon |
| ES8 | Madrid |
| ES9 | Castilla y Leon |
| ES10 | Castilla-la Mancha |
| ES11 | Extremadura |
| ES12 | Cataluna |
| ES13 | Valenciana |
| ES14 | Islas Baleares |
| ES15 | Andalucia |
| ES16 | Murcia |
| ES17 | Ceuta y Melilla |
| ES18 | Canarias |

## Southern Italy

| IT1 | Abbruzzo |
|-----|----------|
| IT2 | Molise |
| IT3 | Campania |
| IT4 | Puglia |
| IT5 | Basilicata |
| IT6 | Calabria |
| IT7 | Sicilia |
| IT8 | Sardegna |

## A.2 The Solow Model [96]

The Solow model is built around two equations, a production function and a capital accumulation equation. The production function describes how inputs produce output. To simplify the model, the inputs are grouped into two categories, capital, $K$, and labour, $L$. $A$ captures technological progress[97] and $Y$ denotes output. The production function is assumed to have the Cobb-Douglas form and is given by

$$Y = K^\alpha L^{1-\alpha} \qquad \text{with } 0 < \alpha < 1 \qquad (1).$$

Defining $k$ as the stock of capital per worker, $k = K/L$, and $y$ as the level of output per worker, $y = Y/L$, the per head production function is the following:

$$(Y/L) = y = k^\alpha \qquad (2).$$

$L$ is assumed to grow exogenously at constant rates $n$ (population growth rate):

$$L(t) = L_0 e^{nt} \qquad (3).$$

The second key equation of the Solow model is an equation that describes how capital accumulates. The capital equation is given by

$$\dot{K} = s\,Y - dK \qquad (4).$$

According to this equation, the change in the capital stock, $\dot{K}$, is equal to the amount of gross investment, $sY$, less the amount of depreciation, $dK$, that occurs during the production process. The term on the left-hand side of equation (4) is the continuous time version of $K_{t+1} - K_t$, that is, the change in the capital stock per "period". The "dot" notation denotes a derivative with respect to time:

$$\dot{K} = dK/dt \qquad (5).$$

The second term of equation (4) represents gross investment. Following Solow, workers/consumers are assumed to save a constant fraction, $s$, of their combined wage and rental income, $Y = wL + rK$ (with $w$ standing for wage, and $r$ for the rent of capital). The economy is closed, so that saving equals investment, and the only use of investment in this economy is to accumulate capital. The consumers rent this capital to firms for use in production. The third term of equation (4) reflects the depreciation of the capital stock that occurs during production. The standard functional form used here implies that a constant fraction, $d$, of the capital stock depreciates every period (regardless of how much output is produced).

---

[96] This chapter builds on Bretschger (1996: 26-57); Barro and Sala-i-Martin (1992: 224-227); Barro and Sala-i-Martin (1995: 14-38); Jones (1998: 20-36); Mankiw, Romer and Weil (409-412); Schmidt (1997: 7-16).

[97] Technological progress is defined as the rise of output $Y$ without increasing the quantity of input factors $K$ and $L$.

To study the evolution of output per person in this economy, the per worker capital accumulation (2) equation is rewritten and combined with (3). The rewriting is accomplished by taking logs and differentiating the equation. This now yields the capital accumulation equation in per worker terms:

$$\dot{k} = s\,y - (n + d)\,k \qquad\qquad (6).$$

This equation says that the change in capital per worker each period is determined by three terms. Investment per worker, $sy$, increases $k$, while depreciation per worker, $dk$, reduces $k$. What is new in this equation is a reduction in $k$ because of population growth, the $nk$ term.

A long-term equilibrium is reached when the growth rate of $y$ is constant. Such an equilibrium is called a steady-state. The steady-state is determined by the condition that $\dot{k} = 0$. Equations (2) and (6) allow us to solve this condition for the steady-state quantities of capital per worker and output per worker. Substituting from (2) into (6),

$$\dot{k} = s\,k^{\alpha} - (n + d)\,k \qquad\qquad (7),$$

and setting this equation equal to zero yields

$$k^* = s/(n + d)^{\,1/(1-\alpha)} \qquad\qquad (8).$$

Substituting this into the production function reveals the steady-state quantity of output per worker, $y^*$:

$$y^* = s/(n + d)^{\,\alpha/(1-\alpha)} \qquad\qquad (9).$$

Now, that the key equations of the Solow model are derived, one can understand the convergence process of economies. On the way to the steady-state, an economy is undergoing a convergence process. Convergence means in this case that an economy (as it is modelled by Solow) is approaching a stable, dynamic equilibrium (=steady-state) for $t \rightarrow \infty$. Figure 13-1 shows this dynamic. According to equation (7), the growth rate of capital intensity, $\dot{k}$, is the difference between $(sk^{\alpha})$ and $(n + d)$. Because of the decreasing marginal return of capital ($\alpha < 1$), this difference is decreasing if the actual capital intensity $k_0$ is smaller than $k^*$. This means that the growth rate of productivity is decreasing as long as an economy converges towards the steady-state.

## Figure 13-1: Convergence in the Solow Model

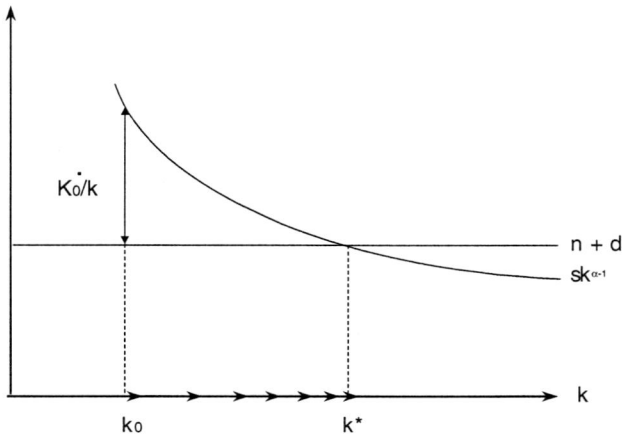

Source: Barro and Sala-i-Martin (1995: 23)

Once the steady-state is reached, only positive exogenous shocks can bring further growth. In the model, this happens by rising $s$ or $A$ and by lowering $n$ and/or $d$. A dynamic towards a new steady-state starts with each shock. As the parameters $s$, $n$ and $d$ are limited in their range, steady growth of productivity depends mainly on an increase of the technological parameter $A$ (Quah 1993).[98]

The neo-classical convergence hypothesis grounds on the following argument. If several economies (countries or regions) differ only in stock of capital per effective unit of labour ($k$), poor economies with small capital intensity will grow faster than rich economies until each economy has reached the (same) steady-state $k*$. During this transitional process, there is a "catching-up" of the less developed economies. This hypothesis - the catching-up of economies among each other - is known as absolute $\beta$-convergence.

---

[98]   In fact, the assumption of steady technological progress is more realistic. This means that there is a steady shift of k* towards the right side in figure 13-1.

## A.3   List of Indicators

| Abbreviation | Full Name | Unit | Notes |
|---|---|---|---|
| DDENSITY | delta[99] of population density | % (of the EU average) | Eurostat data is aggregated to NUTS 2 |
| DEMP2SEC | delta of employment of the 2nd sector | % (of the EU average) | in relation to total employment |
| DLAGUNEM | delta of the lagged unemployment | % (of the EU average) | Eurostat data is aggregated to NUTS 2 |
| DLGLAGGD | delta of Lag of GDP growth t-1 | % (of the EU average) | PPS at 1995 prices |
| DLGSTART | delta GDP per capita at the starting point of the period | % (of the EU average) | PPS at 1995 prices |
| DLOGGROW | delta GDP growth per capita | in log; % (of the EU average) | PPS at 1995 prices |
| DPATAPPL | delta of patent application per capita | % (of the EU average) | in relation to population |
| DTRANCAP | delta of financial transfers per capita | % (of the EU average) | at 1995 prices |
| DUNEMP | delta of unemployment rate | % (of the EU average) | Eurostat data is aggregated to NUTS 2 |
| EMP2SEC | employment of 2nd sector | % | in relation to total employment |
| GREECE, ITALY; PORTUGAL, SPAIN | national dummy | --- | --- |
| LAGUNEMP | lag of unemployment (t-1) | % (of total employment) | Eurostat data is aggregated to NUTS 2 |
| LGGROWTH | GDP growth per capita | % | PPS at 1995 prices |
| LOGSTART | GDP per capita at the starting point of the period | in log | PPS at 1995 prices |
| PATCAP | patent applications per capita | number of applications | patent applications are split up among the researchers who are classed to regions according to their residence |
| Transfers per capita | financial transfers per capita (ESF, ERDF, EAGGF, FIFG, Cohesion Fund) | Euro | at 1995 prices. 13 Greek NUTS 2 regions were merged in 7 administrative regions used for European structural policy |
| Unemployment rate | unemployment rate | % (of total employment) | Eurostat data is aggregated to NUTS 2 |

---

[99]   "Delta" stands for the relative difference between economy i and the European average.

# A.4 Statistical Calculations[100]

## A.4.1 β-Convergence of Regional per Capita GDP

### A.4.1.1 Absolute β-Convergence

**Descriptive Statistics**

|  | Mean | Std. Deviation | N |
|---|---|---|---|
| LGGROWTH [101] | 2.0017975E-02 | 5.6228157E-02 | 200 |
| LGSTART | 4.03733226 | 9.5590145E-02 | 194 |

**Correlations**

|  |  | LGGROWTH | LGSTART |
|---|---|---|---|
| Pearson Correlation | LGGROWTH | 1.000 | -.094 |
|  | LGSTART | -.094 | 1.000 |

**Model Summary(b)**

| Model | R | R Square | Adjusted R Square | Std. Error of the Estimate | F | Sig. |
|---|---|---|---|---|---|---|
| 1 | -.094(a) | .009 | .004 | 5.6100000E-02 | 1.70 | .194 |

a Predictors: (Constant), LGSTART
b Dependent Variable: LGGROWTH

**Coefficients(a)**

| Model | | Unstandardized Coefficients | | Standardized Coefficients | t | Sig. |
|---|---|---|---|---|---|---|
| | | B | Std. Error | Beta | | |
| 1 | (Constant) | .243 | .171 | | 1.421 | .157 |
| | LGSTART | -5.511E-02 | .042 | -.094 | -1.581 | .194 |

a Dependent Variable: LGGROWTH

---

[100] The appendix includes only the calculations of the 3 year average regressions with starting point in 1982.

[101] Appendix A.3 provides a list and description of indicators.

## A.4.1.2 Absolute β-Convergence in Relation to the European Average

**Descriptive Statistics**

|  | Mean | Std. Deviation | N |
|---|---|---|---|
| DLOGGROW | -1.14069588E-03 | 2.3320606E-02 | 194 |
| DLGSTART | -.17031534 | 9.2333363E-02 | 194 |

**Correlations**

|  |  | DLOGGROW | DLGSTART |
|---|---|---|---|
| Pearson Correlation | DLOGGROW | 1.000 | -.148 |
|  | DLGSTART | -.148 | 1.000 |

**Model Summary(b)**

| Model | R | R Square | Adjusted R Square | Std. Error of the Estimate | F | Sig. |
|---|---|---|---|---|---|---|
| 1 | .148(a) | .022 | .017 | 2.3123936E-02 | 4.297 | .400 |

a Predictors: (Constant), DLGSTART
b Dependent Variable: DLOGGROW

**Coefficients(a)**

| Model | | Unstandardized Coefficients | | Standardized Coefficients | t | Sig. |
|---|---|---|---|---|---|---|
| | | B | Std. Error | Beta | | |
| 1 | (Constant) | -7.505E-03 | .003 | | -2.150 | .033 |
| | DLGSTART | -3.737E-02 | .018 | -.148 | -2.073 | .040 |

A Dependent Variable: DLOGGROW

## A.4.2 Impact of European Financial Transfers

### A.4.2.1 *Impact of European Financial Transfers on Regional GDP Growth*

#### Descriptive Statistics

|  | Mean | Std. Deviation | N |
|---|---|---|---|
| LGGROWTH | 2.1717813E-02 | 5.0489496E-02 | 80 |
| T ansfers per capita | .859760 | .942286 | 80 |

#### Correlations

|  |  | LGGROWTH | Transfers per capita |
|---|---|---|---|
| Pearson Correlation | LGGROWTH | 1.000 | .402 |
|  | Transfers per capita | .402 | 1.000 |

#### Model Summary(b)

| Model | R | R Square | Adjusted R Square | Std. Error of the Estimate | F | Sig. |
|---|---|---|---|---|---|---|
| 1 | .402(a) | .162 | .151 | 4.6525828E-02 | 15.034 | .000 |
| a Predictors: (Constant), Transfers per capita | | | | | | |
| b Dependent Variable: LGGROWTH | | | | | | |

#### Coefficients(a)

|  | Model | Unstandardized Coefficients | | Standardized Coefficients | t | Sig. |
|---|---|---|---|---|---|---|
|  |  | B | Std. Error | Beta | | |
| 1 | (Constant) | 3.199E-03 | .007 | | .453 | .652 |
|  | Transfers per capita | 2.154E-02 | .006 | .402 | 3.877 | .000 |
| A Dependent Variable: LGGROWTH | | | | | | |

## A.4.2.2  Impact of European Financial Transfers on Regional Unemployment Rates

### Descriptive Statistics

|                        | Mean       | Std. Deviation | N   |
|------------------------|------------|----------------|-----|
| Unemployment rate      | 14.752867  | 7.711225       | 73  |
| Transfers per capita   | .767253    | .874975        | 73  |

### Correlations

|                     |                        | Unemployment rate | Transfers per capita |
|---------------------|------------------------|-------------------|----------------------|
| Pearson Correlation | Unemployment rate      | 1.000             | -.459                |
|                     | Transfers per capita   | -.459             | 1.000                |

### Model Summary(b)

| Model | R         | R Square | Adjusted R Square | Std. Error of the Estimate | F      | Sig. |
|-------|-----------|----------|-------------------|----------------------------|--------|------|
| 1     | -0.459(a) | .211     | .200              | 6.897335                   | 18.995 | .000 |

A Predictors: (Constant), Transfers per capita
B Dependent Variable: Unemployment rate

### Coefficients(a)

| Model |                      | Unstandardized Coefficients | | Standardized Coefficients | t      | Sig. |
|-------|----------------------|-------|------------|---------------------------|--------|------|
|       |                      | B     | Std. Error | Beta                      |        |      |
| 1     | (Constant)           | 17.859 | 1.077     |                           | 16.584 | .000 |
|       | Transfers per capita | -4.049 | .929      | -.459                     | -4.358 | .000 |

a Dependent Variable: Unemployment rate

## A.4.3 Multivarite Approach (Conditional β-Convergence)

### A.4.3.1 *Impact of European Financial Transfers on Regional GDP Growth in Relation to the European Average*

#### Descriptive Statistics

|  | Mean | Std. Deviation | N |
|---|---|---|---|
| DLOGGROW | -2,13686301E-03 | 1,5494828E-02 | 73 |
| DLGSTART | -,14966833 | 9,1452899E-02 | 73 |
| DDENSITY | 68,10081068 | 452,80714271 | 73 |
| DEMP2SEC | -15,57935404 | 23,97401467 | 73 |
| DPATAPPL | 16822,78010411 | 19961,98689293 | 73 |
| DTRANCAP | 882209,53972603 | 987764,80207237 | 73 |

#### Correlations

|  |  | DLOGGR OW | DLG-START | DDENSIT Y | DEMP-2SEC | DPAT-APPL | DTRANC AP |
|---|---|---|---|---|---|---|---|
| Pearson Correlation | DLOGGR OW | 1.000 | -.208 | -.247 | .305 | -.056 | .188 |
|  | DLG-START | -.208 | 1.000 | .015 | .155 | .675 | -.476 |
|  | DDENSIT Y | -.247 | .015 | 1.000 | -.378 | .004 | .278 |
|  | DEMP-2SEC | .305 | .155 | -.378 | 1.000 | .354 | -.143 |
|  | DPAT-APPL | -.056 | .675 | .004 | .354 | 1.000 | -.342 |
|  | DTRANC AP | .188 | -.476 | .278 | -.143 | -.342 | 1.000 |

#### Model Summary(b)

| Model | R | R Square | Adjusted R Square | Std. Error of the Estimate | F | Sig. |
|---|---|---|---|---|---|---|
| 1 | .458(a) | .210 | .147 | 1,4307009E-02 | 3.490 | .007 |
| a Predictors: (Constant), DTRANCAP, DEMP2SEC, DDENSITY, DPATAPPL, DLGSTART | | | | | | |
| b Dependent Variable: DLOGGROW | | | | | | |

#### Coefficients(a)

| Model |  | U₁ standardized Coefficients | | Standardized Coefficients | t | Sig. |
|---|---|---|---|---|---|---|
|  |  | B | Std. Error | Beta |  |  |
| 1 | (Constant) | -6.624E-03 | .006 |  | -1.099 | .276 |
|  | DLGSTART | -2.855E-02 | .027 | -.169 | -1.880 | .095 |
|  | DDENSITY | -6.854E-06 | .000 | -.200 | -1.591 | .105 |
|  | DEMP2SEC | 1.771E-04 | .000 | .274 | 2.131 | .037 |
|  | DPATAPPL | 2.740E-08 | .000 | .035 | .222 | .825 |
|  | DTRANCAP | 3.376E-09 | .000 | .215 | 1.641 | .106 |
| A Dependent Variable: DLOGGROW | | | | | | |

## A.4.3.2 Impact of European Financial Transfers on Regional Unemployment Rates in Relation to the EU Average

### Descriptive Statistics

|  | Mean | Std. Deviation | N |
|---|---|---|---|
| DUNEMP | 53,49098606 | 75,84636494 | 71 |
| DDENSITY | 128,85820148 | 617,61575196 | 71 |
| DEMP2SEC | -16,87885723 | 23,87989607 | 71 |
| DLGSTART | -,16274249 | ,10009099 | 71 |
| DPATAPPL | 24900343,35211268 | 30461842,28933133 | 71 |
| DTRANCAP | 5963798,34084507 | 6278830,97476553 | 71 |

### Correlations

|  |  | DUNEMP | DDENSITY | DEMP2SEC | DLGSTART | DPATAPPL | DTRANCAP |
|---|---|---|---|---|---|---|---|
| Pearson Correlation | DUNEMP | 1,000 | ,363 | -,263 | ,212 | ,094 | -,231 |
|  | DDENSITY | ,363 | 1,000 | -,384 | ,040 | ,000 | ,384 |
|  | DEMP2SEC | -,263 | -,384 | 1,000 | ,179 | ,321 | -,021 |
|  | DLGSTART | ,212 | ,040 | ,179 | 1,000 | ,613 | -,164 |
|  | DPATAPPL | ,094 | ,000 | ,321 | ,613 | 1,000 | -,227 |
|  | DTRANCAP | -,231 | ,384 | -,021 | -,164 | -,227 | 1,000 |

### Model Summary(b)

| Model | R | R Square | Adjusted R Square | Std. Error of the Estimate | F | Sig. |
|---|---|---|---|---|---|---|
| 1 | ,569(a) | ,323 | ,271 | 64,74989002 | 6,210 | ,000 |

a Predictors: (Constant), DTRANCAP, DEMP2SEC, DLGSTART, DDENSITY, DPATAPPL

b Dependent Variable: DUNEMP

### Coefficients(a)

| Model |  | Unstandardized Coefficients | | Standardized Coefficients | t | Sig. |
|---|---|---|---|---|---|---|
|  |  | B | Std. Error | Beta |  |  |
| 1 | (Constant) | 99,668 | 26,673 |  | 3,737 | ,000 |
|  | DDENSITY | 5,784E-02 | ,015 | ,471 | 3,746 | ,000 |
|  | DEMP2SEC | -,311 | ,387 | -,098 | -,802 | ,425 |
|  | DLGSTART | 150,635 | 98,130 | ,199 | 1,535 | ,130 |
|  | DPATAPPL | -2.185E-07 | ,000 | -,088 | -,634 | ,529 |
|  | DTRANCAP | -4.849E-06 | ,000 | -,401 | -3,398 | ,001 |

A Dependent Variable: DUNEMP

## A.5 List of Interview Partners

### A.5.1 General

*Benito, Miguel*; Head of the Evaluation Unit, DG-16 (European Commission)

### A.5.2 Andalusia (Spain)

*Cáceres, Antonio*; Head of the Sociedad Sevilla Siglo XXI (Diputacion de Sevilla)

*Cuerda, José*; Programme Co-ordinator of the Regional Development Institute (University of Sevilla)

*Del Rio, Juan*; Head of the ESF (Junta de Andalucía, Dirrección General de Fondos Europeos)

*Eguilior, Patricia*; Head of the ERDF (Junta de Andalucía, Dirrección General de Fondos Europeas)

*Fernandez, Romero*; Project Co-ordinator of the Federation of Andalusian Municipalities and Provinces

*García, Villar*; General Assistant of DeputyDirector of ESF (Ministerío de Trabajo y Asuntos Sociales, Unidad Administradora del Fondo Social Europeo (Madrid))

*Gonzalez, Jesus;* Responsible for CSF/OP in Andalusia, DG-16 (European Commission)

*Leon, Mercedes*; Director of the Department for International Affairs of the Andalusian Entrepreneurs' Confederation (Confederation de Empresarios de Andalucía)

*Lozano, Antonio*; Director General of Economic Planning (Junta de Andalucía, Consejeria de Economía y Hacienda)

*Lucena, Miguel*; Representative of the Junta de Andalusia in Brussels

*Muela, Teresa*; Co-ordinator of European Projects of the Federation of Andalusian Municipalities and Provinces

*Muñoz, Angel*; Technical Adviser for the Cohesion Fund (Junta de Andalucía, Dirrección General de Fondos Europeos)

*Orani, Marco*; Head of Cohesion Fund Unit for Spain and Portugal, DG-16 (European Commission)

*Ortiz, Joaquin*; Head of Technical Advisory for the ERDF (Ministerío de Economía y Hacienda (Madrid))

*Pacheco, Alfonso*; Technical Assistant for European Affairs (Junta de Andalucía, Dirrección General de los Asuntos Europeos y Cooperacion Exterior)

*Piñero, Campos;* Deputy Director of the Cohesion Fund (Ministerío de Economía y Hacienda (Madrid))

*Requejo, Juan*; Director of Arenal Grupo Consultor (Sevilla)

*Rivas, Miguel*; Head of Economic Analysis of the Andalusian Institute for Economic Promotion (Instituto de Fomento de Andalucía)

*Ruiz, Carlos*; Head of the Department for European Funds of the Andalusian Institute for Economic Promotion (Instituto de Fomento de Andalucía)

*Serrano, Mercedez*; Technical Adviser for Interreg (Junta de Andalucía, Dirrección General de Fondos Europeos)

### A.5.3   Algarve (Portugal)

*Carvalho, Filomena*; Responsible for the CSF/OP in Algarve, DG-16 (European Commisison)

*Cipriano, Francisco*, Head of the ERDF activities (Ministerio de Equipamento, do Planeamento e da Administração do Território, Direcção Geral do Desenvolvimento Regional (Lisbon))

*Coelho, Filomena*; Director General of Planning and Regional Development Algarve (Comissão de Coordenação Região do Algarve)

*De Sousa, Lucio*; Director of the Regional Delegation Algarve of the Institute of Employment and Professional Training (Delegão Regional do Algarve do Instituto do Emprego e Formação Profissional)

*Gaspar, Jorge*; Director of the Geographic Institute (University of Lisbon) and Director of the CEDRU (Centro de Estudos e Desenvolvimento Regional e Urbano)

*Graça, João*; Administrator of the Association of the Algarve Municipalities (AMAL - Associação de Municípios do Algarve)

*Magalhães, Fátima*; Assistant of the Director General of Regional Development (Ministerio de Equipamento, do Planeamento e da Administração do Território, Direcção Geral do Desenvolvimento Regional (Lisbon))

*Marques, Edite*; Director of Operational Planning of the Regional Institute of Employment and Professional Training (Delegão Regional do Algarve do Instituto do Emprego e Formação Profissional)

*Nunes, Rui*; Professor of Economics (University of Algarve)

*Olivera, Teresa*; Head of the the Cohesion Fund Projects (Ministerio de Equipamento, do Planeamento e da Administração do Território, Direcção Geral do Desenvolvimento Regional (Lisbon))

*Orani, Marco*; Head of Cohesion Fund Unit for Spain and Portugal, DG-16 (European Commission)

*Pimpão, Adriano*; Rector of the University of Algarve and Professor of Economics, former Director for the Structural Funds of the Regional Development Commission (University of Algarve)

*Pinto, Mendonço*; Manager of the Operational Programme Algarve (Comissão de Coordenação Região do Algarve)

*Vitorino, José*; President of the Algarve Entrepreneurs' Confederation (CEAL - Confederação dos Empresarios do Algarve)